CAPPAGHGLASS

CAPPAGHGLASS

PETER SOMERVILLE-LARGE

HAMISH HAMILTON

LONDON

First published in Great Britain 1985
by Hamish Hamilton Ltd
Garden House 57–59 Long Acre London WC2E 9JZ

Copyright © 1985 by Peter Somerville-Large

British Library Cataloguing in Publication Data

Somerville-Large, Peter
   Cappaghglass.
   1. Ireland—Social life and customs—
   20th century
   I. Title
   941.7   DA959.1
   ISBN 0-241-11541-8

Filmset by Rowland Phototypesetting Ltd
Printed in Great Britain by
St Edmundsbury Press, Bury St Edmunds, Suffolk

For Vanessa

CONTENTS

INTRODUCTION

Cappaghglass is a port and market town in the west of Ireland set in spectacular surroundings – a range of jagged blue mountains behind, the sea in front, with a couple of islands and the lighthouse. It is a place that is a lot more beautiful for its setting than for its architecture. A bird's-eye view would show a string of grey roofs cut by the river and dominated by the two churches and the old people's home. The core of the town is the line of Victorian houses and shops running along either side of the main street before it debouches into the market square. On the south side of the square is the harbour and jetty, behind which stood the old station where the emigrant said his last farewell and from where the cattle were shipped eastward and the barrels of salted fish were dispatched to America.

The two churches stand to east and west of the town like bookends. The Catholic church is the enormous Victorian Gothic edifice; the Protestant church, an earlier Gothic shoebox with a tower, is a lot smaller and shabbier, and, to most tastes, prettier. The steady increase of population to over six thousand during the last decade is reflected by the brand new suburbs that have risen to the west. Council housing is mixed with determinedly prosperous bungalows laid out with tarmac-adamed drives, landscaped gardens and plastic urns and ornaments. At the east approach a sad little factory is empty and boarded up. Along the coast where the view is best a thin line of bungalows looks out to sea. Among them is the odd farmhouse, sometimes converted into a comfortable holiday home, sometimes still the home of the small farmer who has sold his land. New Zealand flax and escallonia hedging try to shelter the gardens from the sea wind.

Back in the main street, built for horse traffic, the tractors and lorries laden with supermarket goods try to squeeze between the cars half-parked on the pavement on both sides of the street. You can catch a whiff of the past as you stare at the three storey houses with their lace-curtained Gothic windows, the ruinously big hotel, and the solid bank building, which all recall an age when the street was dust or mud. It is easy to screw up your eyes and imagine 'the appearance of poverty and desertion' described by a nineteenth-century traveller where 'even in well-built and substantial houses every second pane of glass has given way to a board nailed across the window, or a still more offensive paper patching. Bricks or stones or tiles, as they fall from the piles of buildings, which really would constitute a handsome range, if in repair, are suffered to remain where fortune may place them, till the wheels of the heavy carts crush them under the dust which no munificent law controls . . .' That description dates from before the famine. But memories of poverty are a lot more recent, and evident not only in photographs of scenes of forty and fifty years ago where you can see women in shawls, barefoot children and men in raincoats standing with their cattle before the pillared shopfronts. The testimony of old people bring these scenes vividly to life.

Up to twenty years ago Cappaghglass had regular fairs, men and animals thrown together in rowdy chaos beneath the Celtic cross and its list of patriots. The town and country people were set in the old ways, the town an intimate place where crafts and traditional skills flourished – blacksmiths, harness makers, tailors, and all the cobblers making stout hobnailed boots. The few survivors who practise these trades are old men who recall how skills and secrets were passed from father to son until the coming of mass production. You can sometimes come across an old cobbler or harness maker in his shop somewhere in the ramshackle network of old streets and lanes behind the main square.

The gloomy atmospheric old pubs and shops have smartened up. Until the late 'fifties the main store was like an Aladdin's cave, selling everything from sausage to pieces of rope, from underwear to tickets to America. Boots and mackintoshes hung from the wooden ceiling and bolted cash cups ran with your change to the cashier who was sitting in a sort of signal box in the middle. Such trappings have been replaced by supermarket shelves and a delicatessen counter. The old shopfronts, divided up by slender arches, have been exchanged for plate glass stuck with information about baked beans and biscuits, and the black and gilt lettering above has changed to crisper capitals and logos.

The town's past precarious prosperity, such as it was, had its base in fishing and some commerce recalled by the massive shell of the old mill and grain store. In the harbour the trawlers lying at anchor have the place to themselves in winter, although in summer they share the sea with yachts and small pleasure craft. Fishing has declined drastically since the days of the great herring and mackerel shoals – even ten years ago the harbour would be bubbling with mackerel during the late summer. The sea has been a source of employment to the men of the area for over a century, ever since the old currach-type boats were modernized. In the old days the seasonal fish salting industries which employed red-armed girls from Donegal, slitting and salting mackerel and herring, occupied fishermen–farmers all along the coast. Now the bigger and greedier trawlers, both local and intruders from other countries in the EEC, are destroying the fish stocks with frightening rapidity.

Cappaghglass has its share of tourists. There are souvenir shops in the main street, a couple of restaurants that have a three-month summer season, boat trips to the lighthouse, and a singing pub. Visitors stay in the big hotel, in guest houses, farmhouses and B and Bs outside the town or bring their caravans. The number of tourists fluctuates, depending on the situation in the north of Ireland, but there are usually groups of young continentals, yachtsmen in red and yellow anoraks and middle-aged visitors driving along in their Volvos and Audis. A number of outsiders come to the area with the intention of living here permanently. They are mainly middle-class, city people from Dublin, and foreigners, German, Dutch, French and English, artists, potters and writers. Some are still practising self-sufficiency on tiny pieces of land, although enthusiasm for this sort of life has declined. Others came here when Ireland was still cheap, and they planned a pleasant retirement in a beautiful place. Three or four years of wet winters defeat a lot of them, and they depart, to be replaced by a new wave of optimists.

Outside the town the wind and rain fall over the countryside and on the wild flowers along the hedges. The light catches the sea, grey silk in winter, a brilliant blue in the summer sun. On the small country roads there is the sigh of wind in the telephone wires, and the splash from a passing car. In an area like this the good land quickly tails off into hills and mountains. The fields get wetter and more boggy, the fissures of rock stand out above the fields like bones and the only thing that can do well here is the sheep. Everywhere you still see the old potato ridges and broken walls of cottages when the rural population was much denser. Famine and emigration cleared out the land. The majority of farms are still smallholdings of up to thirty acres with solid two-storey farmhouses. Many are lived in by old people, for this is an area with an ageing population. Beside the small old farms, the properties of the more progressive men flourish as they build up their herds of Fresians in this good dairy country. Their activities change the landscape, greening up the wide acres of grass they cut for silage, digging out the thorn hedges, surrounding their farmhouses with shining galvanized sheds. These farmers are usually men under fifty, who recall how as children they watched their mothers cooking over open fires, using candles and oil lamps, and helped to bring water from the nearest well. Such memories are very recent – a number of teenagers told me how during their early childhood their homes were still without electricity. But during the past two decades the changes have been enormous. The modern farmer has achieved most of the creature comforts of his town counterpart; he and his wife no longer talks of the 'slavery' of their lives, he doesn't spend his time jogging each day to the creamery in his horse and cart, and his children don't leave school at fourteen.

The farming revolution is reflected in the demise of the fairs and the rise of the marts in their place. The creameries are still there – among the castles, dolmens and stone circles you see these characteristic landmarks situated strategically at cross-roads attended by piles of blue fertilizer sacks, still providing an essential rural service. Although their function is now changing, during the century they have been one of the most important catalysts of rural progress.

The few big houses in the area are nearly all gone, some burned, most gone to ruin, their land divided up by the Land Commission. One, just outside the town, was taken over by a religious order and is now up for sale with the decrease in vocations. The last of the old estates, situated ten miles away, has survived against great odds. Still screened by deciduous trees and guarded by stone walls, it sits unexpectedly in the wild landscape like an oasis, with the mountains behind waist-high in conifers.

As modern fishing is reducing fish stocks, modern farming techniques have their effects on animals and birds. There is no economic problem in the fact that there are fewer larks, corncrakes and kestrels, some unable to adapt to land conditoned to silage, others poisoned by pesticides; fewer foxes hunted for their pelts; fewer hares captured for coursing; and a dwindling number of otters in the polluted rivers. The lobsters went from the foreshore long ago, and now the salmon is vanishing into the inescapable nylon netting. A constant refrain of the older people is the vanished abundance of the past, and some people believe that the decline and destruction have become irreversible.

A more immediate ground for pessimism is the seemingly permanent nature of rural unemployment. Emigration has ceased to be the automatic and devastating solution to the lack of opportunity. The young people have to struggle on their own. Better educated than their parents, they know that certificates and degrees guarantee them nothing in the way of work. But those I talked to have the same courage and resourcefulness that carried so many of a previous generation to the far corners of the world.

The vast majority of people in Cappaghglass and the surrounding townlands are Roman Catholic. The old religious festivals like Corpus Christi are still widely attended, and in remoter townlands occasional wakes are still held. There used to be a small thriving Protestant community, but this has declined drastically through emigration and mixed marriages. Of the three Protestant denominations, two have congregations under twenty, and ten years ago the Methodist church was closed. If the main arm of the Catholic church continues to be that 'the faithful must remain faithful and follow the religious and moral norms laid down by the church' it is also true that Vatican II has changed old attitudes. Different denominations readily go to each other's weddings and funerals, when in the past they would have to remain outside the churches. Cynics say that ecumenism costs nothing when there are so few to practise it on. The influence of outsiders on the neighbourhood has fostered a degree of tolerance not found in less cosmopolitan places in rural Ireland, as has the growing impatience of the younger generation towards the rigid structures of the church.

I encountered a good many people in and around Cappaghglass, old and young, foreigners, shopkeepers, farmers, craftsmen and professional men. I came to them as a friend, knowing that any knowledge that they gave me could in no way be regarded as a scientific study, only a bagful of memories and opinions. And that is what I pass on.

As elsewhere the memories of the old are the most vivid and beautifully expressed, with the tinge of poetry that derives from a Gaelic heritage. The old are still close to nature and its moods. Their conversation has a natural rhythm and flow which modern education and experience tends to destroy. Almost invariably they are more articulate than the younger, educated generation. Talk to any old man or woman, and the words and descriptions pour out. The changes they have seen, together with the testament of younger people, illuminate what has happened in these past fifty years. Sadly, a number of the older people have died since I spoke to them.

The interviews are not meant to be comprehensive, nor have they any sociological or anthropological intention. They are mainly good talk, and they add up to a portrait of Cappaghglass past and present.

OLD FRIENDS

JOHN REGAN	Farmer, *Aged 80*
EILEEN O'SHEA	Farmer's Wife, *Aged 78*
ANNIE SULLIVAN	Ex-maid, *Aged 82*
MISS HEGARTY	Matron, Old People's Home, *Aged 51*
PAT HICKY	Pensioner in Old People's Home, *Aged 83*
DENIS MURPHY	Pensioner in Old People's Home, *Aged 77*
JERRY O'KEEFE	Pensioner in Old People's Home, *Aged 80*
DAN BRADY	Retired Pensioner, *Aged 74*

Ireland is in many ways an old person's country. Where emigration carries youth away, old age is disproportionally numerous. But that's not all the story, for the rural Irish are long lived and die very old indeed.

The Irish Countryman, M. Arensberg.

. . . your old men shall dream dreams . . .

Joel ii: 28.

My father worked with a horse-plough
His shoulders globed like a full sail strung
Between the shafts and the furrow
The horses strained at his clicking tongue.

. . . The sod rolled over without breaking.
At the headrig, with a single pluck

Of reins, the sweating team turned round
And back into the land. His eye
Narrowed and angled at the ground
Mapping the furrow exactly.

Follower, Seamus Heaney.

John Regan, Farmer. Aged 80.

The long low farmhouse is at the end of a narrow lane that forms part of a network of little roads branching off and losing themselves in the hills. From outside there is a view of the sea, a rich blue in good weather, at other times closed off by cloud. Inside the farm gate, John's cart is stacked away in a shed, while harness hangs from a nearby hook. Through the yard, past a pile of manure where hens are perched, a muddy path leads to the pin-cushion of bright green fields which make up his small acreage. A collarless grey shirt is stretched on a furze bush to dry in the sun.

The house looks empty with curtains drawn and doors tightly shut. A hen chortles, a dog barks and someone pushes open a front door swollen with damp. Inside, the kitchen has a cement floor, two hard wooden settles, a deal kitchen table and an iron stove that replaced the open hearth. On the wall a calendar and a brown spotted holy picture.

John's father and grandfather lived here before him. He was born at the beginning of the century, was it 1903 or 1904? His eyes are very blue, and he is alert and questioning. His sister, who has had a lot of the spring taken out of her by old age, is four years younger than him. She does the housework and cooking, wearing a chequered blue apron, moving very slowly. The only time she leaves the house is to go to Mass on Sunday.

Just inside the gate is an anvil which John still uses to shoe his horse, and the furze machine whose heavy iron wheel he turns to slice up bushes for fodder. He is the last person in the townland to use a horse and cart, but old age is catching up. More and more the nice little animal is wasting in the field, when it could fetch a good price.

His two cows are milked by hand. He has never had a tractor or a car, although when he was younger and his legs stronger he used a bicycle. On farms all around him you can hear the tractors as the hay is cut, but on John's farm there is no sound. Outside is a thick meadow of overseeded grass with the wind rippling through, and inside the little old man talking away, his sister listening and smiling.

Two pensions coming into the house means that money isn't short. Neighbours take them to Mass, and the doctor and the health visitor keep an eye on them. In summer, carloads of tourists, drive regularly down the lane and stop, because the farmhouse is a cul de sac. They say how lucky he is to have such a place . . . such a view. But you don't notice it after sitting on top of it all your life.

★

'I have my memories, my God I have great memories, and you'll never see people now living like I did, anyway. Wait now, and I'll tell you how it was. There is a village back there, a cluster of seven houses, all empty and the roofs gone. In my time between the parents and the children they had plenty there. I had five brothers and two sisters and that was the way of every house.

You know the school house on the coast road that's for sale? I suppose a tourist will buy it. That place is a hundred years old and it had a patchy slate roof that kept dropping off. In my time ninety-five children were going there. Not one of them wore shoes, as they hadn't them. I had a schoolbag which was a pocket of my father's coat, and every day my mother would give us a few slices of bread with some jam for the playhour. Sometimes we had two boiled eggs to keep our hands warm, one in each hand, and we ate the eggs afterwards in school for lunch. In winter we all took a sod of turf under our arms for the fire. When the turf ran out the Master would buy a can of turf from the priest, but it was never enough to heat us. I suppose that old school was the coldest since God made the world, and every step you would go down through the boards and a gale would be coming up through them. In winter it was like spending a night up on the mountain. It was cold as the top of Mangerton.

None of us liked school. I'll tell you the truth, that the teachers in my day were right dogs of men. The Master here would teach you all right, but you got so much of the stick you couldn't learn a bit. All the time he would be slapping our knees and our knuckles and hitting us. He would come at this side of the desk where you were sitting – we'd be six to a desk – and give us the stick across the shinbones. There was not a thing there but the bone, and he would put black stripes across it. A big thorny stick, and God save us, it was sore. He'd cut the hands off you if you hadn't the subject he'd given you to learn.

Sometimes we were able to get our own back. If by chance we heard that that old Master was *scoraiocht*-ing★ we would watch out for him and give him an awful pegging. We would get sods of turf and smear every bit of him as he left the house. You were bound to get him if there were two or three big lads, and I'll tell you he would need a dish of water to wash his head when he went home.

Two or three of us might go to school and the rest stay behind. There would be the cattle to mind and sometimes we picked the potatoes or anything like that. We'd be at a lot of jobs around the farm that didn't amount to much but what you would be lazy to go to. Putting up a fence that had fallen, things like that. I left school when I was about eleven, and helped my father on the farm. Later on in the 'twenties with the School Attendance Act you couldn't do a thing like that. You couldn't leave till you were fourteen, but before that you could leave when you liked.

Sure they lived a fine old graceful life long ago, but there were a lot of people around here who didn't go to school. Patrick Murphy, and he had the brains, never went to school. The same with Con Donovan. But, do you see, we had no back door like the parish priest, or the school teacher or the sergeant. They were big fellow's sons. They would have it all tied up, yerra, they would be half-connected. You can see what good was an ordinary man and his family. Where could they go? We hadn't much education, you know – a natural school.

My father killed himself clearing the land, and I also killed myself afterwards. The farm was gone all wild out with rocks wild to the wind. But it was grand at home. It's hard for me to explain to a man like you just how different everything was, and that although my father had only a small farm of forty acres, we were all content and happy. At that time when I was young you couldn't get near the fire the house was so full.

The mothers of those days were fantastic, and they were good at everything. They made the ganzy† and made the pants and they were good at making a meal out of anything. There was nothing in the house but work, and that's what they thought of – that's what they wanted. There weren't many fancy foods like are going nowadays and other handouts. I can tell you rashers and eggs were out so far as we were concerned.

But there was fine strong food, boy. We would skim the cream off

★ derived from *ag scoraiocht* – visiting neighbours.
† ganzy: a pullover.

with a saucer from the milk and leave it in big pans, and that buttermilk would be grand altogether. People would come out from Cappaghglass to have a drink of it, for it had a grand cure in it. We used to have oaten meal and oaten porridge. There was plenty of home cured bacon and from our own flour my mother would make fine bastible cakes. Potatoes – they were called Champion at that time, and they would be boiled and put on the table with just a little milk and salt and we would eat that. We used to have plenty of fish all the time, and herrings were as plentiful as the grass every day of the year.

Everybody went fishing. My father had a small boat and you would throw out a net at nightfall, and haul it in during the morning, and divide up the catch. Later we would salt them in boxes and barrels and every family around here had their barrel of salt fish. The way we did it was to cut the fish through from head to tail, clean out the insides and flatten him. Then three weeks later dry them out from the pickle and hang them by the gills on a branch of a tree until they dried.

If you went into any farmer's house the teapot was always on the fire. You could be sure of tea and homemade cake and butter, and the food we got was always the best. Pure white skinned bacon and plenty of cabbage, and you could eat a whole bucket of turnips and it would do you no harm. Now it would burst you. The food wasn't grown on artificial and today we are poisoned by the fertilizers. Farmyard manure was the healthiest thing. Today they throw in a dash of nitrogen and grow vegetables up in a week, and when you throw them into a pot they go to nothing.

In those days people dressed a lot more becoming than today. We had one good suit. They were mostly blue, navy blue serge. My father and mother would buy a roll in the draper's shop and bring it to the tailor. The suits would be for Sunday wear and I got my first suit when I was confirmed. It cost five pounds, and after I finished wearing it my brother got it. We never had shoes, for my parents couldn't afford them. My father had two pairs, and when I got bigger I had the same. A Sunday pair and another with hobnails for the farm which would last forever. We tied our Sunday shoes around our necks to preserve them and only put them on entering the church.

Everyone wore a cap or a hat at that time, and I still wear one. If you saw Dev holding a meeting, they'd all wear caps, and that was the way they were brought up. The only person you would see bare-headed would be a clerk in front of a counter.

I helped my father until he died. He died young when he was fifty-two. He was sick for almost a year. Nearly every night the house would be full of people helping my mother. They would say: "Wouldn't you care to go to bed for a few hours and we will talk to him." "Don't trouble yourself with the cooking." When he died there was no such thing as a man working in that townland. They had a big wake here when he was carried out of the house for good. We drank and drank. There was brandy, there was whiskey and everyone in the parish came. They were coming and coming and coming. I counted ninety cars at his funeral. At a wake no one brings anything, the dead man buys the whiskey, some of them go home, but others settle until the morning, you know. It was a big funeral and I went to every funeral until I was too old. I wouldn't be bothered now. Mostly in the winter, for old people die in the winter. It's respect, and you'd shake hands with the buried man, and it's an old friendship custom.

I inherited the farm. He had a will made and I took over. My brothers and sisters had gone, three to England and two to America, and only me and Bridie were left with my mother. That was the way in every house and they didn't stay at home. We lived with our mother. She was a very hard woman, boy, and I had great respect for her. I was mad about my mother, and she was the grandest woman in the world. No one in this world could be fonder of their mother than I was. But anyway she died and we couldn't keep her.

They were bad times then. The best you could get for a cow was fifty shillings. Some were bought by a man for feeding pigs. But they didn't suit the pigs at all and he lost more than they gained. They were the queerest things in the world, and the soup he made for boiling meat was all fat and the pigs used to be queer looking animals.

The first Friday of every month there was a fair at Cappaghglass. It would take us four or five hours to get the cattle over the hills lighting our way with a torch or a carbide lamp. We would start at two in the morning and get there by dawn. But the business of selling them was desperate – you had to get a licence to sell your cattle and they would be tangling all day. A man we called the blocker might come and take your hand. "Give way, give way, he's giving you the right price," he would say if he was favouring the buyer, and another might come up and tell him to bid more. But the difference wasn't great. The buyers sort of boycotted the people. If one buyer came to you and he asked you for your cattle, and you didn't give them to him for the price he offered, he'd go along and tell the next buyer. They were all one. You couldn't get through them at all. You'd have a crack at me, and two or three would be making their living out of one poor farmer.

More often than not we gave the cattle away for fifty shillings or a

pound a piece. Let me tell you one instance of a man who lived
through it all, and can remember the best wagonload of cattle that was
ever loaded, and it went for £16. Eleven bullocks were in the wagon at
Cappaghglass, and they only went for thirty shillings a head. I've seen
a calf no one wanted and they played for her with cards. Half a crown a
piece, and the lad who won her wouldn't take her, and they threw her
down a hole in a quarry.

I've seen men go to the fair, their young families at home, and they
didn't sell their cattle, they couldn't sell their cattle. The worst
situation of all was to take your cattle on a wet morning over the
mountain and not sell them and have to come back again. In very lean
and very poor times it was many the father who came home from the
fair disgusted. They called it an economic war and there was no
economics in it at all.

Sure England was always leaning on us. They didn't want our stuff
– or rather, they wanted it badly but they wouldn't pay us for it. There
was no demand. The cattle would be going at least two or three years
to the fair before they were sold. They'd know how to go when you
put them on the road to Cappaghglass.

But somehow we continued and to tell the truth we all enjoyed
ourselves then. Things were cheap and I'm sorry I didn't drink enough
porter when it was two pence a pint.

You might think listening to me that it was all deprivation and hard
work, but life was better and we had more respect. If only we had a
little more money.

I used to throw the weight and there were tugs of war between
different teams of men. The competitions would be held in the
summer all over the country. There was football and hurling and
dancing and playing cards. The kind of dance called sets with four
boys and four girls. It was good fun all meeting on Sunday afternoon
for a pattern at the cross roads. They used to come long ways to the
country dances, for they weren't in every townland at all. Only in
certain townlands. And we had the balls after threshing in the wintertime. We had them around Christmas and after in the fine long nights.

We'd get maybe forty lads and we'd make up five shillings a man –
would that be six pounds? We'd get eight gallons of porter for eight
shillings and you'd get bread at sixpence a pair – four pound loaves.
We'd buy things, you see, and have a dance in one of the country
houses. They could play the fiddle, melodeon, accordion, mouth-
organ and everything. They were very brilliant like that. A fine old
fling we'd make up for the party. It was a great sight, boy, with the

open fires going up the chimney and a bucket of porter going around. Did you ever see pint basins? Every man would draw a pint basin of porter from the bucket. And we'd have bottles of lemonade, for the girls would drink lemonade or a sup of wine. The dances were great, the ball would be held until six in the morning. We would dance hornpipes and reels and sets, the Walls of Limerick, and the Rakes of Mallow. All those country dances. I used to caper away with the women. I'd do the Stack of Barley and the Barn Dance. The old people would not say a thing in the world. My mother was able to dance a hornpipe at seventy years. People wouldn't go to the country dances at all now. They stopped between the wars and people go to a higher class of society.

In the old days I had a good voice and I was in demand at weddings. When you go to a wedding you can't go with your hands hanging down to you . . . you must bring something for the house . . . a little present to shake hands. And then after the wedding you would be asked for a song. The Old Bog Road was a song, and Killarney's Lakes and Dells, and there was another, The Rose of Tralee. You have big weddings now at hotels, but before they were just at the house. Today people are living beyond their means. Today a wedding would break a farmer because he must keep in time.

They had what they called *seanchaíócht*-ing and the housewives would go around to each other for a chinwag. In the evening we would go *scoraíocht*-ing to a certain house, and each man would bring his own tin of tobacco or what they called twist. We'd play cards – twenty-five, and a lovely game called solo. Did you ever play twenty-five? We might play for a penny on the top of it. Did you ever hear of turkey drives? We'd play for the turkey in cards, mostly twenty-five or thirty-five, a shilling a man or two shillings. Whoever was the best would take up the turkey. Oh, he was alive all right. They got a donkey and car the next day and took him home.

When we grew up our means were so little and we were very happy in small things. Strangely I think we have got more selfish because I think there is not that respect for human life that there was in my time. The children in our days had manners and now they don't have them any more. There was more respect for people and how they lived. You were trained to go into a house and say just inside the door, "God save all here" and they would reply back, "God hear your prayer." That was quite common. If there was an old man in the house you would say "Isn't it a fine day sir, a great day, sir" or whatever the case might be. Now people say "Hi".

Now there is no entertainment in a country place except watching funerals or television. People are not interested in you because they are watching some old picture and don't want to be interrupted. In the old days it was different. People were interested in their relations and their families and today they hardly know them at all.

In the old days old people would always stay in their houses. In Jesus no way would they be sent to a home – may God forgive me for cursing. They were always kept at home, and if you spoke about sending them into a home you would want to be out quick. Oh, you would be kicked outside! The reason for today is the young people won't mind them. Ah, Lord, in the old days it was never done. Even a labouring man in a cottage or travelling people on the road, they would never go into a home. They were called County Homes at that time, now they are called County Hospitals. I wouldn't like to see my father going off to the County Home.

I would prefer to stay in my own house of course, and she would too. When you get old you never want to move. There's no place in the world like your own home, do you know what I mean? You can get a chair by the fire and sit down, but you won't do that in these old people's homes. I suppose the youth of today can't get along with old people and that's it. When we were young old and young played together, and there was nothing wrong in it. But the old won't be looked at today, my dear man. The youth have changed and people have changed.'

Eileen O'Shea, Farmer's Wife. Aged 78.

Eileen O'Shea's family was always long lived; her father turned a hundred. In the parlour a photograph taken on his hundredth birthday shows his children, grandchildren and a couple of great-grandchildren grouped around the resolute old man. Eileen remembers the day well, and says she often comes into the small room with its pink curtains and dusty furniture and old wind-up gramophone with fluted horn to look again at the photograph taken a decade ago.

She is a small woman with pale eyes and a pensive way of talking, combined with a quick laugh when anything takes her fancy. The old miser next door who refuses to take in electricity, the latest scandal about the English people in the small holding down the road. She keeps a critical eye on the neighbourhood as she has done all her life.

The farmhouse has the distinction of having four bedrooms. In the old days it was called the Castle or the Court. It is a substantial building with a rough garden in front and against the wall a luxuriant bed of arums. The inside hasn't changed much since the day she married. It has the same hard floor, now covered with a triangle of bright green linoleum, the same rough wooden table where the family had their meals and the same metal stove. She likes the old style and the old things. Although her daughter has given her a television set, you sense the modern world is an intrusion.

Her husband died five years ago and her two daughters both live in Dublin. She still keeps the farm with the help of a neighbour. All her life she has been busy, and to her mind idleness is the mark of the devil.

★

'I married a farmer, and in those days the work on a farm was pure slavery. You got no holiday and no day off, and the only holiday I got in my whole life was when my daughter got married. Houses are completely changed. T'is for the better to a point because then you had only the well water and the open fire and a crane and all the pots were boiled on it, and the bread made on it. It was a life of hardship to a point, for nothing was got easy from the time you started up the fire in the morning.

The first thing in the summer was to let out the fowl and then make breakfast. After breakfast I hand-milked the cows and then I put milk in buckets and put it into the separator. When I was milking I would leave the child asleep in the cradle, and run in again and see if the child was all right. When they were bigger the girls went to school at nine o'clock. We had no running water and we used to wash them in tin baths with two handles on them. You would first wash the children, and then the clothes. The water was stored in barrels and in wintertime we had shutes around the house.

Every day I would make bread, lovely brown meal bread, and after it was made you would put hot butter floating on top of it . . . it was lovely. The midday meal was called dinner and the evening meal was tea. For dinner I would usually boil bacon and mostly we ate bacon all the time. It was never called pork. A great big pig would last us for most of the year. We would take it out of the pickle after two weeks and I would hang it in good big pieces across the beams. It was common then to have a bonham in the kitchen, and the sow would keep it company and be as quiet as a Christian. She would be like a pet. When a sow was farrowing, you know, I would be feeding her. She wouldn't be too keen for a man to go near her. We also had chickens all over the place. The family liked a roast chicken or a roast duck. We had hens and turkeys and geese and ducks and bonhams. We would always have something special for Sunday. We would have a pudding that day.

In those times people didn't mind hard work or give it any notice. On Wednesday I made the butter. If it was too warm you would be twisting all day and it wouldn't make. You would be putting cold water in it to make it cool. Then it would be made up into rolls and polished over with the butter spades and then covered over with a white cloth.

Next day – Thursday – I brought it to market at Cappaghglass, about sixteen pounds. We had no creameries then and all the country people would come in and sell their produce. People used to be walking in those days. You'd meet them walking. We used to meet the mail car going out west – it was very cheap. For a couple of bob you'd be carted a great distance. It could carry three or four holding on. Then we had covered cars. They always hired covered cars when they were going to a funeral; it was a dark colour with two seats inside it, and he'd be up high driving in the front, and it would carry six people inside.

To get back to those Thursdays. I didn't walk, but I had the car. I would drive the horse from the farm along the road I knew well. Every yard of it familiar, the twist at the broken gate leading in, the lines of trees and so on. As you drove you would listen to the sound of the wheels – they were ironshod in those days. The eggs behind in a big square box and the rolls of butter and messages with them.

After an hour I would see Cappaghglass below. I would tie up in Doyle's yard and it would be a great thing to get a shilling a dozen for the eggs. You'd take what you could get. There were at least four places for buying butter. I would write a list of what I would want and the shopkeeper might take it out of the price of the butter. But sometimes there was no butter bought, and I would have to bring it home and put it in cakes. In every cake we made we would put a lump of butter into it just to get rid of it.

I remember fine Thursdays in the spring of the year around Easter. People coming in ponies and cars and women walking with baskets on their heads. They'd carry messages, butter and eggs and bring home tea and sugar. She'd go with that big heavy load up on her head and back again with another load. She'd wear shoes and have one hand up and a small shawl on her shoulders. The pier road filled with people coming up and down from the island and their boats in the harbour. It was like a small regatta.

Although the men weren't expected to do a turn in the house, we had to help in the farm as well. Women would do all the picking of the potatoes and draw them in afterwards. Milking the cows every day, of course, and rearing the calves. And in the evening after tea doing the mending.

It was all manual work. We had a man at six shillings a week who lived with us and most of the farmers around did the same. Hired help was cheap. He did the ploughing, snagging the potatoes and general work. Sometimes I had a girl to help me, but God knows, more often than not they were poor slatternly creatures and it was more hard work looking after them than any little service they did. Some of the things they did, or rather, didn't do would keep me talking for weeks.

Things are a great deal easier today. The most important change was the creameries and the end of churning your own butter. The electricity didn't come until after the Second War. And later still the water going to your door. We got our first radio in 1934 or was it 1935? But I heard one long before that at Jack Donovan's in 1926, and the people used to go up listening to him on Sunday afternoon for the hurley and football.

I remember the first corn-cutting machine that came in and they were all crowding around to see it working. There would be about thirty men for the threshing, with two or three haggards joined together, you know. The small farmers would join up with the bigger farmers . . . people helped each other then. When farmers worked together it was called "coring" and that's an Irish word, but that sort of thing died out when machinery became plentiful. On threshing day every man was given a glass of whiskey in the morning when he came. The men would work all day and when it was over they would bring in the spade and burn it, and that was a sign of the end of the year. Threshing was their party. I would give them a big meal of meat and cabbage, and basins of porter handed around. When one batch was fed, I would have the next, and so on right into the night. Then when we had all eaten, the dance would be held in the kitchen and all the chairs and tables carted away. An old man would play the fiddle and someone played the concertina. Some twenty of them dancing in the kitchen with the lighted candles and the oil lamps, and later on the

Tilley hissing. Hornpipes and reels, half sets, old and young, but mostly the men and the women were shy. The sun often came up over the fields and they would still be dancing.

I don't complain and I am happy enough living here by myself. When the weather is good I do a little work in the garden. Dahlias were a great favourite of mine, and I used to have the finest chrysanthemums in the world. They were everywhere, all over the garden. You have the feathers of a wild goose, and they were exactly like that, grand furry things.

I go walking a little. The corncrakes have gone. I often listened to them. And what happened to the poor little things I don't know. I suppose they died, and you wouldn't hear them now. I often spent an hour listening to them in the meadows. Oh God, I wouldn't love badgers and foxes at all! But I'm very fond of my birdeens. I feed them every day of the week. I would put the cover out there on top of the hedge, and I've a hundred of them sometimes. I put a power of stuff out there for them. They are nice little creatures and I've been doing that for years and years.

I knit and I watch television. My daughter gave me the television. You know, what I regret most is the company. There's no crowd around. Sometimes I'm disgusted at that thing and I would throw it out of the window. I'm disgusted and I think that television has had a terrible effect, and when you go into a farmer's house at nine o'clock there is no way they are going to talk to you till the news is over.

For all the hard work I miss the crowds and hearing them shouting to each other as they are coming together in the evening. Boys and girls along the road. In the summer time they would be out there with the accordion and sitting on the fence and dancing away on the road. T'was beautiful.

You are only looking at the sides of the road now when you go for a walk, but when I was young our hearts used to be bursting with joy going to meet all the boys and girls who would gather on a summer's evening. See me sitting down on a fence gawking with the other girls at the fellows, and someone would have a fiddle or melodeon and away they would go. And I remember sometimes coming home through the town on a fair day and the cattle were already on the street.'

Annie Sullivan, Ex-maid. Aged 82.

Annie's house is down a boreen thick in fuschia and summer weeds. From the outside it looks much like that of any of her neighbours', a small pretty two-storeyed farm house with four windows and an open door. Some bantams scratch in the dust while a dog greets you, waving its tail uncertainly.

Coming in from the light the visitor takes time to get used to the darkness, but slowly the picture resolves. The small stifling room is buzzing with insects and a trapped bird beats its wings against the dirty glass. An old woman sits crouched in a chair beside an empty grate, her glasses half-fallen from her nose. She has rumpled white hair and rumpled old clothes. Dangling above her head an assortment of tatters is strung on a line across the kitchen, a pair of stockings the only recognizable garments among the mud-coloured pieces of cloth. On the table beside her is a confusion of papers on top of which is scattered a long-opened tin of cat food, broken plates, bottles and a bucket of water. The smell is dreadful.

A staircase leads to unspeakable rooms upstairs. Annie used to indulge in mattress banking until a few weeks ago when a burglar ran up the stairs and stole her savings. She could hear the sound of him but couldn't see anything. Her legs had gone and she couldn't move. 'Who is it?' she called out, but no one answered.

She is almost blind, can walk very little and her body is punctuated with aches which the doctor cannot alleviate. Her legs are wrapped in bandages. She has had a hard life and feels she was born forty years too soon. She tells you about it, speaking very rapidly in a low continuous monolague and you have to bend down to hear anything at all. Much of what she says is without shape or form, just lists of names and places that come tumbling out. So and so and so and so and someone else were good people, and is this man or that man still living or dead?

The Health Authorities keep a close eye on her and kind neighbours visit her regularly and wonder if she would be better off in a Home.

★

'I was born in the most wretched times that could ever be. My mother was dead and gone since I was three months old and my father was a drunkard. Oh, he was drinking every day, and my earliest memory was him stumbling around the kitchen trying to fasten his shoes before going off for a drink. The Dalys used to give it to him, and Mrs Collins, and the Byrnes whenever they got up. He used to be there for days talking nonsense, you know, about racing and that sort of thing, and when he came back he would break up the house. Shove in the door and put me out and everything. He was a confirmed drinker, and once he went into a public house he would never leave it. "How are you, John? Have a drink." He would drink fourteen pints of porter as easy as a baby sipping a bottle of milk and only come home when the money or credit ran out. Oh, he was a blackguard, a drinking blackguard.

"I have two choices to make," he told me one day, "to drink with them or go out of my mind." That's why he drank with them.

I was eight and a half when he sold the farm. The neighbours put him up to it, telling him that he only had a daughter at home and she would be no good. Then we went to Cappaghglass in 1912 and we lived in a rented house. But he hadn't any money, and he was spending more than he was making and wouldn't pay the rent. So they put him out and locked the door and we had no place to stay. He was searching everywhere until he found a small tumbledown house at Clohan and there I lived until I left school.

I must have been about ten years old, and in those days there was no School Act and you could come and go as you pleased. A neighbour's wife took me in, and I helped with the little jobs around: calves and pigs, bringing in the cows and housework of every sort. I tell you that it would be ten o'clock before your eyes were closed and you had your clothes off. You'd be that worn out. But you'd never complain, because there were lots of young people watching out for the first little job that was coming.

I was not unhappy, they were nice and good people. I got ten shillings a month and stayed ten years. They had old style ways then, and I was young and didn't take any notice. It was all washing and scrubbing down the floors, plucking fowl and any other little thing. The Mistress, as I used to call her – may she be in Heaven – treated me well and I was not unhappy. There was plenty if you worked for half nothing and if you were a slave. You would get meat sometimes, and there was plenty of fresh fish. The odd rabbit – but I never liked rabbit. There's the nature of the rat in the rabbit, you know. We had the bastible cake made from the pot hanging over the fire and a sack of flour was only ten shillings. All the farmers used to kill a pig – there was always a man in the district who would do the killing. If there were five or six in the house and you killed the pig in October he would last you till February or March. But I always hated killing, and if I even found a mouse caught by the paws I would take him to the door.

I can remember growing up . . . you were young, and then suddenly you were old and there was little or nothing in between. "Come here, Annie. Go there, Annie." The only free moment in any day was Sunday when I was let off for two hours. "Be back around six," the Mistress would tell me "because of dairying the cows." Oh, I could milk as fast as I could eat so long as they kept quiet and weren't kicking the bucket around the wall. The odd time I could sneak away with Mary Donovan and we used to walk to Cappaghglass for a social at the hall. She's dead and buried before me and she was younger than me.

I stayed there for ten long years before I quit, and I'll tell you how it was. They had a piggery then and there was no other water but the tank, and I had to draw the water south, and honest to God no one would help me. There were three men in the house and a couple of boys, but they wouldn't draw a bucket from the well or help to mix the pigs' food with the shovel. One day the sweat was running off me and I said that's one thing I was going to stop. "Do you know, Annie, girl," the Mistress said when I gave her a week's notice, "I won't stop you, but the devil you know is better than the devil you don't." I remember a week after I left I met Mrs Regan in the street at Cappaghglass. "Annie," she said, "would you ever give me the pleasure of coming back again?" "I don't know," I said, "the work is a bit on the hard side."

Poor Mrs Regan – may she rest in Heaven – it wasn't her fault, but the harsh times in which we were living. I went back to my father and took different jobs, anything I could get. On Mondays I got a shilling for washing from Mrs Donnelly and another shilling from Father McCarthy. I washed baths of clothes in water that would roast your face and then put the pots and everything outside the door. I scrubbed floors, thousands of floors. I worked in Dan Hegarty's shop emptying drawers and putting things on shelves, and I got a pain in my back and my knee. Some of my friends went away and worked in England and some got married. But in Ireland you should have money to get married. If I wanted to marry the son of a farmer, he'd have no regard for the likes of us because we hadn't any land. If we had the land we would be all right, but we were only working class people.

Till my father died I was looking after him. He was against bicycles in case I might get killed, and also false teeth. He wouldn't want you to go to the dentist at all. I got retirement at sixty-six, but it was only three pounds sixpence a week, and now things are much better. At one time people died of different things like the consumption. There was a lot of people getting it. Twenty pupils died of it at school. There used to be dancing every night, going from one little house to another, and they were carrying the disease. A whole family died of it. There was a carpenter and he lived near us and he had twelve children and every one and the father and the mother died of TB. And they were a grand family, you couldn't tell which of them was the nicest. The whole lot died. Cadogan was their name.

Did you hear anything about the Quinns? How the wife had a stroke and was laid up, and now she don't talk too plain at all. They are nice people, good people.

Once they gave you a medicine and a poultice for your chest and some whiskey. Now I'm taking pain killers for this leg. Are you a good judge of tablets? I take five or six of them every day. Put your hand on the dresser and get me a sup of water. Has the cat left his visiting card on the table again? I can't see a lot.

Upstairs is the coat from where they took the money. I had the money in the pocket pinned with a safety pin. Maybe it was ripped before it fell out. It could have brushed into the fire and anything could have happened. I was sitting here and while I was looking for my shoes they climbed upstairs and stole it. Another person would faint, but I didn't. I kept praying all the time to St Anthony and the Sacred Heart of Jesus and I wasn't lost.

When you are over eighty and are getting older you are not looking forward to anything. The neighbours look after me and a nurse comes in two or three times a week and dresses the varicose veins in my legs. Do you see the leg and the bright pink puff all around it? Whist . . . they wanted to put me in hospital. But I tell you I'm a lot happier sitting around here in my own home until I become so bad that no one can look after me. At a hospital I would have to leave the dog behind and the cat and all my clothes. And my sight is nearly gone and I wouldn't make out the other patients. I'd rather stay here. A woman from the Board of Health comes in the morning and gives me breakfast, and plugs in the kettle. And she brings a bucket of spring water and puts a glass on the table. Oh God, what would I do without it? She brings the dinner, now.

I have money, in spite of what they took. I have my pension. Last week I sent some money to a society in Dublin for looking after poor children. I gave a pound and posted the letter on Monday so they must have it by now. The woman who posted it for me is always running to devotions day and night, but I don't believe that people are strong at all in any religion, and although they still go to Mass they haven't the same faith at all. Mr Kelly said to me the other day that religion is gone by the board. Is he right? Today people only believe the things they want. They mightn't believe in St Anthony or they mightn't believe in these things. Sure they are all going to Lourdes to be cured, and if they haven't the belief, there's only one cure in a hundred in anything. And if you were on the road now and had an accident and you escaped, it's only because you believed and trusted in God that he will save you.

When I was young no woman would go into church without having her head covered. Now it makes no difference. Once life was safe, and every fellow was safe, and now you are afraid at every turn.

If I had any money I would leave it to the priests to say prayers for me, and also give money for the poor children and the black babies. That's the best thing to do, and that's what I would do if I had the money.'

Miss Hegarty, Matron, Old People's Home. Aged 51.

In the scrubbed and polished home old men mostly sit or lie on the beds. Sometimes they shuffle on sticks down the gleaming corridor to the day-room where they can watch television. Sometimes they quarrel. When the weather is fine a number of them wander outside and watch the passing cars.

The comfort of the place can be a drawback. In the old days, with harder chairs and less heat, they did a little gardening. Now after five minutes they tend to give up.

'They are all darlings.' But Miss Hegarty admitted that it takes a formidable amount of care and patience to look after them. 'We are doing it for the good Lord, and I hope He's taking note.' The reasons why they are here are as long as the list of their ailments. They are rambling, incoherent, grumbling, sad, happy and discontented.

There's a long waiting list to get in to the home.

★

'Most of the people here are in their seventies and eighties, and they are a bit like children. They need a lot of coaxing, and because everything is free, they get a bit self-centred and demanding. That's always the way. Dealing with the old takes a lot of patience, and it's not a good idea to have nurses straight out of training coming to a place like this. We try and choose our nurses. Sometimes old people might get on their nerves. You might explain something to them, and then they want you back in five minutes, and you would have to do the same thing again. As a local person I feel they have accepted me as one of their own, for it always takes time to get their trust. If you bully them, they will go right against you.

We try and keep people in their own homes if it is at all possible. When they come here we build them up, and perhaps in the summer they can return for a few months. But in most cases they have to remain here. In my experience, once they have settled down they don't want to leave. I have found that people who were born at the turn of the century when times were hard are grateful for the warmth and comfort we can provide.

We have everyone here. There are some who are very old and senile, and when that happens you get hardening of the arteries to the brain. They are living more in the past than in the present. They would be asking you if the cows were milked, and things they would have been doing, and you have to agree with them to keep them happy. A lot of the people we have are farmers, and they are always pottering around and busy. They are still interested in farming, and when any visitor comes in the first question they ask is the price of cattle.

When people get too sick and ill they may give up hope if you tell them they are dying. They are not able to take it. The medicine helps to give them a feeling of euphoria and the priest or rector always comes to visit them. I feel that they all know but don't talk about it. I try and make things easy for everyone.

I can't describe to you the pleasure a job like this gives me. I did it because I wanted to do it, but today it's harder to get people to make the sacrifices. Some of the families are to blame, but then I think so much of modern life makes old people feel discarded like an empty tin. I always like seeing visitors coming in, and so far as my old people are concerned, that's more important than anything else, even the medicine we give them.'

Pat Hicky, Pensioner in Old People's Home. Aged 83.

Wearing his trousers and shirt Pat sits up in bed in the dormitory. Beside him is a man lying immobile who's senile, and doesn't say anything or even blink his eyes like the crocodile in the zoo. It's hard work being old, Pat says. The summer is the worst, for it never seems to end. Other old people stare out of the windows towards the town where the tourists flock around the shops, and the harbour is full of yachts and the rattle of rigging. Pat can't do that because his sight is gone.

'You've too much time in the world, for the days are too long.' The day starts at five in the morning and goes on until three at night.

When his wife died they moved him here far away from the farm where he spent his life. He does not complain. The fortitude that saw him through hard times comes to his aid. And memory is sharp and clear. His pleasure is remembering places and people and friends who have died.

★

'On the first day of May the sun would be dancing around the sky in the rising. It was something that happened, because it wouldn't get up steady at all, and only dancing. And I was delighted by the birds for the music, and for picking up all the worms that would cut the corn on us. The pigeons were the only birds we didn't like, but the seagulls were harmless. You'd be ploughing with the whole fleet of seagulls following behind. They would let no scrape go, and as you reddened the scrape they were right behind you. They were so close you could hit them with the reins.

A scrape is what you do when ploughing, do you understand me? The two horses are taking the same step and know every word you would say. I would say "go" and she was gone, or "wait" and she stopped, and it didn't matter if the scrape was a hundred yards long, for they would follow you to the end.

Ploughing was the biggest thing and took the greatest skill. You had to keep the farrow straight for one thing, and if you turned the horse's tree and made an eighteen inch miss beside the road, you would be the talk of the whole county. Someone at the pub would surely get at you. "You are some ploughman you are," they would say straight out. Today they can plough and harrow sitting on their backsides up on the tractor. In my day it was walking after horses the whole day, and you'd be beat after walking through wet land. It's hard to describe to someone who hasn't worked with horses the companionship they can bring. I loved horses all my life, and only got rid of my last one when I came here. Our whole family was delighted with horses, and we broke our own. For breaking you want patience and love. You have to make him walk first, then you put him in a ring and ring him. Ring him one way, and ring him the other, and the next time he will be quite used to it.

You have to be gentle with him, putting him on a bridle and headstall. If you beat him with a rod he will try and get away from you. Talk is very good for horses, and they have a lot more understanding than a lot of people. You know the horse and you will be talking for the day. But with a tractor, it won't speak to you. The horse and the dog. I would go without my supper and give it to the horse. But they had to go like everything else. In my young days everyone had horses and jennets and traps and spring cars and all that sort of thing. I saw the end of it. It happened in a clap, and one day they were all there, and the next day they had gone. All motorcars in two years, and there wasn't an ass or a pony to be seen at Mass. That would be thirty-five years ago. A man that had a jennet would have a motor.

I am always thinking of those days, lying here in bed, and the cattle I once owned. It was all shorthorns then, and at the fairs I would look for a heifer with two fine hips standing up in front of the tail, and a good round rib not falling off the backbone at all.

It was all the shovel, the pike and the horse when I was young. A lot of the land was rough, but there was also a lot of clean land too. Christ, man, you should see the skin that was once on the land. Now there's nothing but bag manure, but in the old days it was all our own manure from the stables and weed. The weed was best for the land with all the potash in it, while the fertilizer is drying the good out of it. After a storm everyone would go down to the beach for the weed, and get what they liked of it during the winter. They would get the sea sand, and it was also used as a fertilizer then.

We worked from the time we were young. We had to work very hard coming back from school. We'd settle the outhouse for the cows, put bedding in, put hay under their mouths. There were pigs then, and along the road you'd pick green stuff. Crehans they were called. You would bring them home, cut them up and put milk over them. Pigs were made for them, it would fatten them. They had no banks at that time, and the pigs were the banks. Everyone who worked on the farm had pigs.

We had plenty of good times in those days. Often I lie here in bed and think of the sport we had. There was Christmas. When I was a child Christmas was always a big occasion, even though we might only have a penny whistle. We had a lighted tree and candles in every window, and that light is saying everyone is welcome. You'd get a cup of tea and then you would have a talk. Sometimes we got a turkey, but usually it was a goose. And a grand big currant cake and raisins and everything. The ten of us would sit down before the fire, and my father would sing and tell stories that would frighten us.

After Christmas it was the Wren boys. You got old clothes and papers around you and blackened your eyes. Nowadays they are only children, if you like, grabbing the holly bush and singing, the Wren, the Wren. They haven't it right at all. In the old days the men were doing it, a fine crowd of big strong men. They used to have a horse and trap, and there would be a score of them together, and they would travel away through the towns and into the country. They were very nice, all dressed up with ribbons and colours. There was a crowd of men from Parkgarriff, a beautiful crowd. They were very decent fellows. Some of them would have their faces and eyes done, and some had paper masks and you wouldn't know who they would be. At some farmer's house they would go to they'd have a big night after what they would make out of the Wren, and have music and dance and porter. On Stephen's night that would be.

My father's stories were about banshees and ghosts and dead people walking about. When I was young the old men had the finest stories you ever heard about everything like that. Have you ever heard of a banshee? The banshee would give three different cries at three different places and then you knew something would happen and someone would die. Did they hear the cries going through their heads, I wonder, or did they imagine it? You know the song?

The banshee's wail tells a sad, sad tale . . .
For my darling died in his youth and pride
to set old Ireland free.

These old stories were to frighten us as children. They were to destroy us. The fairy tales, all the fairies here and the fairies there. They'd give us such a fright we wouldn't go through the door. All the old people told the stories. They were all lies. One of them was trying to best the other thinking of things and telling them. Jesus, we were frightened. I was waking up crying in the night for the fear of them. They would tell a dead man would come alive, and they hadn't the common sense to know that. You couldn't believe the Lord's Prayer out of them. They'd tell such bare-faced lies, and give a sound name for it, you know. Oh yes, I believed it. 'Tis silly really. I don't like to tell a man like yourself the way we believed in fairies. Most of us believed them a little, anyway. They were like the clouds in the sky, always moving and changing their shape, and you could never catch them no matter how hard you tried.

I had one experience and that put an end to all the talk about fairies. One night I was coming home and wheeling the bike up the hill, when two boys thought they would give me a bit of a lark. One fellow took off his pants, and he had long johns, and then turned his coat inside out and put some newspaper around his hat. I had what they called a "bobby dodger" on my bike, but the light was too weak anyhow, and I could see this thing prancing around the middle of the road. They say your hair will stand with fright, and I can swear that it does. But what gave them away was the hugh . . . hugh of breathing and I soon realized that it was a live person. I said, whoever you are, you are for it, and at that moment the other fellow jumped out of a bush beside the road and I recognized the two of them. After that I never believed in fairies.

A flash in the sky was a fairy. And they had pishogues, a kind of religion handed down to them. They wouldn't even paint a door green. On May Day they put green on the door. Putting green on doors for May Day, that's all over the world wherever you go. You wouldn't let anyone in the house at all on May Day because everyone that came in would be taking away the luck. You couldn't smoke a pipe going into the house on the first of May, that was a very strong belief. You might smoke inside, but you wouldn't be able to go outside with it lighting. Anyone with common sense would know that was crazy.

Monday was a fairy day and you would have no luck. You wouldn't go to a bank on Monday, or take money out, or give your neighbours a pint of milk or get married or anything else like that. They talked about fairies the whole time. The fairies did good and bad. Sure, it was all lies, and we wished to believe them. It's like Santa with a child and gradually you grow out of it.

If you ask me now, what finally killed the fairies around here, it was the Tan War. During the Troubles people were out at all hours planning and moving in the dark, and that broke it up. In spite of all, I don't like to pass a single magpie without calling out "good morning" and crossing myself.

I had an aunt who lived to be more than ninety. We were talking about Adam and Eve and she was positively certain that Adam bit the apple, that Eve gave the apple to Adam. She never believed in the sin of impurity. She never thought at all that Adam rode Eve, she never thought of that. Oh, no. It was the apple, for fuck's sake. The old people believed anything, but it was a genuine belief. There was no doubt about that. They had a one track mind. They'd do anything for priests and nuns, saying prayers and rosaries . . . And a very good way, too.

The station master at Cappaghglass had a red beard and hair, and the fishermen didn't like to see him, for they knew they wouldn't get a fish. They tried to avoid him. I remember one time a woman going for a train and seeing a magpie and coming back home again. All those things, and whistling in a boat. Whistling up a wind, they'd say.

On St John's Eve all the bonfires were lit to protect the potatoes from the blight. They'd light that fire in the country everywhere. We would cut the bushes and put a heap of them together and the smoke would cross the potatoes with the wind. It put a St John's blessing on the potatoes. St John was beheaded, wasn't he? And the blight came that year, and all the people were hungry.

On May night they'd settle down the fire, and they laid down the table cloth. Plenty of bread and butter, jam and cups, and they were sure the fairies would come and enjoy themselves and be gone in the morning. I wouldn't like that idea, would you? Anything for May Day. The women used dew which was meant to give you good looks or something. And the buttermilk. Those people were crazy, going to the well to be the first to get the water and keep it a cure until next May Day. You'd sprinkle yourself with it. We used to collect the holy water from the well and sprinkle it on the seed before you planted it. We kept a bottle inside for the cure, and you could drink it any time. If you didn't have the well water, you'd have the church water. I think that was a bit sensible . . . blessed water. My uncle cured his back with church water.

It's all civilized now, but in the old days they had thatched houses. The thatch came from the wheat and straw, and they had earth floors and an open fire. They had small windows, but they were very warm. The thatch wouldn't last long, and you were always putting on a little all the time. Most of the people near me were farmers in a small way. They would go out with a scythe and cut furze and carry it on their back. They would carry bags of turf and turnips and stuff for the cattle. The roads then were nearly always those muddy old roads kept with stones. In summer the dust of them would be terrible.

Sometimes it was worse than other times. I remember a great drought, it must have been fifty years ago, and the whole country was as white as this sheet – a pure white. We had to buy barrels, you got the two halves, top and bottom, and we'd go to the lakes and fill them up with water. A line of boys and girls back and forwards to the carts. Later the barrels were used for curing crubeens.

In my time people were very poor and they hadn't a bit in the world wide. Do you know I never went to Dublin because I had no shoes? I had only the one pair, and they were an old nailed pair of boots. Mostly people would make their own bit of business themselves or took the emigration to America. I would have liked to have gone to America, for as they say, foreign cows wear long horns, but it didn't work out that way, and I stayed on the farm. I got married, and that's another story.

Mine was a "made" match, like most of the others around here. In those days a love match was quite rare. Anyone who had a girl was interested in a fellow who had a farm. The matchmaker was a shopkeeper who knew both families. I met my wife, God rest her, at the match. Before that there had been quite a few others, and all the time my father was desperate to get me married, because he was losing the old age pension. I had met quite a few girls, but there was always something wrong, and a personality in the way, if you know what I mean. Certain families have personalities, and they don't like other families, and it would be like getting married to a devil with two tails. Your life wouldn't be your own. I suppose in one sense it was a bad system, but people in those days also seemed to get on much better. Most of my friends got married around forty – that was considered quite young and respectable. I was over thirty myself. I suppose you are married yourself, and you know that marriages don't run like a lake without a wind. Naturally there are breezes, and anyone will tell you that a husband and wife don't have a fight, that's a cod as far as I know.

You might think that an old man like myself is living on borrowed time, and a few years more will see me out. My eyes aren't too good now, but my hearing isn't bad. I had a great jolly life all my life. I was always happy, and I'll tell you I had a great life. I lie here in bed and think of the old times.'

Denis Murphy, Pensioner in Old People's Home. Aged 77.

Denis has a handsome saint's face topped by a cloth cap which he wears inside and out. On most fine days he will trot outside and sit in the sun watching the passing traffic. He has a history of illness for much of his life, and perhaps this has made him settle into his kindly prison more easily than many other pensioners. His smile is beatific.

★

'In October 1938 I joined the British Navy, for I hadn't any money. I took a chance. I said goodbye to my mother and away I went. First I went to Devonport, to do my training, and it was very nice all right. I had a uniform, regular money, good grub, and to tell you the truth, after a short time I never missed home.

Occasionally queer things happened to you in the navy. I remember one morning we were on parade doing rifle drilling and this bloke came around to me with a slip from the dentist. He said "Mick" – for all Irishmen were called Mick – "you have to do it. That's what orders are for." So I was forced to see the dentist and it was the first ever time in my life. My God, he was a big man, a three-ringed commander and a face on him that would tame a bull.

When he looked at my teeth he said, "Do you know," he says, "that you have the most marvellous teeth and should treasure them like gold. But you must learn to wash them. Next pay day get a sixpenny toothbrush and paste and wash your teeth before you go to bed at night. Don't brush them across, but up and down . . . God," he says, "I never saw a mouth of teeth like them." I still have them bar one. I regret the one. It was aching and I went to a fool of a dentist in the town. I sat on a chair and he got a pincers and put it in my mouth and turned and twisted and pulled. Oh God it was agony, and he pulled out that good tooth. The dentists in those days didn't give a damn. My brother went, and the man used pincers on him for shooing a horse and gave him a clip with them when he didn't sit still.

I went on convoys to Russia. I was in Russia nine times on nine different convoys patrolling around, mine-sweeping and looking out for submarines. The last convoy was some time in 1942. We sailed from Cape Wrath, that's in the North of Scotland, and the convoy consisted of forty-six ships and they were all attacked by air and submarine. Do you know only six ships got as far as Archangel.

I thought Russia was a strange place. The port of Archangel was all timber and trees, and when we went into a restaurant there was nothing except black bread and meat. They said it was reindeer meat that came down from the mountains, and we didn't eat it at all. Before going ashore we were told by our skipper to take very little vodka, and to make sure they gave us very little money. The Russian people were working class like ourselves, but you couldn't say anything to them not knowing their language.

I remember one Sunday service we had at Archangel. We were all dressed up for it on the quarterdeck, and some fellow would read the prayers – a lieutenant, or skipper or whatever he would be – and the Roman Catholics would fall out. This Sunday they held it ashore on the pier jetty, and when we were told to step forward and fall out, one of the Russians who could speak a little English asked what it was all about. I said "religion", and at that he threw a big spit on the ground and kicked it with his hobnail boot. Then he joined his friends, and they had picks on their shoulders and they marched off in military style. I didn't say anything more, but I always remember that.

Soon after I got ill and was invalided out of the Navy. To tell the truth I didn't mind, I was tired of the war with all the risk. But I have had terrible trouble with my health. The doctors are fine here and so are the old nurses. In the old days the doctors didn't give a damn. I might go at six o'clock. Come back in the morning. Go home again. They didn't give a damn.

Once I went to the bone setter rather than to the old doctor. Old Mick O'Brien put in a bone for me, a couple of bones, I'd say. And his grandson fixed my hand again. 'Tis going down from father to son, and the son will never do anything as long as the father lives. I have had great faith in them. Oh listen . . . 'tis definitely, decidedly and emphatically, 'tis indisputable there was nothing better. But today I would advise anyone who has a hand broke to go to hospital. Because they will X-ray and he will be asleep before the count of fourteen and wake up in bed with his hand in plaster of Paris and no pain. The bone man was painful all right because he had no anaesthetics.

There was a doctor in Cappaghglass called Malone – he gave me old pills, they were no good. I was in Parkgarriff one day, and someone told me to try this Dr Doyle in Parkgarriff. I did, and he sent me for an X-ray. I had a desperate pain in my stomach at the time. I got the result, nothing wrong. I went back to Cappaghglass, and I went to the doctor. He says, "What fault did you find with me?" I told him, I thought a fellow could go where he liked. You can go where you like, he said, and he never bothered with me after.

In the old days you didn't send to the doctor unless you were very sick, because you couldn't bloody well afford him. It was very rare for him to come into your home. The doctor was like King Solomon, and you didn't pop in to see him the way you do now. When he came to your house it was a kind of dread. You know, the houses long ago were untidy, and a hen might come in, and it wouldn't be grand enough for him. Then, in large families, the house was full and you didn't have water and you didn't have toilets or anything.

And, oh, my Christ, things have changed at the hospitals. When I was younger, and that was forty years ago, I had a spell in a big city hospital. It was desperate then, you know, and the nurses were not allowed to talk to the patients. You'd be lying there, and they couldn't give you the time of day. I was there three months, and my God, the cold and the hunger, but it was a bad time at the end of the war. The Sister came in one day, and she said to the nurse, "Turn on the lights," she said, "to keep the place warm."

I went back in seventy-two, and well, I couldn't believe it. It was like home from home. I'd stay there now, if they'd have me. The nurses were so friendly. How are you, Mr Murphy, and they used to call me the Cappaghglass farmer. How's the Cappaghglass farmer today? They were absolutely grand. And the doctors. Doctors in my young days were tyrants. They were semi-gods, like. The parish priest, the doctor and the school-teacher were the three tyrants.

God knows I love the people that is going around now. I'm satisfied with them. They are good to me here, but it's like being in prison, the same as being in jail. You are under orders and have to do what you are told. Oh, I would smoke the devil! I would if I could catch him. The doctor put me off him. I got an old flu in the chest, and I did have to stop it. The doctor won't let you go out until you are fit to go. You get a month in jail if you go out in the road without his sayso.'

Jerry O'Keefe, Pensioner in Old People's Home. Aged 80.

A plump man whose speech is difficult to understand. His teeth fit badly, and they are a distraction, moving about in a rhythm of their own. He is a widower who has been in the home for three years. Before that he was a railway man. The railway line swept past his door, a gleaming steel track on its bed of gravel and wooden sleepers. Two miles up was the old stone bridge and level crossing. He worked on the line until it closed in the early 'fifties. He can remember the names of the old trains, the Nationalist, the Erin and the Mountain Dew, and their different whistles. It's all in his head, waiting to go like the guard's green flag.

★

'I was loading the cattle in Cappaghglass for years into the railway wagons. The wagons would carry four cows, twelve little yearlings and twelve to thirteen pigs. There was a screeching and a roaring, but you took no notice. I used to hold a flag out when the train was coming. A small piece of timber with a red flag, a little red cloth tacked on to the end of the stick and the other was a green. And if the coast was clear you'd hold out the green one and if there was anything on the line it would be the red one.

At one time there there were four trains a day into Cappaghglass. They had one first class carriage with a soft seat and a couple of second class carriages as well. They were quite nice with varnished wooden seats. There would be a big line of carts, hackney cars and ponies and the hauliers who used to draw the stuff all waiting at the station. And the man with a handcart from the hotel to collect the guests' luggage. On fair days especially there would be extra business and there might be fifteen carriages and wagons, and I never thought they would come around the bend. A lot of people took the train to the fairs, but in the last years they used to run it on turf and you might as well walk.

It was a grand ride from Cappaghglass to Curragheen. You'd be about an hour and a half doing the fifteen miles. It was slow all right. You'd go beyond to Cork and that was the way of the emigrants. A ticket to America cost twenty pounds. There were a few out of every family. There were four out of our family, there were four out of the Sullivans beside us. In 1923 they had a very good football team in the town, a team of fine strong young men. And in 1924 half the team went to America together, and that was the end of it. There was the Murphy boy going from Cappard and his brother came down to see him off. And he was very lonesome for his brother going away on the train. And when the train pulled out of the station he said, "Blast you, Smokey Hole, East, many a good man you've carried away!"

They went by train to Cobh. And then you'd see the liners passing up here every Sunday. The Cunard mostly, and the White Star was there too. You'd know the liner might leave Cobh at a certain time and pass here a few hours later. You would look out for them, if there was anyone belonging to you on them. Some lit bonfires on the hill so that their people could see the smoke from the deck of the ship.

The islanders used to watch their people go and emigrate, and all the island women falling down on the ground and they are never again to see their sons. They'd start that hullagoing★. They'd do it anytime. I remember the people buried from the island. They'd come out to Lisheen and down to Cappaghglass and they'd keep up the hullagoing, hullagoing, all the way along. One time two men were going out to the island and the boat was sinking – they were bringing out potatoes to sow. And when they threw out the seed, the boat was capsized and one man was drowned. And his brother went out the way of this place where I was standing, going south with the body to the strand. Well, you'd hear him, such a hullagoing, you could hear it going away to Carrolaska.

I was told in the old days when a landlord put people out they started that hullagoing and they'd keep it up for days.

It was nice to see the old train coming up the hill. But all these things have changed and I suppose we change too. They have done away with all the railways. The railway stopped and then there was only the bus. They took everything away. It was all collected. Even a nut they didn't leave behind.

There's a carriage that survives over in a yard at Curragheen. It's got two seats left in it. They say if you sit on it and have six or seven pints it starts to move.'

★ Probable derivation agualohfairt – grieving, keening.

Dan Brady, Retired Pensioner. Aged 74.

Another who will end his days in the Home. Arthritis brought him here at a comparatively early age. There is a desperation in the way he progresses down the passages on his two sticks. He is a very small man with a very undershot jaw and has given up any attempt to shave it.

★

'I am just old enough to remember the First World War and the lads who went off to fight. They were all mad. There was a man by the name of Johnny Sullivan and when he returned you couldn't put down sixpence on his body with the marks of the bullet holes that were on him. Sure he was stone mad. Another man by the name of Tim Donovan was shell-shocked and could only look at you. He was lying there in bed all the time.

It was terrible the First War. There used to be a lot of wreck coming in on the shore – bits and pieces. I dream it.

The Black and Tans were very busy here because of the coast guard station. I remember when the coast guard station was taken by the IRA from the coast guards. It was a Sunday morning. I remember listening to the rifle fire outside the station. The navy then came into the harbour, and rounded up all the men in the whole parish of Cappaghglass into a field. Some of them were old men, and some were young men. They rounded them into a field near the coastguard station, and they questioned them all. The Black and Tans came over the hills in hundreds.

They came and searched the house. I remember being stretched in bed and hearing them come about two in the morning to the door. They banged at the door with the butt end of a rifle and came to search the house. At that time there had to be a notice. You had to write down all the members of the family. My father was in bed, and he asked them to give him time to dress himself, and they kept butting the door anyway till he let them in. I remember them coming upstairs to us. We were inside the bed and I remember them running their hands along our legs to see if we had our legs crippled up – to see how tall we were –

to see if we were men or boys. I remember that. To see if men were there. I was nine or ten at the time. Its very hard to forget things, especially the Irish. I think we were trampled by the English for far too long.

You didn't know what was going to get you. First it was the Tans banging away, and then it was our own lads. The Free State soldiers, and what we called "the boys" or Irregulars, and many times I lay in a ditch with the bullets flying above. Fighting and ambushing and killing each other, that's how it was and still is in Ireland today. We can't stop it.

In the Second World War a German plane came in low and hit the mountain. I went up to look at it with a group of lads, and it was dreadful to see the bodies thrown around – a bit of a leg here or an ankle there, they were all blown to bits or roasted. When we were going up I met a fellow called Dinny Hickey coming down. He had something in his hands, and I said "What's that you've got?" And he said, "I have a boot, man, a German boot. Do you see, a flyer's boot?" So I said, "Give me a look at it. What happened to the other one?" "Oh, I couldn't find the other one." So he handed it to me, and I had a look at this boot, and the next thing I saw was a fellow's shin bone at the bottom of it. I said, "Dinny, did you look into the boot?" "No," he said. "Have a look inside it now," says I. So he looked. Oh God! and he threw it away as far as he could. I didn't follow it either, and for all I know it's still lying where he threw it on the mountain.

I think that when the next war comes it will be worse again. The stuff is made, and the chances are that it will be thrown. What are you going to do with it, leave it to air? I'd say that the danger is hanging there, and if there was any intrusion on America she will throw it. She will throw it sooner than Russia. Sure, they threw it on the Japs, and it was horrid.'

THE TOWN

PETER DOYLE	Shopkeeper, *Aged 55*
WINNIE O'DWYER	Publican, *Aged 60*
PRONSIAS REGAN	Hotel Keeper, *Aged 55*
JOE MACNEIL	Butcher, *Aged 56*
TIM HARRINGTON	Baker, *Aged 58*
MICHAEL O'SHEA	Postmaster, *Aged 58*
PETER CORKERY	Postman, *Aged 72*
NOEL KENNEDY	Garda Sergeant, *Aged 55*
GERARD WHITE	Solicitor, *Aged 38*
LIAM HEGARTY	Republican, *Aged 84*
MICK O'KEEFE	Stone Mason, *Aged 62*

In many ways the town is an alien world, even a hostile one to the countryman. He feels its scorn for his rusticity and dislikes its urbane ways. Yet the town has also an attraction for him. It weans away his sons and daughters – it brings him a breath of the outside world.

The Irish Countryman,
M. Arensberg.

Peter Doyle, Shopkeeper. Aged 55.

The draper and haberdashery stands prominently in the main street. Once known as an emporium, it used to sell everything from hob-nailed boots to sticky black oilskins, sides of bacon, tin openers and ladies' lingerie. The boast of Peter's father and grandfather was that at Doyle's you could buy anything from a thimble to an engine, and a person could be fitted out from the cradle to the grave.

His grandfather came from an immense 19th century family that scattered its progeny all over the civilized world. Half a dozen or so went to America, a couple went to Australia where one vanished, and several sailed for England. Old Mr Doyle stayed behind, took his chance, abandoned farming and started the business.

It really started to flourish after the Treaty. Many of the shopkeepers in Cappaghglass were Protestant, and in spite of their good standing, they decided to emigrate. This left a commercial vacuum in the town which Doyle's filled up.

Peter has an old photograph showing the old solid front of the shop; you can see shawled figures, barefoot boys and some carts drawn up in the muddy street. It was taken in 1925, by which year his father was in charge. In that year he bought one of the first Model T Fords in Cappaghglass. Because of the bad roads almost every journey meant a broken spring or a puncture.

Peter is a small thin eager man, whom contemporaries regard as having been born with a silver spoon in his mouth. When he was young he had the opportunity of entering his father's business, and didn't have to take the boat. They forgot that good fortune was thrust upon him and was hard to push aside. There was a dynastic feeling about his situation. That didn't stop him being started off behind the counter.

★

'My grandfather opened the place in September, 1900. I know that date because my father was born in the same month in the following year. I was born myself in 1928, and my earliest impression of the shop was that it was like a palace. There was the carving over the main door, the great gold scroll with our name, and inside the pitch-pine panelling and the big pitch-pine counters and what we called the "sling" that carried the change. I used to spend hours watching the assistants undo the screw top and give it a pull and make it go whizzing over people's heads.

When you first came into the shop then, you saw everything. It would be hard to believe the stock that my father carried. Just inside the door were the groceries. Everything was loose, and it's packed today. The sugar was loose, the dried fruit was loose and we had to pack them all. We hadn't the variety of fruit you have today – we had bananas, all right, but, for instance, no grapefruit. I didn't know what a grapefruit was like, and the first I ever saw was one floating into the strand. I was a kid then, and I remember thinking it was some kind of seaweed.

We would also sell bacon and general groceries. I remember on fair days when the whole town was chock-a-block, we used to have a special counter at the end of the shop where we didn't do anything except sell pigs' heads. We'd sell about four barrels of heads, and there was three hundredweight in a barrel in a day. We had three people behind this counter selling heads which will give you an idea. Have you never eaten a pig's head? Pig's head and cabbage was the poor man's food, and it was damn good. We used to buy what they called Danish heads. They were very small little heads, and we imported them. They were a penny-halfpenny a pound and tuppence, and people would argue like blazes. We had those big hanging scales behind the counter, the sort of thing that is considered an antique nowadays.

Then there was the drapery and footwear, and further down, bits of rope and hardware. Many things were parcelled up in boxes then, or in packets with the size and numbering on it. There was a lovely old sign across the shop which we still have, and it says, *No Second Price*. It meant that the prices were fixed, and there was no haggling. Many people used to be famous for haggling, and a lot of other traders used to put up their prices, so that they could bring them down. But my grandfather said he had a fixed price, and that was that.

In those days they were advertising the Cunard and White Star lines, and my father acted as a sort of agent. I can remember the old billheads around the place. Passages to America, £29 Second Class, £35 Return, Tourist Class, and the names of the different ships. Of course, it was only a small part of the business, and now that I look back on it, a very sad part. Almost every day a train was leaving packed with men and women carrying their cases to the boat.

I can remember how the conversation used to be, "Who's gone today?" for everyone was leaving in batches in the 'forties and 'fifties. I think the year they closed the railway was a sort of peak, because by then so many people had already left it was almost a ghost town. You had the publicans and shopkeepers all right, and very few others. Of course the old people seemed like a wave about to engulf the young ones. So any young person growing up at that stage didn't wait around, and they were usually gone when they would jump from the cradle. Those that were left would be people like myself who inherited a business or a farm, or had to look after an old father or mother, and there was no way out. You could say, if you were trying to analyze them, that they were more loyal than the ones who left, but an awful lot of them grew bitter. For they in their turn were left sitting in their houses, and when they grew old there was no one to look after them.

I've thought about emigration a good deal, and I can see the other side of it. What is going to happen now there's no escape? This country is completely bankrupt. It frightened me when I was in Curragheen the other day and there were eight or nine buses with school children . . . and where are these kids going to get jobs? They haven't the option to emigrate – no country wants us. It's all very well talking about the haemorrhage of people, the way we used to, and which was maybe a load of rubbish, for it's a grand thing to be able to emigrate and send money home. I was saying to my nephew the other day, you'll see the day, I mightn't see it, when you'll be having doctors driving your van because they can't get jobs. As a matter of fact, and I shouldn't say it, the more educated they are the more troublesome they are going to be, because they are going to get very dissatisfied and they won't settle down on the farms like they did before. My cousin's farm in Waterford has five hundred acres, and two fellows are running it with the aid of machinery where there used to be fifteen employed. You can't regiment educated people.

We've rather got off the subject. Pig's heads . . . I'll tell you about the drapery now. In fact most of the money we made came from the drapery and footwear side, and that was always regarded as very important. We sold stockings, ladies' underwear, trousers, shirts, hats and men's underwear and the heavy grey working sock that used to be three and eleven. That would be the equivalent of one pound thirty pence today. The shoes and boots were of the heavy hobnailed variety, and were sold from one pound fifteen shillings to two pounds during the 'forties. I can always remember the red flanelette, and the old women coming in and chewing it to test it for quality. When I took over from my father, and closed down part of the business, there were volumes and volumes of knickers, and in the name of Christ, what did they need that collection for?

I think most of the other shopkeepers in a place like Cappaghglass can say like myself that their grandparents came off the sod. When my grandfather was young he never wore shoes. When he got a new pair from his father to come into town, he brought them on his back until he came to the first shop. He could remember the long cars and the mail coaches, and how before the road was tarred you could see them coming miles away by the clouds of dust. When he ran the shop he had a big cart with big wheels on it, which would go around making deliveries, and the man who drove it was called Jack the Mail.

When I left school and entered the shop, the place was still very much the old style Irish town: the mountains behind it and the sea in front, and bugger all else, you know. I was sort of apprenticed to the business, and at that time there must have been half a dozen other men working in the shop. We opened at eight in the morning, we had no holidays as such, and we worked six days a week. When I started, someone would tell me what to do. "You go and clean the windows. You go down and sweep the floor. Make sure that all the doors are shut at night and the windows closed." The older people didn't trust the young to do anything right, and when customers came in, they would always say, "I want Mr Dempsey," or "I want such-a-one," for those were the ones they knew and trusted. We were only the young fellows, and I'd say that was the general rule.

I served my time four years learning the trade of shop assistant to my father, and I don't think I ever qualified in his eyes, for he was that discerning. The slightest fault would mean a good thumping, and you were expected to be twenty-four hours on your feet and always smiling. I learnt a bit about everything and was master of nothing. How to sell women's hats or yellow meal that was stronger and harder to digest than porridge, or the salted ling we had hanging from the ceiling. In damp weather it would run a bit, but in nice weather it would keep hard and dry. People liked nothing better than a feed of ling, particularly before Christmas. It's still best served with a thick milk and onion sauce.

I suppose where the training – if you can call it that – helped was on the drapery. How to trim a suit so that it could be made up by a local tailor, and there must have been about a dozen of them around the town. You would have to know if it was a two-piece or a three-piece, and how many buttons he would want on the jacket. Normally a two-piece suit took three and a quarter yards, and then there was the lining, pocketing linen and buttons. Everything would be correct with the old crowd, and more formal. When I started they wore the plain navy serge suit or the plain dark grey, and for work it would be heavy frieze trousers, a ganzy and tweed cap. My grandfather always wore a navy blue suit which was called a Crisdale, and a black bowler. We also had ready made shoes, plain shoes with the toecap and no fancy gimmicks. They were all leather soled.

Certain times of the year would be especially important. Just before Christmas the island people would stock up the shops after selling their cattle. It was always a grand moment when they would come in carrying half-sacks and take away a couple of hundred pounds' worth of stuff. Things like blankets, clothes and caps, and there was always a bag of flour and a bottle of rum and a bottle of whiskey. You'd wrap them specially so that they wouldn't get broken.

The other main thing was the fairs. On a good fair day the cattle would stretch down the street from one end of the town to the other. It was always a busy time; the farmers had money in their pockets and would pay their accounts. There was no such thing as going off to lunch, and you were expected to be everywhere at once. The old farming expression was "I'll pay you on fair day."

It's hard today just to realize how short money was for nearly everyone. My father says that he remembered the time when there was not a hundred pounds between Cappaghglass and Galway or Cork. It just wasn't there. For shopkeepers this meant that everything was put on credit. Most people thought that my father, John Doyle, was made of money, and you had to wait. Although they were basically honest, and their word was their bond, they didn't understand the credit system. People came in and were charged up, there was no question of ever refusing them. Only very rarely did they pay in cash.

I could show you ledgers with hundreds of accounts for even a penny. I was looking at one of them recently and was wondering if I should throw it away, and saw that a fellow bought a big china jug for two and sixpence sometime in the 'twenties, and he only put down tuppence on it two years later. As they say down here, "my father carried many a family" and he sent them to America by giving them credit. It was accepted that you would take a chance on them and let the children grow up, for at that time there was nearly always a priest in the family who could be relied on to pay the debt.

The trouble was, of course, that no one seemed to realize how difficult it was for the shopkeepers. When I gave up the animal feedstuffs in 1965 you had only a shilling profit on a hundredweight of meal, and you couldn't make money out of it. My father got into very heavy debt, for there was a lot of money owing, and because of this he was forced to sell the farm.

Even now I sometimes get people who owe us money. Last year an American family, who were tourists down here, told me that their parents had left an account that was never paid. It dated back even before the war. They knew it was there and wanted to settle things. I think the total bill was around ten or eleven pounds. When I gave them the receipt they picked out twenty dollars and said, 'You bring your wife out to dinner tonight, and thank you for the patience,' and the rest of it.

Everybody used to come in with their shopping list and hand it to the girl who gathered everything and that was written into your account book. There was no question of you paying cash. In that way the shop could become the larder for the whole village. And everything delivered – the doctor's wife and the bank manager's wife and people like that used to get their big lumps of butter, about eleven pounds. They didn't even have to come to the shop unless they wished. But you'd see them, holding up a candle to the eggs to check each one was all right and wouldn't be blurred. There were times when we carried them along with everyone else. The whole town was on credit. It was a hell of a system to get out from, and in the 'sixties when I said enough is enough, many people took it as an insult.

So much has happened in Ireland, and so much in Cappaghglass and even in our old shop. The old style commercial traveller with his bowler hat, spats and umbrella who used to call in and take orders has gone. Deliveries have gone. But the biggest change has been the arrival of tourists. When I was a boy growing up here they were like Tibetans, and everyone would come out of their houses to stare. But it didn't take long for things to change. At first tourists were a chancy business. The great thing was to come in the summer, draw like hell, and at the end of the day say "Post me the bill."

In the late 'fifties we began to get the first trickle of English tourists, the sort of people who thought that all the Irish were absolutely charming, and who liked being waited on in their cars and being called titles like Captain and Major. I remember one particular Englishman, and we were deciding in the shop whether we would call him Captain, and two years later everyone was calling him Captain, although I knew for a fact that he had never been in the navy or army. It was the sort of thing to do. Even today you still get a trace of the landlord-tenant bit when a doctor comes in and we will say, "Yes doctor, no doctor, we will have it for you in two minutes, doctor . . ." and he will be looked after first, for the doctor is still looked up to and respected.

I must say I'm in favour of it, and I'll be the first to demonstrate what you might call servility. I think the old politeness which I remember and which was once taken for granted is vanishing. There isn't the proper respect for people today, let him be your priest or whatever. OK, I suppose the business of calling people Captain and so on was pretty ridiculous, but standards have slipped too much altogether. This thing of people twice your age saying "Call me Frank" when you haven't the slightest interest in calling him Frank. A man came in the other day and asked me for the address of Eddy Humphries, the rector. I looked at him and said, "Do you mean Mr Humphries?", but he didn't get the message. I hate that tendency among the younger doctors and vets, and they are called Denis or Pat or the other. I'm very much with the older people calling a doctor – Dr such-a-fellow. It won't be long before the priests are all Denis and Pat as well.

As I was saying about tourists, the English were the first to arrive, and now we have seen the lot of them, you can say the English were by far the most popular. They spent their money and enjoyed them-selves. There's no way of understanding the Germans, French or Dutch, and as for buying anything, they are as mean as hell. They have the money all right, but we don't know what they do with it.

Quite a few of the English stayed. Retired people, a lot of them, and younger ones as well who bought houses in the area. They were liked well enough, but they have never integrated, even those who have been living here for years. It's sad that when people have been in a place twenty years they are still called "the Englishman up there", and you'd think that in a rural place like this people would mix better. But they don't. Oh, they are very polite on the surface, and there is no question of antagonism, but they are still identified as English or Protestant. There's one old woman who lives here and has a fruity English voice, and she swears she is Irish, but nobody believes her unless they know about her. The ordinary person listening thinks, Irish, my eye, because they judge by accent.

I must be honest about this, for I am talking of the basics, English versus Irish, and there is a very strong feeling under the surface. When I was at school the Irish history books were an absolute disgrace. Anything English was bad, and everything Irish had to be good. It's ridiculous, and now that I am older this sort of thing makes me angry. We have a lot in common, the same language, not to mention eight hundred years of tearing one another asunder. All right, the Irish integrate better in England than the English do in Ireland, but that's no reason for keeping any antagonism going. If you look at the map of Europe, we are all on our own on the left hand side, and we should be able to get on together – and we can't, really.

In other ways things are changing more positively. I think television has a lot to do with it, and people today are much more open and not afraid to speak their minds. A man will talk about something like divorce or contraception, and ten years ago this couldn't have happened. You had this battle of wits between the clergy and people. The clergy were afraid to ease up, because they would have had old ladies coming up and saying, just look what he is allowing in his parish, and then you had the people running to the priest about things, and the priest looking over his shoulder because the bishop was right behind him. I suppose I can speak for the Catholic religion, for I was brought up that way when religion and nationalism went together, and everyone was suffering from Jansenism and the Church of Ireland people felt the same siege way.

Mind you I also think that in some ways we have gone too far. I don't know if it is the effect of television or tourism, or what, but the younger people are a different crowd. They are all boozing, and I'm sure some of them are on drugs, and they don't know what to do with their money, and they are all sleeping around.'

Winnie O'Dwyer, Publican. Aged 60.

There are twenty-two licensed premises in Cappaghglass, a fraction of what there used to be. One of them is O'Dwyer's, a corner pub with an exterior whose woodwork is painted ox-blood, and the name in black and gold over the door. In the window a large ginger cat dozes in the sun beside a bunch of plastic flowers. Inside there is a sense of warmth and cosiness about the bar and shop, the kitchen behind and the room which they still call the snug. The stranger to Cappaghglass makes an instinctive step towards O'Dwyer's and, seduced by the friendliness, will keep coming back.

The place is run by a brother and sister. Winnie is the more dominant of the pair, a determined looking woman who is generally regarded as a source of information about the whole area. She knows the times of buses, the reasons for family quarrels, the latest rise in prices, and will give you an opinion about most senior members of the government. She has a small sharp face, grey eyes and untidy white hair round her head like a collapsed halo. Jerry is small and bald, and you wouldn't be taking much notice of him. Winnie gives me tea in the kitchen and a piece of Christmas cake, while a couple of farmers lounge in the bar, and across the room a woman is buying groceries, preferring to do her 'messages' here than in the tempting ease of the supermarket. Jerry is giving a sweet to her child.

★

'In the old days there would be a dozen women shopping, not just the one like now. They would come in on Thursday which was market day, and they would usually go to the grocery side. If they wanted a drink they would go into the kitchen or the snug. The men all stayed at the bar. You would get the half gallon of porter and you'd give them three glasses, and they would divide it up, and that was the cheapest way, it was.

The barrels of porter came in on the train or boat, and there were a couple of ponies and cars which brought them from the station. They were very big, and they were put into the shop, and they were the seats. You would sit on them, and they would give the place an old smell.

We had oil lamps and candles, and only when we got a bit grander bought the Tilleys that you pumped up. We had two old hanging lamps – those ones there beside the door. When you got up in the morning the first thing you did was to light the fire, take up the ashes and clean the range, and boil the water. My mother was grand altogether, and when we grew up a little, we always helped her.

The shop side was always an important part of the business, and even today you couldn't do without it. The drapery was mostly for farmers. We sold those flanelette shirts – they wear them now for style – and coarse frieze trousers in sizes four, five, six and seven, and the only things we didn't carry were boots. We had hooks from which you would hang the meat, and there was always what they called American bacon. We also kept a barrel of pigs' heads which everyone ate. My God, did you never eat pigs' heads? 'Tis the nicest part of the pig, lovely and sweet, and when they killed the pigs, they took off the heads, and pickled them in a barrel. They used to be sold for four pence and sixpence a pound. For the children we had big jars full of sherbert and sweets, and what they called Fizz. The men would want lumps of tobacco and you'd cut two ounces off them.

Apart from the pub we also had a small farm that my father worked, but we only went there for the holidays. Because we lived here, my mother was very strict with us, and I suppose working in a bar made you that way with children. We were always up to tricks. When the commercial traveller came in to be paid, we would go out with him into the street looking for a penny or something, and she'd tell them that we didn't belong to her at all, but were little ones from across the street. She didn't want them giving us money, you see. When we got bigger she wouldn't want us out at night at all, and if we were out she would put two or three chairs against the door so that she could hear us coming in, and then maybe she would give us a belting for coming back late. She was very strict.

I don't mean to criticize her, for we always enjoyed ourselves, and there was always something to see or do. There were the fairs and market days and the men came in their horses and cars, and the women wearing cloaks or shawls. There was a little window at the back, and they would tie the horse to the latch of the door and knock, and they would ask you for a drink through the window. Their favourite was a pint and a half, and that meant a pint of porter and a half of whiskey, and he would always have the half whiskey first. They didn't drink an awful lot, but there were more people to drink at that time.

Then there were the special occasions like Christmas. A week before, the farmers and their wives would come in, and the whole place would be taken up with baskets for carrying things. The kitchen and the bar would always be full, and people had a habit of going around to the different houses and getting presents from the shop-keepers. People thought shopkeepers better than themselves and very "uppish", and because of this we were expected to give something, even small.

You know the old Christmas candle – what we called the pound candles? They would get loads of them, all right, and start lighting them up. Christmas was always considered good for getting credit. I have the books where everything was written down, all the groceries and even the drinks went down into that book, and you would have to write them down straight. When you were looking for the bad debts, you wouldn't get them, and maybe they wouldn't come in any more and that sort of thing. But the older people were very honest. They would come in and say to you, "I can only give you that much now . . . you'll have to wait until I sell something" and at Christmas time they would have a few extra pounds.

If a stranger came along you would be all curiosity to know who he was and what he was doing, and the main sport was meeting the train, or just walking up and down the street. Everyone did it, young boys and girls, and down at the forge the older men would tell stories to each other under the chestnut. Sometimes there would be a storm, and the islanders might be in Cappaghglass doing their shopping, and they couldn't row back. My mother would fix them with plates of meat from the big timber safe, and they would spend the night talking away in the kitchen.

When my mother and father died, I never had any trouble in looking after things, and now that Jerry is back from England it makes things a lot easier. My mother served in the bar, and I still think that a woman has an advantage here with men, for they will never fight a woman. Things have changed, and you can't make a proper living from a pub here – and you never could. We always had a bit of land. Today every time cigarettes and drink go up in price, the sale goes down, and then you have all the new pubs with music, and they take the business away from you.

The worst thing, I find, is that you can't trust people any more, and leave them around the bar. You have to keep an eye on them, and if they didn't pay you for a drink, it wouldn't worry them. And there is another thing about it. We left all our doors open and nothing would ever be stolen, but you couldn't leave anything open today. That's another thing you have to watch. When we go to bed at night, we put trays against the door in case anyone would come in. It wouldn't be locals, but someone from the outside.'

Pronsias Regan, Hotel Keeper. Aged 55.

The hotel stands at the top of the street facing the bank, a white Victorian edifice four storeys high, the biggest building in Cappagh-glass except for the Catholic church. Inside it is typical of a country hotel with its patterned carpets, a great oasis of a bar smelling of stout, cigarettes and dirty glasses, adorned with the colour TV flickering against a wall. Behind the bar is the new function room, another huge space, and the thickly carpeted dining room where you cannot hear the footsteps of the waitresses. Upstairs are scores of bedrooms.

The place has been in the family for two generations, or as Pronsias says more picturesquely, we have been in the trade for a million years. It is something he often regrets. No one would run such a white elephant from choice.

★

'I came home from roaming around the world, and my brother upped and went to Canada and left me with the business. I hadn't a clue of what I was taking on, and even after thirty years running a place like this, it's still almost as much a mystery. All I knew when I started was that I wanted to get married and didn't want to emigrate, and the hotel was there waiting for me. Another bride, a great fat white bride.

I still think that the most important quality you can have for this sort of business is a high degree of stupidity. Perhaps stupidity isn't quite the word. Unworldliness or something. You need to feel yourself terribly involved with people and their problems and try to be helpful all the time. We are selling food and shelter for the night, and hopefully companionship.

Running a family hotel is nightmare country. When I started we had a staff of fifteen. You could get a first class chef at £25 a week, now you'd pay £200. We inherited some faithful people from my father, who were receiving the famous stamp. Their cards were stamped, which I think cost three and six at the time, and after their board had been taken out they received the princely sum of one pound and ten shillings. Of course they were working impossible hours, but in the main they were well looked after, in so much as if they came and said to you at short notice, "Look, there's been the death of a first cousin – I really want to go away for a couple of days" – you felt an obligation as the boss to let them go.

As a novice greenhorn my mistake was to raise their salary to three pounds and to bring the whole town on my back. "We appreciate what you are trying to do and you must help them, for fair is fair. But you have overshot the runway in giving them three pounds, and it's debatable whether your business will stand it." I became more cautious after that. I introduced the service charge, and that was pooled in September between them. And that held them, because if they left before then they wouldn't get a share.

If you want to make a success of the hotel business, you have to work very hard and the hours are crazy. You must be the first up at half-past five or six o'clock and the last to go to bed. As the boss you are expected to be seen around the place and to check everything. Check the toilets and bars, supervise the different meals. I do the reception as well as the bar in the afternoon and let the staff off. Between half past three and six is the casual booking-in-time, and I am watching out for that. For dinner I have to put on a dress suit and my wife has to help. "Did you enjoy the dinner?" she will ask after me sweating three hours to get it properly fixed. "Are you enjoying your stay?" And in the evening she will go over the books.

When we started we worked very hard and made a bit of money, and in that way we couldn't complain. People told me that I had the broadest spectrum of customers in town, anyone from purple blood to Baluba. It was a long way on from the time when I was growing up. During the war we only had a small commercial trade and the occasional Dublin families coming down by train for their summer holiday. They would double up, and my father gave them a special price for around £6 a week and the children for half.

In winter time the "commercials" were our bread and butter. There were travellers from the main distilleries and from everywhere else. They are long gone. I'm speaking of the death of a generation of nice gracious old well-worn men who only had to do a little writing and present their charm and appearance. They would stay in the hotel overnight, eat their steaks – nothing but a steak would do – and drink whatever money they were making. Next morning, suitably plummy and taking little orders, they would get into their Ford cars and move to the next town. They were highly respectable gentlemen, and by the late 'sixties they were wiped out and replaced by a young lad in a fast car. Three became one and then the computer took over.

After the war the English visitors began slipping back, and by the first fortnight in January we had all our bookings. You knew that you were going to be full for June, July, August and half of September and that was a fixed fact of life. It seemed that if only we could extend the season to April and May, you were on your way to having almost no winter.

We had about eighty per cent English staying here, and Mr Englishman was the best friend you ever had, and he was the one that filled your hotel. Although I am native born Irish and my family have been here since Brian Boru and that kind of thing, I still think the English are marvellous people. Compared to the Continentals they are vastly superior. The Englishman spent his money, there was no language barrier and all he wanted was good plain food. If they came with a hundred pounds in their pockets, they would spend a hundred pounds, whereas the Frenchman will take back fifty if he can. And if the Frenchman is spending, he is buying things like Aran sweaters and Waterford glass, and making sure of every penny. Oh, the burning of the British Embassy! Before that you lived.

When the first English came over after the war, how they were charmed by the warmth and hospitality. They didn't just like it, they wallowed in it. They set out to enjoy themselves. They had morning tea – Oh, yes, at seven, if you please – and they would be sitting up there waiting for it at seven o'clock, and after a few days they would get acclimatized and give it up. Then they would be only waiting for breakfast. They had a fixed way of life which nothing could alter. At say, twenty-to-twelve he would come into the bar with his wife for the coffee thing, and there would be a little pause in the conversation and in the middle of the silence he would say, "You know darling . . . I'm going to have a whiskey." I think there's a warmth and spontaneity about that.

Today Mr English Visitor is only about five per cent of what he used to be, and what with the troubles and all those signs plastered round the country saying Brits Out, I can't blame him. The ones that do arrive here are well educated about the present situation. They are preaching back home: "But they are not shooting each other in the south, I promise you." The education gap is in England, and for years they seemed to be under the impression that the British Isles meant just that. You had Scotland, you had Wales, you had Ireland and it was all one. During the 'fifties they found out that here was a magical country full of warm generous people, and no sooner had they begun to come in vast numbers, than suddenly the whole thing burst asunder under their feet.

One of the big problems in running a hotel is the cooking. Before we started doing dinners, we employed a lady cook who did high teas. When we got more sophisticated we got a chef. Salmon was only half a crown a pound, and honest to God, people staying had salmon every evening and never got tired of it. Poached salmon with a nice salad – they were mad for it, and of course we plugged it, because it was so easy to do. The salmon's mainly gone and they are skin diving for the lobster, and now we have crab salad and prawns. Every day I put the menu outside the front door. When I started doing this it was something new for Cappaghglass, and it used to amuse me to watch the people discussing the different dishes, and of course these had to be changed every day.

The tourist is much more demanding than he used to be. Fifty years ago, when the country was born, you didn't think of putting up anything tasty, and as for things like garlic, you didn't know how to spell the word. Nowadays anyone who has dinner orders wine, and they also want late night drinks served till all hours of the morning and every night of the week. Because they are on holiday, they forget you are working.

A fairly new phenomenon is the visiting yachtsman, and he is generally considered the worst. People say to me, "Don't let them walk all over you; they probably have no more money than you have, and the banks own the yacht." We dread them. Maybe they are tired, cold and dirty, but they will still come in and expect to take over. The worst thing we ever had was a yacht party who asked for eighteen Irish coffees, and because we could not produce them fast enough they created an almighty scene.

The Continentals have their own mentality. Their life style is so different to our own. Only recently I tumbled to the fact that a certain group of Dutch who come to the hotel every year didn't want to do anything. After shopping in the town they would sit at my bar counter sipping half pints of Guinness. I have a tendency to organize people, and this had been going on for some time before I said to them, "Listen you lot, you are in the middle of some superb scenery, there are marvellous things to see and do . . . wouldn't you think of going out?" And they kind of jointly nodded and said, "It's a nice idea, but it's very pleasant here" . . . and it slowly dawned on me that their pleasure in life was to sit at a counter drinking very slowly with their minds in a neutral blank. And when you threaten them with it – that's the wrong phrase – point out things to them, they say, "But of course, Mr Regan, you don't know where we are coming from." And then they tell you how in a place like Holland people live in apartments and you don't know your neighbour in ten years and the person beyond him is a complete blank. You run on steel rails that take you to work and steel rails bring you home again, and there's no vestige of grace in living in Holland any more. And that brings them to Ireland and sitting at the bar, perhaps susceptible to the humour behind the bar and some of it in front, but just deliberately and pointedly doing nothing. What can you say?

Apart from the hotel there is the bar, and from making a living they are twins. One couldn't do without the other. The bar side is worse than the hotel side, because you are all things to all men, and you've a twenty-four hour day and a seven day week – that's what the bar means. People come in and you are the barman, and they want to talk with someone and be amused. Anyone with a problem comes in and expects you to listen and perhaps give advice. People don't talk at home, this is where all serious talking is done and it's much the safest place.

Oh, definitely, the pub and the bar is the place where you get a person's innermost thoughts, those that he wouldn't reveal to his wife. And he would have to know a friend a very long time before he will open up to him in the same way as the man behind the bar counter. Every publican in the country is a father confessor, and he is automatically ruling what's fit for publication and what's not. Because he has seen similar people placed as yourself, his advice is very sound. Whatever he says to you, even to the point of chiding you because you are drinking too much, it's never done in a personal way. He is looking around like a lighthouse beam in all directions all the time. An interest in people can be cultivated, it's not necessarily a God-given thing. I've often said to my family, I can't think of any job in which I can make a living and do as many simple inexpensive good turns for mankind at large as running a pub.

One of the things that has vanished is the old fair day. The damn thing used to start at daylight, and unless you would tear yourself out of bed it would be practically over by nine o'clock. We got an early morning extension to enable us to open at 7:30. It was a very common occurrence to go down to the kitchen and help to eject a cow. You would even see a horse's head poked in at the bar while the owner held him with a piece of scruffy rope and charged the counter and said, "Give me one and a half neat."

But in fact the drinking pattern varied on fair days, insomuch as anyone who enjoyed the leisurely whiskey followed by a pint changed his habits. He didn't want to be too drunk, and he didn't want to stay too long in one place, so he would be eternally asking for half pints of Guinness. That would give him an excuse to be there and look around, to catch his breath and hang on the counter and go out again. The great phrase that broke our hearts was, "Missy, Missy, I'm in a fierce hurry" – rapping with his cane. There would be a hundred little deals going on, and everybody hoped to connect to make a bargain.

People dressed down for fair days so as not to be thought too wealthy or respectable and that you couldn't strike his arm. They would allow two days of growth of beard to appear on an otherwise clean-shaven man, and he would wear a scruffy overcoat, with a rag tied around the thing holding it together. I remember a usually well-dressed person coming in one fair day in a most outrageous condition in this torn raincoat with a cut at the back. I said, "Jimmy . . . am I seeing right?" and he looked at me rather sheepish. "It's the fair, you know, Frank, and you can't afford to put on an image of wealth, and I have to appear poorer than the next man."

I like nothing better than seeing people drink and enjoy themselves. But I also admit that here in Ireland there is a terrible curse in the drink. In the old days it was terrible. Some people drank from what I called "the drunkenness of desperation", the feeling that there just wasn't any hope . . . no jobs, no social services or anything, and when a man got into trouble he went straight to the bar. I remember, you would say to yourself "There's been no fighting in the last two weeks . . . good gracious me, that's not so good . . . There will be two fights in the next three week period." When I say a fight, I mean it would be broken jaws.

Today thankfully that's mostly gone, and the young fellow can hold his drink much better. But as for making money, the truth of the matter is that at the present moment the cost of a drink is mind-bending, and the people who take a drink have gone down forty per cent. I know only one person in Cappaghglass who is making a living out of a bar and I think he has money coming in on the side.

We are too expensive. Nowadays people stay for a few nights and move on. I think we had only three families altogether last summer for the whole season. With rates and things like electricity and even fireproof curtains at nine pounds a yard – that's what they cost –

running a hotel like this is uneconomic. Which is why every second hotel in Ireland is up for sale.

There is no such thing as a winter season and the only way we can keep going is by holding discos and functions. Of course there will always be a few wealthy business people who are able to charge everything to expenses. Last year a group of Frenchmen came in, and I was able to give them porbeagle shark – and that's a fact. They caught a shark and put it in the freezer and it tasted like fresh pork without the apple sauce.

Sometimes I feel that the recession might even be good for people if it doesn't last too long. By the time we have tourists back again, we might appreciate them and not fleece them. Oh yes, that happened. When the tourists first came everybody was delighted. Then it was like the goose and the golden eggs – we got greedy and killed it. Then there was the oil crisis and the recession and now we have no tourists – no tourists that spend money, anyway. But I also happen to think that when sanity returns and when this country lurches slowly and unsteadily through the awful depression, Ireland will score massively as a place where people will want to come. We have all around here an unlimited quantity of Europe's most precious commodities – empty spaces, peace and quiet roads.'

Joe MacNeil, Butcher. Aged 56.

Do you remember the old butcher's shop with the lines of carcasses hanging outside on hooks, and how the occasional crow landed on their sides and pecked away? Joe was a young butcher during that era. He is a big man in every sense of the word, known for his wit and sharp tongue. The business, once so primitive, is now thriving and modern; Joe has his shop in Cappaghglass, and, like the majority of small rural butchers, his own small farm where he runs store animals for slaughter. If he is critical of some aspects of modern meat production – particularly the overuse of antibiotics and growth promoters – he is also quick to acknowledge that butchering is a much cleaner and more profitable business today than it was thirty years ago.

*

'My first job from coming back from school was killing the white calves. At that time they only cost two and sixpence, and after killing them we would sell the skin. I remember killing my first animal at seven years of age with the maul, a four pound hammer, for that was the way of doing it before the humane killer came in. You would tie the animal to a pole in the house, and you'd make a fluke with him between the eyes and knock him out. I became good at throwing him down with the first clout. Then you just cut the two jugular veins and he'd kick the blood out of himself. Skinning the animal was the next thing, and you'd start from the front legs; it was always important to be clean in taking the skin off, and if, say, the blood of a sheep got on your hands, you would be in trouble. It was important to wash your hands very often.

It was quite a different place when I started, and the shop had only shutters which were bolted inside, while in summertime a wire mesh kept the place cool and helped to stop the flies. In the country there was no training at all, and you'd start straight away, although in the cities it was always different. We used to be called "quack" butchers, because there were no licences or government regulations, and if your father owned the shop, as eldest son you naturally followed the business.

When I was fourteen I left school and began helping my father. We used to open at half past nine, and the first job was always to hang the meat on the hooks on the bar outside the window sill, all the quarters and a couple of sheep in between them. Then I had to clean the boards and the beechwood block before the cutting. There was no electric saw, and it was terrible hard work, not the skilled business like it is today. Only the knife, cleaver, and chopper and the boning knives.

My father had his own farm and during the wintertime we went to the fairs, when you wouldn't have your own cattle. My father employed drovers and I used to walk back with them over the hills driving the sheep and cattle. I enjoyed that. Then, one of my most important jobs was selling meat. I bought a postman's carrier bike, and put two small boxes in the front and back, and in these I could carry a whole sheep. I would cut it up in eight or ten small pieces, and put a white cloth over them before cycling off.

Later on we had a mare and round trap with seats inside it, and a flat board on top for carrying the meat. God rest my father, he used to come with me, and we'd go off together for a radius of six or seven miles around the town. You had to have your wits sharpened, for it was all bargaining then. "Do you want any meat, Missus?" I would shout as the woman would come out from her house. She would pick up a piece and have a good look at it, and if we came to anything, I would take up the balance or scales and make a bargain. The price of meat might be twelve and sixpence, and she might only give you nine shillings. And you had to take it, for there was no refrigeration, and otherwise you might throw the meat away.

When my father died I took over the business and have been at it ever since. It was quite different then. Those heavy rails were there, and there was a desk for marking down the accounts, and there was always one big barrel for corned beef. Behind the shop we had a room where the blocks of ice my father got from a ship were kept. They were brought up from the pier by horse and cart. The trouble always was that with no proper refrigeration there would be a lot of waste. If an animal was too big, the flies might eat him. You would kill him on a Thursday, and he would be black on Monday morning. On a hot summer's day the flies were all over the meat, and we kept at them with a leather strap, if you had it. They would drive you up the wall at times, and you would be watching them night and day. There were no sprays, and you had to drive them off, and that would be the whole summer.

What I used to do was to cut down the meat and get some pieces of newspaper, and then put gauze sheets over the carcass. But even then we had to throw so much away. There was the dust from the streets blowing in, the heat, and all those insects and flies.

At the time I am talking of, the most popular meat by far was boiling meat, and that's all people could afford. The price was one and six a pound, old money, and two shillings for steak. But of course in the summertime steak was too fresh, and had to be boiled down. One of my jobs was to kill pigs for farmers all over the country, and they would give me a piece of the meat for my pains. Making black puddings and sausages was something else. I used to take the blood in a bucket and put a fistful of salt into it, clean a small piece of gut and make the pudding. They were beautiful. You're talking about taste and flavour now, but you couldn't get that sort of stuff today. Nothing ever equalled that delicious black pudding.

The improvements began to come in about thirty years ago, back about the time of my first fridge. Then there was the humane killer, and things like the electric saw and sharpener. Before that we used a little emery stone inside a little box, with water and a little handle.

Killing is just supply and demand, and the problem was always the shortage of money. On the desk we had two ledgers and a day book for marking down the accounts. Mrs So-and-so would have a balance of five shillings, every week the doctor would spend a pound, and the priest and other regular clients paid by monthly accounts. I have their lists off by heart: Mrs Desmond, a leg of mutton, half a dozen chops for Mrs O'Sullivan, and I would sell as far away as the lighthouse.

The other ledger was for casuals, and that was another system, and a much smaller book. If they had the money they paid you, and if they hadn't you hoped they would come back sometime and pay something off. Everyone wrote things up on the slate.

Our most important day of all was Thursday when they had a market. I would put my kitchen table outside the shop and sell bits of meat from it. "Buy a piece of meat, Sir?" I would shout out as the crowds walked up and down. Later in the day people might come in for a few drinks and start talking. There might be a row all right, but it could always be sorted out.

The difference now is that people have a lot of money, but they are all strangers to each other. In spite of the recession they come in their Mercedes and spend fifteen pounds a week, and sometimes more. A leg of mutton or steak or chops, and if they have a freezer, a whole carcass of beef that would cost two hundred pounds. They will eat meat five or six days a week.

It used to be old cows and old sheep we were selling, but today we are mincing meat which was stewed before. It's all lamb now, and good heifer meat, and every week I kill about five animals. But you wouldn't know them, and they don't taste the same. Now you have a year and a half heifer killing as a three-year-old before. Or you could have a ten-month-old animal killing as a two-year-old, and they've been driven with the needle and the growth promoter.'

Tim Harrington, Baker. Aged 58.

Like so many other tradesmen in the town he has inherited his position. There is nothing easy about being apprenticed to your father, Tim will tell you with a smile, and many a son has taken the boat.

He is a quiet methodical man who goes to the bakery at the same early hour every day and finishes his work at the same time. Everyone likes his bread. There was consternation some years ago at the rumour that the bakery might close and the crisp still-warm loaves would become unavailable each morning. He has continued out of popular demand, although baking requires endless hard work and early rising.

★

'Do you want the story of my life? It will take a good ten minutes. I was born into the business if you like, it went from father to son and I have two brothers who are baking in England. When we were children my father also had a small mill and a shed for carding wool. Corn and wool came from all over the place – of course there was a much bigger population. Every farmer seemed to grow his own patch of corn and they all had sheep on the mountain. You might think that between the three different businesses my father was a wealthy man, but to tell you the truth we only scraped along like everyone else.

One of the first things I can remember was being in our bedroom above the mill and waking when the island boats would be coming in with their load of corn. The men spoke Gaelic which we didn't know, and the first sound we heard was the clapping of their hands trying to keep warm. Later in the day they began the grinding when the water was switched on and the large wheel outside began to turn. That set in motion the different wheels inside. To us children it seemed as good as magic, and we would watch the large stone quern begin to rotate and the crushed yellow-grain falling down the shute in a shower into the waiting sacks. We never got tired of it.

That was how it was done and perhaps it's no wonder I should have become a baker. Corn and flour, ground oats and barley. And the mill was full of grey dust that covered everything. The wheel sent us to sleep, a quiet sound, like that of a big boat and nothing sharp.

The other thing was the carding. I never found out how my father had got into it, and by the time we were growing up it was dying away. Wool was everything then; and a lot of men wore outside jackets called "Wrappers" in natural white, and their trousers were also made from the same *bainin*★ cloth. There was one old man who went on wearing a white wrapper and they called him White Jack.

If the mill had this rumble of the quern stone grinding away, the carding had also a number of wheels which were set in motion, and they teased the wool as it went along. I can remember my father pouring a gallon or maybe two of water on the vat of raw wool which

★ Coarse cream-coloured woollen cloth.

had been washed and collected, and it came out on the other side like Christmas candles, one roll into another, and it was put in sacks and brought home.

There was an old lady who came in who had a spinning wheel, and she used to put the ends together and spin it into thread which was rather like knitting wool. It must have been thirsty work, for Bridgy, for that was her name, was crazy for her drop of whiskey, and sometimes we would get it for her. If our mother knew what we were doing we would have all been murdered. There was also an old weaver at that time with the name of Cock of the Horn, and he had a house at the end of what was once called the weaver's wall. It was called by us the waver's wall, because the waves would rush in and beat it. As children we called him a waver, not a weaver.

These are the sort of things you remember, things like bringing pigs down to the fair in a common cart. We also had a small farm of twelve acres, and as a boy I always fiddled around with the farmers while my father worked away at the bakery. Our mother cooked for us, and being out in the country you had a better appetite. It was plain simple food of the kind that everyone ate then. A piece of pig's head or bacon with a fine big head of white cabbage, and you might get a bit of goat at times. I remember you would see goat in every butcher's shop hanging down skinned.

I couldn't tell you how different things are since I was growing up. We had electricity in Cappaghglass in 1950, and it made people lazy because they were used to the lamps. Before running water came in I remember there were two pumps that kept the whole town going. They'd get a bucket of water in the morning and another in the evening.

Getting back to bread, the pot oven bread made from milk was the best. They also used yellow meal or maize, and you put a fistful or so into a cake, or you would have it in the morning as a gruel with a slash of milk; I'm not afraid to say it, either.

We had four bakers in Cappaghglass then, for everyone was eating bread. The fishermen lived on it. They would go into a shop and that was their meal then, a pint of porter and a lump of bread. You could get a single loaf for tuppence halfpenny. In bread making you can always fall in for bad flour, and that's the only thing that can go wrong. The flour used to arrive by boat, and the Manitoba flour was always considered the best. Dulcey white, not like the Irish stuff that nobody wants.

My father was the boss, and I had to work under his direction. The first job he gave me was to carry a basket containing fifteen pairs of loaves down the main street knocking on people's doors. That was during the war when petrol was scarce and the bread was horrible because there was no imported flour. Later I got baking. I would go down at about seven o'clock in the evening and put so much yeast, water and flour together. Then at six next morning you'd break up all this batter again, and add more flour and more water. The same as we do now. The oven we use was built in 1900 and uses coke. There was a coal oven before that. She is lit in the morning, and takes about an hour to heat. In summertime it can become very hot indeed, and you are only wearing a shirt or vest and an apron over it.

There can be so much moisture in Irish wheat, and in the old days there were no mixers. It was very hard work and still is pretty hard. We used to make two batches, and each batch had about a hundred and twenty loaves, or sixty pairs, "the lumps", pans, and turnovers. When I took over the business I bought a van, but otherwise the business of making bread has stayed much the same.

People are so choosy, they don't know what they want. After the war there was the new white bread and everyone was delighted to get it. Now they are shouting for the brown. Before the war a lot had their own meal, which we got ground like I said, and they would only buy a loaf for a novelty and a bit of a change. Then the big bakeries began coming in, although now the price of petrol and the high cost of deliveries has them discouraged. The old hand-made bread is coming back fast, and my business is booming.'

Michael O'Shea, Postmaster. Aged 58.

The post office is part of a general store. In the old days the long narrow room was not divided up, and the wooden counter ran from end to end. It seemed that there were almost as many goods hanging from the ceiling as stacked on the shelves. Somewhere in the centre the work of the Post Office was done.

In the 'thirties, at a time when the townspeople considered themselves socially above the farmers, Michael's father was known for his kindness. During the long economic war, when the farmers put everything down on the slate, he trusted them and was rarely disappointed. "Throw in that bag of meal," he would say to some impecunious countryman, and sooner or later it would be paid for.

Michael is a small portly man with a reputation for honesty and seeing things are done. His wife, Eileen, stands by his side, and their children help in the shop and behind the grill. Although there is a tradition that rural post offices are run by single women, in Cappaghglass it has always been a family concern. Michael will recite the different generations: Joe, his father, Michael his grandfather, and his great grandfather, too, all of whom acted as stamp dispensers, honorary father confessors and bank managers. In recent years the role of postmaster has declined. The 'phone has gone automatic, people don't write letters any more, and the American mail has lost its importance. Much of Michael's grocery business has gone to the new supermarket down the road.

★

'When I first started helping my father, having the Post Office and shop meant that you had an enormous advantage over an ordinary farmer, who was regarded with a sort of contempt. A farmer was a fellow who was hunted off the street on fair days because his cows had fouled the kerbstone. Having said that, I hasten to add that we were farmers too, and knew exactly what was involved. But then we had the business as well, and therefore some sort of cash flow, and this enabled my father to educate us beyond the normal primary level.

It used to be said that the job of running a post office was given as some sort of political perk. I could never see that. It was regarded as a great prize by other shopkeepers, but now most people feel that it ties them down too much. When the Postmistress in Curragheen retired, she hadn't saved one penny after twenty-five years. You are not in a well-paid or pensionable position, and you only get the old age pension. We were paid on a contractual basis, and every three years there would be a review. The shop and the post office were absolutely complementary. In no way could one work without the other.

When I took over from my father it was an archaic system, and as I've said, the pay was sub-standard for all the work you were expected to do. You had to give all your time to it, and I'd still say that the post office in this country is the last in the world to develop and get modernized. Even today we don't have Giro banking.

When I began I was always running down with messages. You would get a halfpenny for going to the doctor's house and down to the station. We were the centre of the town, if you like, an information centre, with a knowledge of every single person within the district. People would come in here for directions, or to make some other arrangements. "I'll meet you in the Post Office" was what everybody said to each other when they wanted to meet.

I can just remember my father using the morse code and what he called the "sounder" before the telephone came in and the manual exchange. At first we only had three telephones in the town. The first was the Post Office, the second was the Barracks, and the third one was the Bank Manager. Then after about 1940 it sort of exploded. It had to be manned day and night, and the veins weren't big enough to carry the flow of business. At first people couldn't do it at all, and when I got married, Eileen had to teach them how to use it. They were shouting and were very uneducated.

If you wanted to call Galway or Limerick, we had to take the number and pass it on to the next biggest town, and there would always be long delays. I can remember the callers coming in here and sitting on the counter and just waiting, and you'd be giving it a turn.

Handling the switch board was always what they call today "labour intensive." The first call might start at six forty-four, and I remember the clergyman reading out his sermons every Sunday morning from about seven o'clock to nine or thereabouts, and I cursing. I knew everything that passed. Then at night-times I had to sleep very light, and always be ready to get up and answer the 'phone. After twelve o'clock you had a non-attendance system and what was described as a non-wakeful system. It wasn't at all modern until 1960 onwards. Finally last year it became automatic. Only recently were we emancipated.

A twenty-four hour job, yes. Mind you, it was a more wakeful service than a watchful service. You'd sleep, and like the man on the lighthouse – it is when the fog guns stop going off that he jumps out of bed and says, "What's that?" You were aware of it the whole time, and this very loud bell in your ear. Now its an enormous relief, but it paid us about six times what we are getting paid at present. It was a salary which was quite respectable. It's lucky that at our requirement of life we don't need that much money now.

You didn't need any training for post office work, you trained at your mother's knee. I saw my parents doing it, and that's the time you became familiar with it. When I started the people here were un-educated, and when they left primary school and went off to work on a farm, it made them unable to write at all. Sunday used to be the great day for pensions, and practically all the signatures had to be filled in by ourselves. The people who owned the books would leave them with you, and you would fill in the names, John Murphy, Denis Sullivan and so on. Nowadays people can write all their own stuff.

In fact they got more educated over the years. When the postage for a letter was only tuppence, they wrote regularly to each other. If you had five children in England, every fortnight the parents would get five letters, and they would send five letters in return. Of course the biggest thing was always the arrival of the American mail. In my father's time December the eighth was always the big day for paying American money. Usually the writing from America in this part of the world took the form of dollar drafts with the name of payee and sender – very little in the way of letters.

I think the coming of the electric light had an influence on letter writing. There was no electricity until 1952, and people used candles and oil lamps, and if they were better off, the Tilley. The reading was governed by the light available to them. I certainly think so. I think that was why socializing and chatting and what they called *scoraiocht*-ing was so important.

One of our chief jobs was the pensions. The old age was only introduced in 1908, the Widows came in about 1935, and there was no Childrens' Allowance until about 1950. In the small post offices like this one we pay the dole as well. Today, if you took the payments out of it, there wouldn't be a bit to do.

In the old days, if you were efficient enough to cater for the people, the post office was certainly an avenue for business. You could even have a pub in a post office, but it had to be in a different room. Things were a good deal more primitive then. I can remember when the roads were untarred and there was yellow dust flying about. Fair days were a terror. Do you know that the ladies of the town would go out with their buckets and brush, and they would be raging because a cow would turn her backside and do her whole thing around in the street? And the shopkeepers would be driving the animals away.

Never mind the people who keep telling you how good it was in the old days. It was dire. There were dire standards of living. The children now think torture and hell was the sort of existence I can remember older people having. And they had to, for they didn't know anything else. If you throw in with that a very uninteresting diet, ragged clothes, bad shoes or no shoes – and walking for miles with your cattle to the fair – that was hard, all right.

The role of the Post Office has declined in importance and I know that none of my children wishes to take it on. There are just too many snags for modern people. Did you know that every penny you lose on the counter through some mistake you are accountable for? As recently as 1970 you had to take annual leave at your own expense. And no pension at the end of it. The people today wouldn't stand for it. Another thing, although I could transfer it to my children, there's no such thing as selling. After four generations of my family serving the public I must give three months notice to the Department, and they advertise it, that's all.'

Peter Corkery, Postman. Aged 72.

Peter retired two years ago, having walked and cycled, he reckons, something like forty thousand miles during his life-time. Can he be right? Half a century of constant regular exercise has left him blooming with health. He is a small compact man who was never seriously ill and has never seen a doctor. He still has the postman's tan, red where the sun caught it and white streaks where his forehead was shielded by his cap. He misses the round that covered an area of some twenty-five miles, not including the sea crowd when he took mail to the islands.

★

'When I got my job as postman there was no examination and I was just given the job. It was very small money then, and I was delighted to get it. I was never without money since that day, and that's the truth. My first pay was eight and ninepence, and I brought home every penny to my mother. It was a one day week then, and they were going to change me to two. I think they would make it a pound – but eighteen shillings was what I finished up with. The job was too small for a uniform, and it was up to yourself to get around. When I was a young fellow I might walk twenty-four miles in a day and there might be a couple of hundred letters in a delivery.

Before my time the mail used to come into Cappaghglass on a jaunting car, but when I started the motor had come in. The postman always used to walk on his rounds, but since then they have got very lazy and motorized. At one time you used to have to get special permission to have a bike. I can remember when the roads were untarred. There were no steam rollers, and in summer there was yellow dust flying around all the time, and in winter great muddy pools of water. The men used to fill in the potholes with baskets of stones, but it never seemed to make any difference. A few gales would see to it. My route led me over big open country which was very wild in winter time.

There was a much larger population then and all the houses were occupied. Have you been down the road to Battery Point? In my time I have seen sixteen houses closed in that short three mile run, and they all contained big families. The people were always watching out for you – there were no telephones or radio at that time . . . and you were always expected to bring the news and answer a few questions too, and bring messages anyhow. Sometime later I took a horse, and it was good sport to take a shortcut across the fields and hedges, the bag of mail on my back.

I had the post for the island for one day a week. I had a small boat and later I was given an outboard engine. On calm summer days there was no trouble, but if there was a south-east wind you would be hammered, and there wasn't much talk of keeping dry in that sort of weather. I knew all the people on the island and they knew me. I used the donkey from the pier to carry the mail to the small shop where I would sort out the parcels and letters and then walk around.

The people were very good to me. You were always brought in and given tea and something to eat, and the house was always full of children. Christmas was an especially important time on the island, and I would get almost as much mail then as for the rest of the year. Especially they were watching out for the little green thing you had to sign for the registered mail, for that would mean money from America – some few pounds, like. They were expecting a little money to come all the time, and it would be hard to blame them. Around Christmas it was customary for people to give the postman a present and they were very kind in that way too. I remember getting a pound from the bank, but it was usually a little token. Big or small, it didn't matter, you felt better.

There's an awful change in the population since I started and they are down to one third roughly. They didn't all emigrate, and I'll tell you what happened to them. A lot of people never got married over the years. I don't know in the name of God why they didn't. They lived their lives there, and that was the end.

When people go away there is nothing, and it doesn't matter who is there as long as there is someone. I was delighted when the foreigners started coming in. If a man builds a house for a million pounds I wouldn't give a continental except they were nice people.

I never thought I'd miss it so much when I gave it up, for there was all that neighbourhood and meeting people. In the old days they would say a man was old when he was seventy. He was finished. But I'm seventy-two November last, and that's old enough. I still do a little fishing and a bit of crabbing, and last year was the first year I didn't drop out a line. To be honest with you I'd rather go back a score of years and come up again. But there's no second chance. I'd like to be young again and go through all the hardships and everything that I went through, and I'd still enjoy the hardest of them. It was lovely to be young. If the sky fell behind you it would make a lot of noise, but you wouldn't look back to where it was. But now if it fell, you would just drop.'

Noel Kennedy, Garda Sergeant. Aged 55.

His car, like the Doctor's or Priest's, is recognized everywhere. He can usually be found either at the local station, a slab of a building near the main square, or in his bungalow which he built for himself and his family. He is a big burly man with a countryman's open face and a reputation for not suffering fools gladly.

★

'Although I went to secondary school, when I joined, most of the other lads going into the force had only been to primary school. I think there was this feeling that as the criminal came from a lower class and hadn't a great deal of brain, if you know what I mean, there was no need for us Garda officers to be well-educated. Now they have things like Leaving Cert and even degrees from a university.

My father was one of the first recruits into the force after the disbanding of the old RIC. Obviously being a Guard's son must have helped my chances of getting taken on, for there was always the feeling of belonging to the same organization and having a lot in common with each other. Things like that follow down the line.

I spent six months in the Training Depot and I was lucky I wasn't sacked. They were glad to get rid of me. After training you could be posted anywhere in Ireland. The only general rule was that you could never leave a man closer then thirty miles from his home town. I went to my first small town for plain ordinary police work. You had no running-in period, and were put straight on the street. I think you're as nervous as bedammed, but after six months police work hammered into you, a certain amount of unarmed combat, square bashing and everything, I suppose you are ready for all eventualities.

The big difference between what happens today and what happened in the 'fifties is that people didn't eat then. They would never think of going out and paying for a meal. On fair days there was always an extra man drafted in, and you saw a lot of drunken people at that time. When I mean drunken people I mean people that could hardly stand on their feet, because they had been drinking all day and without a single bite. If I could get them home, that's what I did, and the very worst thing that could happen was for them to be locked up for the night.

Looking back on things, it seemed a much simpler and more honest world. The majority of people prided themselves on their honesty, and they would hate to take anything belonging to somebody. That was ninety-nine per cent. Only occasionally would you get a man known as light-fingered, who might take a shovel from a field or some other trifle like that. The most common offence at the time would generally be under the Road Traffic Act, unlighted bicycles or carts, or perhaps forgetting to buy a licence.

When I started first the Garda usually lived above the barracks. I think that one of the reasons for this was that you had no time off anyway. They could work you 24 hours a day, and there was no such thing as overtime. You had two days off a month at the discretion of the sergeant, and if you didn't get along with the sergeant, you mightn't get your two days off. And when you left the Force and retired you had no house. And that's why it began to change.

Nowadays when the Guards are young they stand a chance of being shifted, depending on where the demand is, but once a man settles in and is married and has a house, they will rarely shift him. That's what has happened to me, and I can't see myself ever moving from Cappaghglass. I like to think of myself as part of the community.

In a city you get big areas that are just concrete jungles, and the young people growing up there are not only alienated from the Guards, but from society. The Guard in the city works for eight hours and goes home and is anonymous. He is probably living in an area that he doesn't police anyway and a lot of his neighbours don't even know he's a policeman. That's to his advantage, because in places like Dublin it was somehow always accepted from the old RIC days that the police weren't Irishmen at all, but a different breed. I wouldn't enjoy it. But I know that the Guards do a lot of good work in these places and it is often overlooked.

Down here it's quite a different thing. Perhaps I'm boasting when I say I regard most people as my friends. In a country area like this I regard my duty more as social work then police work, and that's quite honestly what it boils down to. There is no doubt at all of the fact. I'm always away calling on old people and taking messages – the doctor will bear me out – and because of this I get to know everyone and their problems.

It's no use the government setting down rules and regulations. "Oh yes, you can work your eight hours and go home." The people won't face it. If you know what I mean. They expect your presence. Do you think any man in the town with any kind of problem won't come and see me because I am technically off duty? I'm telling you, that sort of thing never works. They expect you to be there on call for them and I would expect them to call me out. Last week I was called out at night by two 'phone calls to my home, and they were both genuine cases. I think the guard that is not involved in communities is a bad guard, and it's as simple as that. You hope that people feel you are doing a fair job, and I think if you have a conscience anyway, you are.

There's a lot of new laws coming in, and we are supposed to have them off on our fingertips, but of course that's virtually impossible. We are meant to know our powers and to react immediately, and arrest or not arrest, and you can't go back and look up the book. But people today are better educated. What had made our job harder is that they know so much about the different laws. Every young fellow from fourteen upwards can tell you his rights so far as the Guards are concerned, and, literally, if we have a house broken into up the street, and we meet two suspects walking along, unless we have evidence against them, we can't take them to the station for questioning.

I maintain that if the policeman is faced by a situation on the street tonight or tomorrow, and he has to react and do things, the barristers will look up their books and see whether he did right or wrong. They have to go to their law books. We have definitely worse powers than any other police force in Europe for arrest and questioning.

When I first came to Cappaghglass more years ago than I like to remember, every second house looked a ruin. People didn't have paint, and if they had the money for paint, they would put it somewhere else. Because of this most small towns in Ireland looked very shabby. The money just wasn't there. I remember when I was going to school and the only way I could go to the cinema was by hunting rabbits. A few rabbits gave me the price of the picture. If you went up the street corner you'd have a group of lads just standing around talking because there was no television and there were very few radios. All that changed with money.

The value of life has gone down. I think the real violence started around 1969 before the troubles in the North got going. We were an unarmed force, because even the crminals in the south never carried arms. Now the guns are commonplace. I think television also has had something to do with the growth of violence; when young people see bombs going off and people being injured they lose the value of human life. During the 'fifties you never expected to have to face up to a man with a gun; at one stage it was recognized that the IRA wouldn't shoot. Today in any town in Ireland you can have a bank raid with shooting.

If you ask me why this has happened I would put a fair share of blame on this new liberalism. There's a lot of bleeding hearts and people saying, "Ah yes, the poor fellow may have murdered him because he flew into a rage," and that kind of thing. But really, unless the person can be caught, unless they feel they will be caught and punished, crime is going to get worse and worse. Our set of values has been completely overturned.

I also blame much of this on the drift away from religion. The country people really believed in religion, and it went very deep into their lives, and when it goes it leaves a big hole. I am not a terribly religious man myself, but the people must have something, and it's being discarded too rapidly. They all go rushing to Mass on Sunday and at the same time they are all living around. Look at all the things on TV about abortion and every God-damm thing. Now they don't bother thinking, for the television does it for them. There was something the other week about making the homosexual thing legal. And the Judge said, "No Way." They should do exactly the same about abortion. It's out. I think the young people are so anti-everything that they want to see everything changed. But recently I've noticed that there is a big swing back by the young, and it's nothing to do with being afraid of the priest. The priests and the clergy have changed with the times.

When I first came down here I remember saying, "It's a grand place for the summer, but in God's name, what are you going to do in the winter"? But the truth is that I have become so busy I haven't half the time for all the things I want to do apart from the job. I enjoy things in nature like walking and fishing, and there's always something to be done. And I can honestly say that I have a better social life than I would have in any of the big cities.

I think this is partly because I was brought up in the country and I'm a countryman at heart. I respect the small farmer with his thirty stony acres who has to work bloody hard to bring up his family. I respect him a hell of a lot more than these hippies who are coming in and who I think are quite mad. They expect to come in and buy seven or eight acres and grow all their food and vegetables and put themselves in a shack where you would hardly put pigs. That sort of thing is crazy.

Of course it's not only the fellows from the city who have problems getting employment. Down here too there's a shortage of jobs. Young fellows even talk of entering the Guards, but now there is a long waiting list for anything so secure. The problem about Ireland is that so many people have a relative in the Guards or you are married to one and this gives them a certain say. Politicians will always tell you that they are entitled to make representations through the Force but all I can say is that I have never been pressurized.

It seems funny to me that when I started off all I got was my pay of six pounds six shillings a week, and from that I had to deduct my digs and laundry. I didn't drink or smoke at that stage. Nowadays anyone lucky enough to be chosen as a Guard has a relatively well-paid job, on parity with the male nurses and prison officers roughly. I suppose some people might think we are privileged, but to me the most important thing about the Garda Siochana is that its members are by and large still drawn from the ordinary people of the country, and they still reflect their opinions.'

Gerard White, Solicitor. Aged 38.

Before modernization the office was Dickensian in its gloom and clutter. Behind the brass plate the first thing you saw was the high topped desk and then the two old ladies sitting among scrolls and documents scribbling or tapping at an ancient Underwood. Beyond them sat the senior partner in a large untidy room, where the roll-top desk and table were covered with papers and black deed boxes were stacked against the wall. Above the desk was a print of Grattan's parliament and a photograph of Gladstone.

That has all been swept away, including Grattan and Gladstone. The carpeted office is very modern and tidy now, with recording machines and such-like on the steel desk, signalling the age of communications. The crisp girl in the waiting room who takes messages and types silently onto a large electric typewriter with the aid of earphones is about forty years younger than the ladies who used to work here. All the changes have taken place since Gerard took over from his uncle.

He is plump and cheerful, a family man who enjoys his profession. He is on a number of prominent committees, a leading member of the golf club and a pillar of society. He likes to consider his work and his relationship to his clients as parallel to that of the family doctor. He is generally liked, although some people are critical that he makes too much money negotiating house sales and encouraging outsiders to come and live in the area.

★

'You can start a practice from scratch. Any man can go into a country town and put up his plate. Against that it takes a very long time to build your practice up. Many are called, but few are chosen. I came here straight away after finishing my law degree, because, like most countrymen, I had a relative in the business. If you like, "the uncle" handed his mantle to me. It wasn't all plain sailing. The simple fact is that people don't like going to a solicitor's office any more than they like going to a dentist's waiting room. But once they choose you, they keep coming back again and again.

When I started things were more leisurely. Everything was more formal and things were still done in longhand. It's not possible to modernize in the same way as, say, you could smarten up a group practice of doctors. Everything takes time, and if a man comes to see me, it will very likely mean a return visit, if not a third, while the documents are being prepared.

The most important quality you can have in dealing with people and the law is common sense. Perhaps they come in and tell you about some accident they have had, over which they are seeking compensation. You can't always accept what a client is telling you, because he is telling it from his own point of view, and all the time you must maintain an objectivity and be alert for attention to detail. It requires a hell of a lot of patience. Working with people in this way you often become aware of their most intimate and financial arrangements, and they tell you some things they wouldn't tell their best friend.

When I started the older solicitors spent most of their time dealing with disputes between neighbours. They could be outlandish, not only the usual quarrels about rights of way, but also rows about dowries for married daughters and even about a seat in the local church. That sort of thing is vanishing, thankfully. Those old disputes brought the solicitor little money and lots of problems. Dissatisfied losers often led to feuding in the neighbourhood, and feuding could last for generations and get handed down from father to son.

A city solicitor coming down here would find it very difficult to acclimitize himself without knowing the people and the area. About eighty-five per cent of my clients must be farmers. I don't have a farm myself, but I come from farming stock, and they would expect me to understand what they are talking about. Things like farm tax and the administration and inheritance.

Let's take a particular example, say a family who are handing over a place and may have a history of squabbling among themselves, and you are aware of this. You have to be. Perhaps the last settlement in another generation didn't work out too well, and you are automatically on guard in case the same thing happens again. You write down every syllable to the smallest detail like making sure that the old person has a right to have fuel in his kitchen for himself and his wife. You write that down. It sounds a bit daft saying that the transferee covenants to make sufficient fuel available for the winter for the transferer's kitchen, for the benefit of his old parents. But I have seen it happen where young people actually leave the kitchen fire unlit in the winter to freeze the old people out of it. It doesn't happen very often, but it's very important to know at the settlement.

Another thing is that people expect to be guided how to avoid litigation. There is hardly a week without some person coming into my office and I have to tell them, "Look, you may succeed in your action, but I would advise you not to take it, because you are only going to incur expense and create bad feeling without any material benefit." Nowadays the general trend would be to try and settle things and resolve the conflicting problems without going to court. Of course that makes sense.

There was this boundary between my client's land and his neighbours which was a stream, and the neighbour had erected a barbed wire fence in the stream. It sounded a bit unusual to me, since barbed wire can be a dangerous thing for cattle, and my client was rather concerned about it. He came into me, but instead of saying "Can I get the barbed wire removed?" he said, "I wonder, is he right?" And that question typified a change that has occurred in my experience over the past twenty years. Only a few years ago that same farmer would have said, "I want that barbed wire fence removed, or else," and it would have been a case of writing a letter, and giving the neighbour fourteen days to get rid of it. If he didn't, there would have been a full blown action in the circuit court.

When I went to see the boundary it seemed to me that the course of the stream had changed, and the farmer on the opposite side was quite entitled to have the boundary changed, because of the change of the stream. This had happened because the County Council had built a new bridge and created a different volume of water. The change had happened gradually, not overnight. So my client was quite happy with this, and went over to the neighbour and said, "Gerard White and I thought we were going to have law, but I'm glad we didn't . . . we'll shake hands on it."

And that typifies a big change. People are more clever now, and willing to listen to the other man's point of view. I think they read a lot more and see things on television. Young farmers now have more interest in getting on with farming and less inclination to get steamed up over problems with the neighbour. Now its nearly all car accidents. There are so many cases involving accidents listed in the courts that they can't be heard.

I always attended the District Court until I could afford a young assistant to spend the time in court. It takes up a lot of time and it doesn't pay. But a lot of the people who are up in the District Court are poor, so we have to make sure that any client is properly represented. Then there are things like the buying and selling of property, the administration of estates, and wills. There are several new statutes like capital gains and acquisition tax, and you always have to keep up to date or you can make serious errors.

There used to be a tradition of having Protestant and Catholic solicitors, like the shops. Catholics would regard the Protestant as a "gentry-type" office, and the Protestants would go there. That's mostly died away. The only occasion it might come into play would be in a mixed marriage, and the sort of settlement that might take place involving the father of a daughter who is marrying into a Protestant family.

In point of fact, it's not work involving mixed marriages that you are most likely to come across today. It's far more often marriage break-up. That's something we rarely had before. Sometimes the split occurs between newcomers to the area, say one of those authors who are residing in Ireland for tax benefits. The irony is that you've come to a tax haven and you are actually losing out on the community. The chances of your marriage foundering in the Emerald Isle are quite a bit higher than if you had stayed at home. People aren't aware of the stresses before they come to live here.

Among local people marriage break-up is mostly a compromise arrangement. I find the whole trend most distressing. You have seminars on it, the social worker and priest. You don't get any middle-aged people coming in, it's invariably something that happens in the first ten years of marriage. I suppose there is a social obligation to sort it out, and I think a lot of work is done down here by fellow parishioners in the church. Everyone knows it's a pity about Mary, she came from a good family . . . and they look after her and give her moral strength.

We have another problem here, and that's the infirm and old. The doctor and the Health Board may try and look after their health, but the solicitor has to look after their legal affairs, and these can become very complicated. You know that one of the great characteristics of the old Brehon law system was that there was no specific provision whereby younger people had to look after older people. There was no need for anything like that since it was a natural trait, apparently, that the older people were taken care of.

You probably don't remember, Peter, but at one time Dev made a speech in County Clare in which he advocated the "Dower House" system. And what he proposed was to give the older people a grant so that they could build a little two-roomed annex off the gable of the old farmhouse, so they could keep in touch with the family. They would be able to look after the grandchildren and tell them stories, and they could always have the safety valve of going back to their own place. It seemed a wonderful system, but unfortunately it never worked.

In an area of such a preponderance of old people the problem arises over the position of parents when they hand over the farm. When a farmer reaches the age of sixty-six, in order to qualify for something like an old age pension he has to transfer the farm over to his son and must pass a means test. But what I find a bit strange is that so often the old man is very slow to keep a right of maintenance. That's natural, but not very wise. It works like this; in order to get the pension he is going to transfer the farm to his son. You understand? He will keep the right of residence but won't keep any right of maintenance, because if he does they would cut his pension down by fifty pence a week, and he is not prepared for that. Well, say the son marries then, and the young woman comes into the kitchen. The young woman and the old woman don't hit it off well and the maintenance goes bang. And you are then asked why the maintenance wasn't worked out beforehand. You'd be surprised how often this can happen. Now I would advise any older farmer to get down in writing the rights he needs for his declining years and for the declining years of his widow.

From a practical point of view I have tremendous loyalty to the farmers around the area. I know their lives and they give me my bread and butter. The recession has affected everyone, so that when farming suffers we suffer too. Running an office like this requires a considerable amount of business. While the city fellow maybe analyses his income, tracking down how many hours he spends on a case, and how much an hour he can charge, in the country we would usually be a year behind in our fees. If you came in to me here to administer your father's estate, I know very well its going to be at least twelve months before I get paid.

That makes things especially difficult in a time when jobs are scarce. Recently we put an ad in the paper saying we needed someone, and we got fifty replies. And quite a lot of the solicitors replying volunteered to work for nothing in exchange for the experience they would get.

Generally I am well satisfied. I inherited a job I like in a place I like. I enjoy living in Cappaghglass. The pleasures of country living is in small things. If your child is sick, a neighbour will say "You know where we are if you want help." They don't push themselves into helping, but they do care. I like the fact that so many country ways survive. Television may have killed the *scoraicht*-ing but the old people still praise God in Irish if they bang their foot against the door. My work offers a permanent challenge – just keeping up with the new regulations and statutes keeps me busy. The great satisfaction about my work is that you know your job and can do it well, and people come back afterwards and tell you that was a watertight arrangement you made.'

Liam Hegarty, Republican. Aged 84.

He is an impressive man, well over six foot tall, with a shock of white hair. He joined the Volunteers in 1918 and subsequently fought in the Civil War on the Free State side. In his sitting room are photographs of old comrades in slouched hats, young soldiers in Free State uniform and an idealized portrait of Michael Collins. A framed Tricolour sits above a cabinet filled with presentation plate.

★

'My family has been in the same area for six or seven generations farming the same bit of land. My grandfather, who died in 1922, was born before the famine. I remember him pointing out a field in which he remembered people travelling about "aimlessly together" and that's how he described it. They were wandering around looking for food, and he said he saw the green of the grass in their mouths from eating the weeds among the corn. He said they died more from cholera than they did from hunger. He said that his family had a bit of wheat so the famine didn't hit them so hard. The wheat was grown to pay your rent.

In those days you couldn't put a big window in your house or they raised your rent, and before the Land Acts came about our parents walked with the rent, because if you had a good horse the landlords thought you were too prosperous. Wheat was a very important thing for Britain, because 'twas before the American prairies opened up. The farmers sowed so much wheat to make sure they had the money for the rent. It was a money thing. My family had this bit of wheat, enough to carry on. My grandfather said the fright was in every house. God Almighty, it was a very difficult time.

I'll tell you about it. Do you see, Britain was a great power for colonialism, and Ireland was one of the first of their conquests. And it was conquered by one of the English kings siding up with the McMurroughs, and it was they who invited over the Normans. But when the Normans came they became more Irish than the Irish themselves. I suspect the first lot of settlers got on better than anyone else. Of course later on you had all those divisions. Each generation had its own insurrection, if you like, but people still went along under that old Irish maxim, "in the shelter of each other's lives people live." I think that's a very apt expression of how people lived in the country. We learnt to cope with each other over the years, and there was no feeling of bitterness. Although there were landlords down here, we always got on with our Protestant neighbours. One of the sad anomalies of Irish history is that while the landlords kept to them-selves – I suppose they had to, there was little option – the greatest patriots were also Protestant, and that's a well-known fact.

When I was a boy I knew an old lady who lived at the crossroads here, and she told me that she had gone to America at the age of sixteen and she was ninety-two when she died. She went a few years after the famine. In those days you went on a sailing ship and the voyage took six weeks. All she carried with her was a "kerchief" . . . that was the old way . . . a red bandana, you know, with the four corners tied up together and you put the stick through it. They only paid for transport and water, and she lived on boiled potatoes and engine meal porridge until she arrived in America. To think today that you would send your little girl on such an arduous voyage for three thousand miles across the toughest ocean in the world. I remember her telling me that they used to go forward for a week, and be blown back the same distance the next week. It's the sort of story that you never forget, and I think it helped me to become a Republican. In those days about ninety per cent of people went off into the wilderness. Everyone was leaving the land, and they went by horse and car and on foot. All that history and suffering made us want our own freedom.

Anyway when we had the chance both myself and my brother decided to join the Volunteers against the English. Our parents were with us in principle, but in their judgement, they really laughed at us that we would take on Britain after beating Germany and the bloody world. We were going to be the fools that our people had been before and end up with the hangman's rope. They were just as patriotic as ourselves, but they hadn't the courage.

There were two different movements in Ireland then. You had the Ascendency, and they were conservative and Tory, and on the Irish side a liberal movement which supported Redmond. Redmond said that when the war was over Britain would give us a greater share of things, but of course he was overtaken by events. I still think that if the British government had given us Home Rule it would probably have avoided all the fighting. But it didn't happen that way.

So far as I was concerned fighting for your freedom is an inherited natural thing in every blooming country. It makes no difference where you are born. You are a unit, then you are a family, then you are a parish and then you are a country. You don't want to be told by someone else to obey foreign rules and regulations. You want to run your own country.

It was a tough enough war and everyone suffered. My father was badly wounded and he wasn't even fighting. When the barracks down here was blown up, a policeman picked up a bomb and threw it at my father's direction, and it killed the man he was talking to, and he got it in the back. One time I was arrested, and the soldiers and RIC men were going to burn down our house when they were stopped by a major in the British army who turned out to be our family doctor. He stopped them because there was nobody in the house, except one wounded man who was my father. He said what they should be doing was to take him away for treatment. That's the way things went.

In this area here we obeyed the rules of warfare. We didn't do the deeds that were done by individuals in other places. I maintain we had a different outlook then to what the IRA in the North have today. I didn't go out to fight the War of Independence just to do to the Ascendency what they did to us. I didn't go out to exterminate everyone that was against me – that wasn't our motto. Every town I took over I saw that the Protestant people had safety just the same as ourselves.

Later we got as bitter fighting each other as we got against the English. What the Civil War lost for us was our spirit of sacrifice. Before the Civil War we wanted nothing, only our freedom. Number one. And we were prepared to sacrifice everything, our homes, our lives and families in pursuit of that.

I followed Michael Collins, and I could still cry to think of his death. He was a man brought up like myself out of a little farm, and he had grown up with a highly patriotic sort of background. Those sort of men meant business. I still believe that the idea Michael Collins had was to build this country into a position that the North would have been anxious to join in. We would have done it, only for the Civil War, for it killed that, and brought into the North schisms of every sort. It all ended badly, and I suffered because I was always an independent spirit.

When we got back to sanity after the Civil War it wasn't long before we had to endure the ravages of the economic war. It started because Dev kept the annuities that were going to England to buy out the

Land Act. He didn't pay them and kept them for budgetary purposes. England retaliated by refusing to take our cattle. The big farmer and the small farmer were all hit together and the price of cattle fell to nothing. It caused terrible unrest. Farmers stopped paying their rates, and they started a special police force which went around collecting their cattle from them. They had a sale then and brought in fellows from the North to do the job.

I remember one case when there was a seizure of cattle in Cappagh-glass, and there was a birth in the house and they asked if one cow could be kept for the mother and child. But the police even threatened to burn the house and take everything away. I can tell you all this made me feel very bitter. The bloody man who was in the army with me, and was carrying out this business, never flashed me a look of recognition because he thought it would interfere with his progress.

To tell the truth I didn't see that much of the economic war because I was locked up in Arbour Hill prison for three and a half years and never saw a newspaper. Before, it had been Out the British, but the moment Dev and his crew came into power in 1932 it was Out anyone who took part in the Civil War against them.

The first time I was arrested it was by an old comrade. He said, "Liam, I have a warrant for your arrest, but you've been a good friend to me and I'll give you a chance to get rid of anything in your possession. I have the house surrounded so don't try to escape." He gave me five minutes to get rid of everything. There was a little window, do you see, too small to climb out of until I got hold of the frame and pulled it back into the room. The river was outside and I went out. Down I went in the branches and trees of the river, and lay in the bank below, and later I was picked up by friends. But they got me in the end. Best not to give that time too much thought.

I believe that while Irishmen and Englishmen should learn to live with each other, both sides should realize how different our cultures and way of life are. That's what's been the trouble. Look how different they are. The Irishman is a religious animal, and the Englishman is largely a godless person. In England the tendency of the serf was to change his style and get into industry. Here you didn't have that. Here you made do with what you had or emigrated. I have heard a person say that there are about ten classes in England and they put a lot of store on it. The people in the middle class tend to segregate themselves into upper-middle class and lower-middle class and other footling sub-divisions. In Ireland it isn't altogether a classless society, but it's more clear cut. You can divide people up into those who have and those who haven't. It's not just money, but things like education and tradition.

Take the way an average Englishman behaves when he comes here. Although he wants to be friendly and means well, nine times out of ten he gets it all wrong and makes a complete cockup of things. He has the wrong attitudes completely. That's the way I see it, and I've watched it for years. Perhaps he stops the car and prattles on about the weather to someone who has twelve acres of hay lying flat on the ground. Take something as basic as Sunday afternoon. The Englishman will spend his time gardening or washing the car, while the man down here is waiting to get a couple of pints in the bar.

I remember an Englishman who was staying in a house down the road, and he hadn't got a car license. The Guard told him, "Ah, sure, it's only a pound, and the fine would be only a pound," as if, Don't bother to get it. He could never understand. And then there's the punctuality bit. If he asks a man to fix the window at nine o'clock in the morning, he expects him to be there at nine o'clock – and they don't do that sort of thing here.

I'm not blaming either race, but we must recognize how different our cultures and traditions are. Hopefully we will go on from there and people will be able to come to terms with each other.

I'm still what you might call an old-fashioned Republican. I've no time for the way they go killing up in the North. As a matter of fact, I'd rather lose my life than do that. They like to say it was the same with the old IRA, but it wasn't. I was talking just now about the English and the differences between them and the Irish. But the same is true of the Northerners. Do you know what a friend told me lately? Listen, he said, you've tried to get the Northerners down here long enough, but if they come they will have the whole bloody country to themselves. They are a hard-hearted business crowd, and business is their way of life. Whether Catholic or Protestant, they all have the same sort of hard attitude. And, he said, they are a bloody different type of tribe to ye here.'

Mick O'Keefe, Stone Mason. Aged 62.

He is small and wiry with a humorous face and eyes that quickly size you up. A number of missing teeth. His farmhouse stands right up on top of a hill between sea and sky. He escaped the slavery of farming by turning to building and working with stone. The farm has always come second in his mind.

Recently he demonstrated his skill as a stone worker, when a man from the city bought up the ruin of a castle. Six hundred years of weather had reduced the building to a shell, and Mick made it good as new.

He tells stories of the old landlords without much malice. About the tenant who received money from an American relation and paid her debt before it was due – next year the rent was upped. How any old shipwreck or piece of salvage was claimed as a feudal right. Now the big house is knocked, the great ballroom dismantled – by Mick – and the trees that cloaked the estate have gone. Instead of landlords you get city people and foreigners coming. Until the recession converting cottages was a pastime of theirs which brought Mick profit. He regards the newcomers as valuable additions to the community, welcoming them as neighbours and friends.

*

'My house is mud. The old people around here who built the houses we still live in mostly used mud. They would dig a hole in the garden, pile up the earth, throw water on it and make a mortar. It was as simple as that. The only cement they would ever use was one bag for the chimney, and the rest would be mud with a lime mortar finish. I remember one old man telling me how he heard his father tell a man, "Don't spare the mortar, for the stones are hard to get." That was always the way of things, and quarrying and finding stones took much harder work. At the seaside, at the cliffs they used to quarry them.

I have always been interested in building with stone, and when I was a boy I used to watch the men cutting away and chiselling, for you know all the walls around this part of the country are made from stone. The first job I ever had was repairing the old pier below the big house, and for that I got fifty-seven shillings.

When I started, it was expected that I would help on the farm until the big rush was over in October, and then I would be free to go until the spring. "I go away working and come back at the cuckoo," that's what I would say. I tiled roofs, I built walls all over the three parishes. And lately I restored that old castle.

It was a difficult old thing, and there was always a fierce pressure on you to think things out. I'd lie awake at night. After a couple of hours going to bed I'd ponder and think, and things would fall into place, and next morning I could walk back to the job with no bother. I got ideas as I went along. The architect said to me now, I see a lot of things up in the tower. When he saw me started, he maintained that I had done a better job than he had planned, so he let me go ahead. When you work you get better ideas, and a lot of his ideas were changed.

In working with stones you have to watch out for certain things. Some stones have a soft nature, and you can dress them, while others are as hard as a smith's anvil and you could do nothing with them. Take something simple like a stone wall. You can't put down one stone over the next and have the seams in a straight line. When you strike the first block, the next stone should be only half the length so that you cover every joint. A lot of the farmers would like to build a wall with a pattern, but its more troublesome and harder to do. Things like that take a lot of patience, and time, and the young people today wouldn't want any of it.

The thing I want to tell you about building, Peter, is that it's the gift. It's the same with building and the blacksmith, the shoemaker and the carpenter. It doesn't matter if you can't write a word, if you have the gift. You can learn, but if you have the gift you will be better. You are better off than the man who has served his time.'

THE LAND

JOHN GAHAN	Dairy Farmer, *Aged 48*
MARTIN FITZGERALD	Dairy Farmer, *Aged 36*
FRANK GANLY	Pig Farmer, *Aged 55*
JOE McCARTHY	Shopkeeper, *Aged 52*
BRENDAN SLATTERY	Publican, *Mid-fifties*

In the years most brilliant weather
heifers low
through green fields, not driven nor beaten,
tranquil, slow.

Song of the hermit, Marbhan.
Trans. Frank O'Connor.

What land means to a peasant people, that love of it, can be more jealous than love of a woman and more steadfast because it is embedded in the past.

Woodbrook, David Thompson.

John Gahan, Dairy Farmer. Aged 48.

Every morning and evening the Friesians make their way along the
lane to the yard and milking parlour. The lolling procession takes its
own time and comes its own way. Each cow, eager to unload her
gallons of rich milk, had a numbered tag pierced in her ear. They total
over fifty. When John took over the farm from his father there were
six. He has seen not only the numbers grow, but the milk yield from
each cow almost double. The sixty acre farm is now achieving what
John considers an optimum of production, but in spite of the large
turnover he insists the profit margin is very small.

He works hard, winter and summer, always seeming to be riding
a tractor, often with his children perched up beside him. He never
went to an agricultural college, but learned the hard way from
experience.

He didn't want to be a farmer, but he didn't have a choice. There
was no work outside the twenty-five acre holding he inherited from
his father. Although people may envy his prosperity and happy family
life, he has some regrets that he never enjoyed a secondary education.
He takes an interest in local history, enjoys reading and if he had the
time and money, would like to travel. He sees his generation as
forming the great divide in Irish farming. His lifetime has seen the
changes. He learned to plough with a horse and remembers the old
farmhouse with its open fire, and how every evening neighbours used
to call in to play cards and talk.

The old place is transformed from the way it was in his father's day.
It has grown so much bigger, and the yard is full of machinery. It used
to be a sour old joke that the Irish farmer was more interested in the
well-being of his cows than of his wife. The Gahans' modernized
farmhouse is streamlined and well-appointed; John's wife, Breda, has
washing and drying machines and a freezer. The television aerial
hovers over the slate roof.

John has had to learn to keep proper accounts. His father kept
figures in his head. He feels that farming in Ireland is undergoing
a Darwinian struggle, and only the fittest will survive. The less

progressive farmer will be eased out by competition and high costs. You have to be part business man and part everything else.

Nothing is easy about dairy farming and John finds so many things have to be done that he hardly has the time to read the papers. The cows have to be brought in and milked every day, and then there is the run down to the creamery. The silage and hay, the dry stock, and countless other demands need his attention.

The EEC grants have dried up, and the problems of the Levy loom. Prices are bad and expenses are soaring. But John wouldn't leave farming now. For one thing, he has the security of owning his own farm, for another the pleasure of rearing his own cattle and raising his milk yield. You keep at it, he says, smiling at you. Of course, many farmers will go to the wall, and many of these were on the way out anyway. He is critical of the farmer's dole and easy handouts, but he will be the first to defend the rights of the small farmer.

From the hill behind his house he can see seven different parishes, and all around are the scattered farmsteads of his neighbours. The first man who arrived here three thousand years ago, John will tell you, was a farmer, and he sees himself carrying on that very ancient tradition.

★

'I was attached to this place all my life and I was farming from the day I began to walk. This isn't a grain growing area, cows have always been the thing. The climate is suitable for them and grass is the best crop grown. You have the cows, and also the calves, and the dairying is the foundation of the dry stock industry as well.

Our house is an old one. I can just remember the open fire before the first range was brought in. I used to blow the bellows when I was small before going to school, and was always delighted to see the sparks going up the chimney. My great-great-grandfather had the first farm here, and that would have been around 1830. I can remember my grandfather talking about the famine; when he mentioned it he would take off his hat in memory of the dead. I met an old woman once who said her grandmother told her she used to take the children when they died on her back to be buried while they were hot, before they became stiff. It was tough, you know.

We only had one horse, which did all the ploughing and harrowing. I ploughed at ten or eleven years old. The drills hadn't come in then for the potatoes, and ridging was very tough work. The horse was called Paddy, and he got more care than anyone in the house. People were more enterprising then, with their sows and hens and everything, and they used to grow a little corn. That seems to be going out now, which is a great pity. Before the creamery came we had our own separator, and my mother did the churning. I cannot remember that, but I do remember bringing the wheat over to the mill for grinding. Younger people won't believe me when I tell them that today. I also used to take the horse to the forge for shoeing. There were great tradesmen then – masons and carpenters, and I remember John Sullivan whose job was to kill the local pigs. He would walk up to our house through the fields with his bag in which he kept two knives and a thing called a jugget. Then the day came when I had to hold a pig for him.

Our school was three miles down the road, and we walked there whatever the weather. The National Schools then were very strict and Miss Donovan, the teacher, was a genius. We learnt the basics, English, Irish and maths. After we left almost everyone was forced to take the boat. There were six boys and three girls in my class at school, and I am the only one of them living in Cappaghglass today.

The truth was that unless you had some scholarship or some wealthy friends or relations, there was no hope of any other training in life. You were stuck with the farm. I would have preferred to go away, but the opportunity wasn't there. My brother, who should have been the farmer, went to a secondary school. I think part of the trouble was the tradition that if Michael or Jim was bright he was told "the farm is no place for you." It was the dull chap who was kept on as a farmer, and that in itself contributed to the backward attitude and decline in farming. But I was fortunate that my father was probably a good deal ahead of his contemporaries in his ideas about farming. He would come up with what would be called today the right ideas – getting in good grass seed, getting the yield per cow up, getting good cows, and making the most out of them. He was also keen on reclaiming land and digging drains. I used to take tea to him after school, and you couldn't see him at all, as he was often down six feet underground with a pick and shovel making drains. There were no grants whatever then.

It was pretty quiet when we were growing up in the late 'forties. We knew every passing car by the sound of its engine, because anyway there were only three or four. You would know whether it was Paddy Lyons, the vet, who had an old V8, or the doctor in his Vauxhall. On the farm we only had the few cows. Prices were always bad. I remember once in the fair at Cappaghglass we sold a line of calves for twenty-five pounds. They were lovely animals, but you had to get rid of them, especially when you were nearing the time to pay the rates. That cost eight pounds half-yearly. It sounds small, but I assure you it wasn't easy to have it. Another time we sold a fine Hereford calf for four pounds fifty. If I sold one today, it would be for a hundred and eighty pounds, and that's the difference.

I remember as a young lad going to fairs with my father and walking about six miles to Cappaghglass. We would often be running after a few cattle, and they wouldn't be used to traffic. If they met any lorry, they would go over a ditch and across two or three fields, and you had to get them out on the road again. I remember it always seemed to be soaking wet. There's no doubt the buyers broke the hearts of poor farmers. They had the money and could do what they liked. A lot of them had big ranches up in the country, and you'd know any buyer would be well padded in comparison with the farmer. And you might be standing in the rain for hours – it was a tough racket.

One of the big changes in my life has been the change from the fair to the Mart. In a fair you had to know the value of your beast, but the tangling is not yet gone and the buyers are still doing the rings. The Marts are meant to send in someone if the man isn't getting near the value of the animal he is selling. A farmer can also go in and ask a neighbour to bid up for him. A lot of dishonesty, I call it, still goes on in the Mart, but not to the same extent as at the fair.

I got the farm in 1950 when my father died. He was a great man, but stuck in a bad time. If he was alive today, I don't think he'd recognize the place. I think that in the last ten or fifteen years our milk yields have gone up thirty-five per cent. I remember my father coming home from the fair with maybe twenty pounds for a couple of cattle, and on the way out of the town he'd go into the shop and pay off his debt, and maybe go home with only a pound or two in his pocket, for he would owe the shopkeeper that much. You paid off your debt on the fair day.

I was the first generation to see the improvements, and I have seen nearly both sides of it. I remember doing things the hard way when potatoes were struck with the spade. The old people used to aim at having about fourteen pounds saved every November, which would last until the following March. They wouldn't be making anything on the farm, you see, and would have to buy tea and sugar. We weren't as pinched as that by any means, but things weren't easy.

Electricity came in the early 'fifties, and it's amazing how we take it for granted. You have forgotten the time when you had to get the paraffin when you had lights in the evening. If it happened tomorrow morning that there was no more oil – remember the scare ten years ago? – half the new generation would die from starvation. They couldn't tackle a horse, for example or plough with one. At least I could go back to that if I had to. But I feel if there was some disaster, all the younger generation would end up in the mental home.

After the electricity, you had the water grants. I got my first tractor in the mid-'fifties, and after that the farming boom had started. If you had eight cows in 1950, you would have thirty today. The turn came when the farmer's house was on a par with the town house. Before that the farming people were tolerated in the towns, but there was a bit of class distinction, all right.

I can't imagine that there will ever again be such changes as I have seen in my lifetime. We have seen the big break through. Labouring has gone, there's no doubt of that. In the old days they worked hard for very little reward. It was also to some extent a way of life. They were not concerned in profit margins and keeping accounts. Money wasn't a very big thing with them. I remember as a very small boy stooking corn and turning hay with a fork. Nowadays if a man wants to do something with a shovel, he does it because he wants to keep fit or extend his yard, or something.

I get up about six, and my first job in the morning is to bring in the cows. If it is winter time they are already in the yard. I am still delivering milk to the creamery, although that business is going out. I am yet to make the decision to pay to get the bulk carrier to come this way. Most of the big farms have the bulk tanks. Going to the creamery isn't much of a time-waster these days. In the old days, it was a big occasion when you met everyone, but now I do it in ten minutes and there's no delay. No waiting for the separated milk to come through.

Of all the jobs I have to do I think one of the hardest in dairying today is harvesting the silage. You need help for that. You have to plan how many acres you are going to have for silage or early grass, and so on. The important thing about dairying is the monthly cheque, and if you also do dry cattle you probably get another cheque three times a year.

I think in farming you must like what you are doing. If you don't like working with cows, there is not much point in doing it, even if you are making money. Of course that applies to most things in life – you are lucky to get the work you like.

One of the problems that affects me is trying to get more land. It isn't easy. Although there is a lot of waste land around here that isn't being farmed effectively, you can't get your hands on it. Everything has an owner, and with dairying you must have land adjoining your farm. Being a farmer myself I can understand the old attitudes about owning your own piece of land. My father was born at the turn of the century when the Land Purchase Acts were coming in and landlordism was a dirty word. People still talk about how tenants were charged excessive rents and how they could be dispossessed at the drop of a hat or because someone was in a bad mood or temper. Because of all that, security of tenure became terribly important to people. It wasn't just a question of working the land efficiently or anything like that. Just to have it and own it. That's why there is still a fierce hunger for the land. I don't know what it is, for it's like a disease in some people.

I wouldn't blame anyone if he misuses the resources he has, because people in Ireland won their freedom to do their own thing, and nobody is going to take that away again. But I also think that people like myself who were born since the foundation of the state have a more practical and business-like approach than the generation further back. My reaction to the thing is not emotional.

I think we will have to move to a situation where the farms become larger and more efficient. It will not happen overnight, but there will be a gradual progression. People will retire or sell up, and they will lose the incentive for doing this kind of thing. I think the forces that will bring pressure upon them will be economic forces, and that's the best way to do it. That way people have time to get themselves sorted out. It's happening already. The hard facts are that over twenty to thirty years there has been a big drop in the number of small farmers. I don't mean by this to be anyway critical of the small farmer – I am one myself.

I dislike laws saying that you cannot do this or that as a means of running the country, and I tend to agree with Ronald Reagan about reducing government in people's lives. I also agree to some extent with Mrs Thatcher that if people are lame ducks they can't be helped over stiles.

I would never like to see the sort of factory farming business you have in England, because it takes all the attraction out of farming. If small farmers go altogether, if that happens in Ireland, the land won't be worth living on. If we lose our people, what good are big empty spaces to us? To have a viable farm income today you need at least twenty-five to thirty cows, or something in that region. I'd say roughly a quarter of the farmers around here have this. If you will do a cow on one acre, you will do it on twenty-five or thirty acres of reasonably good land.

With minimum assets in a place like this of over a hundred thousand

pounds, it's very important to keep careful accounts. If you don't
know where you are going, how can you know where you are going
to arrive? But I also think that a dairy farmer is a farmer first of all, and
after that part-accountant, part-mechanic, part-builder and everything. I've told you that fifty cows are not a great liability so far as
labour is concerned, and it's not heavy work. You are just moving
around morning and evening. What you are doing is washing cows,
which is a very light job, putting on milking machines and taking
them off. The milk goes into the tank automatically.

It's a one man job, and one man can manage up to seventy cows. A
second man would be no use there. The only time I need help is in
harvesting silage. I think we have reached a sort of plateau in regard to
any more great changes. I know farmers who have automatic cleaning
equipment in their houses. They press a button in their cow houses
and they are automatically cleaned. If you can afford that, fair enough.
But it doesn't push the yield up any more, and you are talking about a
situation where you are going beyond the necessary things.

But it's essential to have your dairy modernized with good equipment if you are ever to get away. Nobody is going to do relief milking
on an antiquated system. I'm not talking about anything very elaborate. I'm talking about a milking parlour, and collecting yards. I'm
talking about a tank to put milk into. They are simple but essential
things that'll set you back around £15,000 for that set-up. You have to
have it, if you want to beat the old, old problem with cows. They
require a seven day week and there's no escaping that. But the relief
milking has been another factor that has changed our lives. My
generation again will be the first generation of farmers who take
holidays – even if it is only for a week in the year.

I don't envy people the move to early retirement, and I like to be
always busy. I wonder if this early retirement isn't a disaster? No one
should retire and do nothing. It must be very hard to tell someone that
at any stage of their lives they are redundant and not wanted any more.
I think that the greatest pleasure of farming is being your own boss,
and that you are basically working for yourself. You can work very
largely in your own time and are not answerable to anybody. Last
week an American cousin came to stay whom I hadn't seen for years,
and I only did the minimum of things and had a very pleasant week.
And that's something I personally value.

It's opened up. People have had a much more complete education
and have more need to fulfil their lives than just working around the
house and farm all day. Of course there is the TV, but you also want a

balance of reading and other things. I'm interested in local history. At one time there was a fright for tracing one's relations, but now people don't care. The old people always talked about history. There's hardly a parish in Ireland where the history goes back further than here. We have castles and stone circles, and many of these things should be in State care. Two years ago we had this lovely stone alignment and the farmer on whose land it was got it into his head that he'd knock it down, and he hired a bulldozer. I will always remember that as being the blackest day.

I voted against the EEC in the referendum, for I think as the years go by it will become a rich man's club. Ireland produces about five per cent of the dairy products within the community, and the history of the EEC has been that whatever proposals come forward, the final solution is never the same. They have had mountains of butter and lakes of milk, but you'll find that they will suddenly vanish, no one knows where. To feed the Russians or old age pensioners in the Pacific Isles. The problems with the Levy haven't affected anyone I know in this area – I haven't had to make any cutbacks yet, and nor had anyone else around here.

If my son wants to take over the farm when he grows up, more power to him. But I wouldn't divide up the land like they did fifty or sixty years ago. I certainly think there is a big future for the progressive farmer in this part of Ireland. My own feeling is that you are seeing the last of the old-style farmers who for whatever reason don't want to change. But you had better get your camera and tape recorder out quickly before its too late.

Is it worth it? Many visitors come down here in summer and tell me how lucky I am to live in such a place. They talk about the sea and the mountains, but of course they only see it for a couple of weeks. But they are right in some ways. I think we'd miss the things around us if they weren't there – the seasons and changes of scenery. They are part of you, and I am aware of them, anyway. The land is important for me and my family in this way – I like living here. It's a very attractive place. If one just had a house here and no land, it's an attractive place to live.'

Martin Fitzgerald, Dairy Farmer. Aged 36.

The farmhouse, a miniature Georgian replica with traditional door-way under a fanlight and windows whose tops are curved like eyebrows, was built by Martin's great-grandfather exactly a hundred years ago. Architectural style was slow to change in this area. There is a ringfort on the nearby hill surrounded by the brilliant green grass of the vast field that Martin has enlarged and sprinkled with all the correct fertilizers. The rural charm of the scene is dissipated by the huge tin barn erected with the aid of a grant. The milking parlour and concrete yard have been added in the last couple of years.

Martin is small, dark, deeply serious – passionate when he discusses farming matters. He sees to his cows and pastures with an intensity that suggests a general on the eve of battle. His wife, Anne, who was a nurse before she married, grows flowers and vegetables which she sells through the ICA* each week and also to hotels during the tourist season. They have two small children.

*

'You can walk into a dairy farm quite easily if you are brought up to it. Of course you have to inherit it or have the money, and you haven't a hope on God's earth of getting into farming otherwise. I inherited the farm twelve years ago when my father died. I was an only child and it was a foregone conclusion. I'm lucky, I suppose – farmers rely as much on succession as kings. Otherwise you have to win the pools if you want to buy land. The Land Commission is dead, a has-been – it never had any clout to divide up farms. You'd need about a hundred thousand for a start – I'd say that would go a long way to set someone up. It also helps to have been to college the way I did, but it's by no means essential.

Here we have a hundred and eighty or a hundred and ninety acres. When I started off there were fifty acres that you could cut hay off, and we've reclaimed about a hundred and twenty acres, I should say. It's a

*Irish Countrywomen's Association.

fact that any boggy looking land around here can be reclaimed. There is no land that you can't actually grow grass on. You can grow grass on anything unless it is a rock.

I couldn't have done it without the EEC grants. There is no point in going after these things in a Mickey Mouse way, and you have to get in the big machines. That way I have doubled the farm in the past six years. We did the bog five years ago. We found stuff on that bog, you know. We found old houses, we found trees that had trunks on them four feet wide.

It means that when we started we had twenty-five cows, and now we can support over a hundred. We haven't reached maximum yet, but the land has been reclaimed, and you can talk about a hundred and fifty acres of farmland now. I'd say it was worth about eight hundred to nine hundred and acre, and as a unit would push a thousand an acre.

We have a few pieces of land that simply can't be reclaimed because the rocks would kill you, and there we've planted trees, little patches of them all around the place. The fields are the biggest change. You have to knock out a whole lot of fences and change sizes and shapes. It's got to be done if you want to get contractors in for work. And if you are cutting a field for hay and there's half an acre of fences, that could go across the good hay. It's much easier also to turn inside a big field.

There's no real argument for keeping small fields. If you are doing it efficiently you will take the cattle off the land for the winter. They will be in from the end of November to the beginning of March so that you don't need shelter the way you did in the old days. Small fields are out because maintenance is too high, and by taking out fences you get all the extra acreage. A four acre field is about the smallest you would be wanting now.

I reckon our cows have come from about four hundred gallons to nine hundred pushing a thousand now. That's all in twelve years. The improvement is from a combination of factors – different wintering, feeding them properly and using good AI bulls – inseminating the cows from the best bulls in Europe. And we are still light years behind Britain. There are a lot of cows in Britain around the two thousand gallons mark, while the average quality farmer over there is pushing twelve hundred.

The minimum acreage for an economic farm would be sixty acres and that's not owing the bank anything, so that you are not paying back capital. That would mean you can make an income for two kids and build up your machinery slowly. Grants have all been stopped since the EEC has run out of money, and subsidies have been cut down drastically. Germany has been supplying the EEC and they are not exactly flush themselves. Anyway farmers can make enough money for themselves if they want to. We're on our own now. There are plenty of Irish farmers who can hold their own with any in Europe bar the Dutch. The Danes are better for housing for pigs and things like that, and can produce food on a small holding a lot more efficiently than we can. But we are down to a cow per acre, and that's a thousand to fifteen hundred gallons off that one acre. At fifty pence per gallon which is the very minimum acceptable price after collection, that acre is doing its bit.

You don't do farming for the money. If I was to get overtime for the work I do I'd be a rich man. Money doesn't enter into everything. The only time I have money in my pocket is when I go into a pub. But you have massive security as a start. The farm itself is a hell of a security. If we were to sell this place with all the stock we'd do well. Of course you have credit. If you want to do something you have this incredible credit. You have the stock to back it up, you have machinery to back it up.

There's pleasure in the way of life, and something else. People talk about land being the sacred Irish thing, and there have been more feuds and fights over tiny square feet of land and things like water rights and rights of way. Our place has been tied up over the years, so we're lucky and there are no loose ends any more. But if someone was driving their cows through our yard or if they had a right of way to a field at the top, I would go crazy.

People are entitled to do what they like with their land, even if they aren't using it correctly. There's no doubt about that. The way I look at it, the less that people are producing of what you produce, the better. If they are inefficient they are contributing less to the milk surplus, the butter surplus and the beef surplus. I know that sounds a bit cynical and makes farming seem like something pointless. But if we're driven to it, we'll have to diversify. If the Super Levy comes about, we'll go into other things. I've been thinking of cheese as a way of making milk into a solid, and that's just one example of getting something different going.

If you want to farm efficiently it's in your own interest to look after the land and make it more fertile, building up the fertility year by year. You can make mistakes of course, and then some farmers go very wrong. I think insecticides are lethal in the wrong hands. They can just wipe out wildlife. A lot of people use them and don't even read the label. Some fellow in a shop told them about it. People tend to be too lavish about the sprays. There's a spray for every bloody thing now, gorse, fern, briars. Fern is a poison to animals – the male fern, that is. When the grass is getting scarce and they look lovely and juicy the animal will eat then and will start bleeding internally from haemophilia.

The chemicals make life a lot easier, of course. If you are getting a combine to cut your grain, now, you have to rely on the spray. It was all right with the old hand machine when you hand picked the old docks out of it, but now the seeds are spread back behind the combine, so you are covering the ground with all your weed seeds. Whereas if you spray it in time the weeds are screened out perfectly.

The paperwork is hell. We've had to worry about book work for the last ten years. The first five years were bad, the next two worse and the last two have been hell. We have our own accountant now and he's brilliant. I used to spend four or five working hours a week in an office and a couple of hours on Sunday tidying up when a new lot would come in. I hate the sight of it, and the accountant is a godsend. He's someone my father never had. My father had everything he wanted to know inside his head. We had to get into proper accounting at the £50 valuation which brought us into the tax bracket. As well as that we've been breeding pedigree cattle for ten years now, and you have to remember the grandparents and the pedigrees – all that has to be recorded.

Even if we are making a hundred thousand, we are only getting six thousand out of the whole thing. We are probably sitting on half a million to make six thousand, and that's ridiculous if you think about it. Until Anne started this vegetable thing we never got cash in our hands. You got a creamery cheque and normally you would pay the bills in the middle of the month, and they hot things up at the bank the same time as the cheque is due. Then the cheque goes in and you take out £200 to keep you going as long as possible. It's crazy, no matter what stage you are, you are never solvent.

I worked out that until last year for every pound you made you got about ninety pence back on it. Last year you made forty-nine pence in every pound. In real terms your income has halved, although technically your income has doubled. We have to double our output to maintain our level, and are able to do so because we had the raw materials to build up stock. We had the breeding stock there and the machinery. We put in a cattle shed for the cattle, and that cost £20,000.

We'll be offered a grant of £4,000 for that on condition that we build a slurry pit that will cost £5,000. The grants were incredible when we first went into the EEC, but no longer.

If you have enough land you can work the whole farm from an office. The other day I was talking to a man who has four hundred acres, and he doesn't step outside. I could do the same if I was in a grain growing area with a nice tillage farm. But in dairying it's night and morning. There's no way you could grow grain here, you'd be picking stones for the rest of your life.

We had a guy to help for a time. We had him for six months and it cost me five hundred pounds in stamps and he was taking £75 a week in his hand. We were paying his petrol bill and that was another £10, so that was £85. He was costing £110 a week for five days, nine to six, and missing both milkings. But he could have gone to a building site and made easier money.

I think the small farms will sell out and the big farms will get bigger. If you have a big farm, you can buy a smaller farm and make it productive and have a bigger farm still. And that's the way it's happening. You can buy the new farm in your son's name.

I wouldn't like my weekends free. Christ, now, I wouldn't know what to do with them. Normally we take off a couple of weeks in the year. The trouble is always the money – you always need it. The list price of the tractor we're using at the moment is sixteen and a half thousand pounds. I often go out in the morning and spread something like fifteen hundred quid of bag manure on the ground, and in the evening I will be scraping my pocket for a few pounds. But we like the life. This house is as busy as Regan's hotel most days. Once people have cars they are not missing out on anything. There is no loneliness about it.'

Frank Ganly, Pig Farmer. Aged 55.

From far away you can see the feed silos sticking out over the hedges, bright galvanized cylinders gleaming silver in the sun. The piggery is like an old-fashioned hotel – but hardly the Ritz – where a continual stream of guests is given constant adequate food. Frank's set-up is a model of its kind, spotlessly clean and well maintained. The slurry falls through slats and goes to some secret tank from where it is carried away. There are no obnoxious fumes. The pigs loll like great white pillows beside an endless stream of foodstuff pouring into their troughs night and day. The temperature is set, everything is done to facilitate growth and feeding, and the rapidly fattening guests eat and sleep oblivious of their approaching fate.

Frank buys them young, fattens them and sells them to the factory. He still has a few pigs in old pig houses with straw covered floors, stench and dirt, but those places are antediluvian compared to the new heated pens. He believes that the pigs in their luxury premises are happy and contented. If they weren't, he would soon go out of business. They have to put on steady weight and become fat, and this they do consistently.

He went into the business determined to make a go of it. He has seen too many small farmers and other pig farmers go to the wall as a result of the fluctuating market – the pig cycle. At one time the pigs are very good and then they are very bad. Pigs get too plentiful and the price goes down. Pig farming requires a farmer's feeling and love of animals, together with an aptitude for figures. The margin between profit and loss is terrifyingly slim; what he calls the 'conversion rate' is crucial to his success or failure. His wife complains that any money they make goes back to pigs rather than to their home and children. Frank says isn't that always the Irish way?

*

'Our farm is only a small one of about sixty acres and early on I realized that if I was to continue in farming the only thing was to specialize. Since I was a lad my father encouraged me and I have been rearing and selling pigs from the time I was fourteen. I started with two, and then I got eight, and today I have fifteen hundred, and soon that figure will be topped.

The aim is to make more money out of them than you would by farming the land. You have to spend a lot of money and invest a lot of time and acquire a knowledge of pigs. If you are not going to do that, you are only wasting your time. When you are putting up these units and buildings you have a declining asset, because they will only last about ten years. If you put your money into buying more land, the land is always there. So in order to make pig farming pay, it is essential to get higher profits.

When I was young it was done in a casual easy way. You always had a sow rooting around the yard, and when she was farrowing she was always brought in next door to the kitchen. My mother would spend the night with her until the litter was born. It was principally a woman's business. Our food and the food for the majority of people around here was nearly always pork. A neighbour would come over whose job was to kill the animal, and it would be cut up and salted. Everybody got a piece. There was the barrel of crubeens and pig's head. I still enjoy crubeens and pig's head.

But when I started out the old way of doing things was already going. It just didn't pay, and the pigs and hens were beginning to vanish from the farm. Now you're lucky to see any at all. The hens have gone inside into the battery and in the case of pigs, everything has been taken over by the big breeder. Quite early on I realized about specialization. For instance that cows and pigs didn't mix. If you do pigs twice a day and cows twice a day, they are clashing. That's milking cows – dry cattle don't clash and you can keep them all right.

It's very hard to generalize on anything, but I think people go wrong by not keeping up with things. The more I learned about pigs, the more I realized that every detail of the whole enterprise has to be pared down and worked on like an accountant at his books. You must take a hundred different things into consideration, the ratio between feeding and weight, the temperature in which they live, the house, the way you feed them, the amount you feed them, the breed of pig, the number of pigs you have in the pen. Things like that.

When I started back in 1967 there were eight dealers around this area buying pigs from the farmers. They had a monopoly and the farmers didn't have a chance. One man would bid you a certain price, and his friend half a crown more, but of course they were in cahoots with each other. It wasn't until years later that a group of us approached a factory and bargained a price that will go up and down with market conditions. If the factory wants extra pigs now, they just ring up our secretary.

I think what I learnt most from all of this is that it's no use thinking of your neighbour as some enemy. The way I look on it now is that by selling together we are much more valuable. In the old days it was all individuals. The pigs themselves have changed. I can remember when the only pigs around the farm were Yorks or Large Whites, but now in Ireland we breed a bacon pig that is leaner. In Denmark they are stuck with this Landrace, a pig that produces beautiful bacon, but their conversion rate is much higher. The Landrace doesn't convert as well as other breeds.

I'll tell you a story that will illustrate the pig breeder's main problem. An old man said to me some years back: "You are in pigs, boy?" "I am," I said. "A chancy business, boy . . . the pig has his snout in your pocket all the time, and every day he is eating, you have to pay for it. Now if you have a cow or bullock you can give him a bit of grass, and you aren't paying for it straight away."

He was right, of course; the bag of rations is there and the pig is eating it all the time. If something goes wrong like a pig is sick or not converting the food, you will soon go out of business. To give you some idea of cost, at present I use about three tons of food a day, and each ton costs me about a hundred and eighty pounds. You just chuck it out. The old yellow meal on which they used to feed pigs has gone, and now they have a ration with barley, soya beans from America and all sorts of vitamins and minerals. The conversion rate has been brought right down, and this is the whole thing in the business – getting as much meat made with as little ration as possible. If I can't do that I am out of business. It used to be four to one – four pounds of meal to one pound of live weight gained, and now in the past ten years it has come down to about three to one. The conversion rate is always a knife-edge business.

As I told you I started in a small way and gradually built up. Only when I was over two hundred pigs, I went automatic. This was a very big step. Firstly I had to borrow a great deal of money for new sheds and new equipment, but now that it's automatic I have more free time for other things. Everything is taken care of, the temperature, the feeding and the cleaning. I am lucky in having two neighbours who take the slurry for their land, and that solves a big problem.

Apart from the worry and pressure of looking after pigs, it's nothing like the hard work in the way we once used to know. I do about an hour in the morning and an hour in the evening, apart from things like putting them into pens and sending them each week to the factory. That can be a tough day. I don't breed the pigs, but just do the finishing end of it. I buy them when they are twelve weeks old and I usually sell them at twenty-three or twenty-four weeks – if all goes well. But they can be tricky. Last year we got swine dysentery – that's blood scour – which means that the food just runs through them, and they get thinner and thinner. It's a horrible disease – the pig's stomach comes out with it – but modern technology has it beat.

Pigs are intelligent animals. You can train them to keep clean and when it gets warm they like lying in the muck to cool themselves. But I don't believe in any false sentimentality about animals. You have to look at it rationally. They talk about poultry in cages, about intensive breeding and factory farming, but the simple truth is that animals won't do well unless they are contented. If I put pigs in wet and cold conditions, it's just a waste of time and money throwing away the food.

Rearing and selling pigs is like anything else these days, and the inefficient farmer gets out. You have to do things well, and besides all that you have to enjoy what you are doing. My aim is to produce an animal that's wanted, and you must concentrate on something and do it right. It's not an easy thing to get into and many people who saw us expand and do well, and tried to do the same, got burnt going into it. Accounts, accounts, that's important. If you are on the balance, you have to be on the right side of it all the time. There's no room for amateurs.

In 1969 our small group of farmers sold about 500 pigs. This year we have sold over sixty-five thousand. That's how big it has become. It's an up and down business and you have this cycle. When pigs get plentiful the price goes down. This happens on a very regular basis. You want to be sure that the things you buy are less than sales at any given time. If they are not, you have to wear it out until things get a big scarcer and the prices go up again. I don't believe intervention is the answer to this problem. Unlike cattle, pigs breed so fast and you would have the whole thing filled up very quickly. I think water finds its own level. The main market is still England, and after that you are just dabbling. You have to sell to the best price, and where there is a vacuum like there is in Japan at the moment you try and fill it up.

In today's Ireland you need at least £10,000 a year to live comfortably, to support a family and run a car. That's why I am in pigs. I think it's a good life. My son has pigs now, and he is only fourteen, the same age as when I started. He keeps them in the old house. Now that there are many more people trained in the business, you can hire a man to run it. You couldn't do that ten years ago. And when you do them yourselves, you can have Sundays free – you can get away with feeding them thirteen times a week. You couldn't skip Sundays with cows. And a pig can take advantage of the new technology in drugs, hygiene and husbandry that wasn't available ten or fifteen years ago.

I often go over to England in October and look at their pigs, and they come over to look at ours and pass on the new technology. Although we are in a sense competitors, we regard each other as the best in the business. Even the Danes can't compete. We are doing the job better than nearly any country. I have confidence in the future of the country and in my own farm and in my own skill.'

Joe McCarthy, Shopkeeper. Aged 52.

'Somebody said to me the other day, "Do you know that the biggest crowd of crooks in the world are the farmers?" And I asked why, and he said, "They're fiddling every blasted thing, even the dole." I must be very stupid, because I saw a lot of cars going down one morning, and I thought there must be a funeral or something. Then after a time I saw all the cars come back again. So I asked somebody. "God help you," says he, "they are the farmers going to the barracks to collect the dole." All in cars, in nice smart cars. The dole was a good thing when it was needed, but put the beggar on horseback and he'll take it to hell. He'll break your back.

A lot of the emigration was caused by bad politics and the economic war, we all know that. It's all turned around now. Twenty years ago when you went to church there was only one car or two cars. Now every fellow has a car or two cars and he used to have a horse and cart. There's a fellow over at the Point, he's had three cars in the last four years. Isn't that dreadful and demoralizing?

I'm not criticizing the farmer who puts in a lot of work, but what I am criticizing is the way they take advantage of cheating. He's fiddling everything with no taxes, and if he needs a tractor that will cost £5000 or £6000, all he has to do is to put his hand in his hip pocket and bring out the notes. Another thing, the Credit Corporation is responsible for the high price of land by lending money to farmers at a fierce rate. Last year there were fourteen acres came up at Ballymore, and sold for £3000 an acre because the Credit Corporation came around and said, we'll give you the money. But with sixteen per cent the man is tied up for life.

The other thing I notice is how all the fields are full of briars and bracken. When I was a child I saw potatoes growing in them and the hedges were cut. It's all gone wild. Now they have tractors and they do nothing, they don't have to work. The dole takes the character from the people, and they go to the bar after collecting it. That's the unfortunate part of it. I think the dole has the country ruined. Everything for nothing is bad.'

Brendan Slattery, Publican. Aged mid-fifties.

'I always believe in the saying of being a happy tractor driver rather than a frustrated professor. What amazes me down here is what tremendous workers they are, and how constant they are. They will go out in the morning, rain or snow, and even in the middle of the nights. They will get up if the cows are calving, and the weather can be fierce and severe, and they will still do it. They get up in the rain and the frost and the wind, and they milk their cows and feed them seven days a week. They are such hardy tough people, that they might go to a wedding or funeral and have a massive skinful, and be back at seven to milk all the cows and make sure they are perfect. I find the people are so happy and nice, and they are not interested in world affairs. Eighty per cent of them, if you talk to them about world affairs and people like Margaret Thatcher and President Reagan, they are just not interested. They are massive workers, for the country fellows who are brought up on a farm have to get up at six and work all day. I have worked on the farm, and I was a hard worker, and you feel a great satisfaction from doing a good day's work, and it's a medicine to you.'

THE SEA

JOHNNY HARRINGTON	Ex-Mackerel Skipper, *Aged 75*
JERRY O'SHEA	Farmer and Fishseller, *Aged 67*
TOMMY CONNOLLY	Island Man, *Aged 82*
CAPTAIN SLATTERY	Retired Skipper, *Aged 89*
DANNY SULLIVAN	Farmer and Seine Fisherman, *Aged 71*
MARTIN HARTY	Trawlerman and Fisherman, *Aged 25*
CATHERINE KEARNEY	Fisherman's Wife, *Aged 25*
JACK JOBSON	Retired Shopkeeper and Story-teller, *Aged 65*

When the wind is from the west
All the waves that cannot rest
To the east must thunder on
Where the bright tree of the sun
Is rooted in the ocean's breast.

> *Tumann, son of Colman, 8th Century.*
> Trans. Frank O'Connor.

The young generation today don't know anything at all about
the hard life I and my like had when we were young. When I
hear them find fault with life today I don't say a word to them
. . . but I think if I had such a life when I was young I would
consider myself the king of Ireland.

> *The Man from Cape Clear*,
> Conchúr. Ó Siocháin

It has always been said that the worst of all livings is to be made
from the sea.

> *Ibid.*

Johnny Harrington, Ex-Mackerel Skipper. Aged 75.

His small house looks down over the harbour and from the kitchen window he has seen many of the changes. When he was young it was all sail except for the small coasters that brought in coal. Today there is still plenty of sail – the pleasure boats that jam the harbour in summer.

He has detailed knowledge of local conditions and will recite the names of every harbour and port along a two hundred mile stretch of coast. He is consulted about wind and tides, the sky at night, the names of ships, local regattas and anything to do with fishing.

The sea seems to have moulded him; his eyes are watery blue and he has the massiveness of some great sea animal. He still leads an active life, and can be seen most days at the harbour. If his familiar figure was not there people would be afraid that something was wrong. 'Where's Johnny?' they would ask, as if the sun or moon was absent.

★

'There is great excitement in the sea, and I was born and reared up to it. The first thing I can remember was a dog pulling me out from it. I had fallen in, and my mother was screaming. I got a wallop that night and a big fright, and after that I was more careful.

In those days ships were always coming into Cappaghglass, and you couldn't see the people for the amount of spars and rigging. We had the sailing schooners which carried mostly flour and coal to all the little places around the coast. Everything depended on coal at that time. A hundredweight of coal was as low as one shilling, and you paid two pounds a ton. Two tons, four pounds, and you couldn't understand why they were cutting the turf. I don't think there was that much turf, not in the town anyway. The farmers had it, but coal was cheap. I suppose it was hard to get the four pounds.

It was always interesting to see the boats coming in. I can remember the names of them all right. There was the Star of the Sea, the Shamrock, the Veronica, the Finbarr. The St Dominic – she was the biggest, about thirty-five feet. Most of them were what we called sailing yawls, with a working crew of two men. They were small open boats of around thirty feet, although some of them could be bigger. They carried a gaff-rig and bowspit, a mainsail, jib and topsail, and they would tack anywhere like little yachts.

I think nearly everyone in those days had a little boat. The islanders all had them of course, and on Sunday you'd see four or five of them coming in from the island with little lug sails, all going to Mass. And two or three coming from the far islands. They'd spend the day here and go home about two or three o'clock.

My earliest memories are sitting with my father in the boat, and it always seemed a holiday. There was a great deal of flat fish in the bays everywhere, because they weren't at that time overfished. My father was a very smart man and a very great scholar, and from him I got the interest in the sea. On a nice fine day it's a different world out fishing and you are out of all harm's way, and there's no one to annoy you. I tell you we enjoyed ourselves to perfection.

When I was a boy it was the First World War with Germany, and I can remember bits of it. They thought the Germans were going to invade us, and there was an old RIC policeman who used to go around to all the houses telling us if the invasion took place what we should do. He told us we would have to burn everything and go to the mountain behind and then strike out for Curraheen. These were the only orders we got, and I don't know what we would do when we got there.

I can remember the piles of oranges that were washed in from ships that were sunk after being torpedoed. Once there was a rumour of a German submarine out in the harbour, and my father took a crowd of young fellows to see it. She was for all the world like a great steel barrel rusted over. The Germans inside her were brought away to England. All the time a lot of British Navy boats used to come in here every evening, mine sweepers and that sort of thing, and spend the night and get away in the morning. I remember going to the coastguard station and seeing about forty bodies lying side by side in a shed which were washed up from the Lusitania and were later brought to Queenstown for burial. What struck us more than anything else was to see the grand brown shoes they had on them after being sunk, for to us at that time shoes were the greatest luxury.

I was under thirteen when I stopped school. The ordinary rule for working boys was to stop school when they were confirmed. A boy like me was expected to work out his own salvation. My first job was with the mackerel. I was working with a man called Dan the Wire who had us splitting and curing mackerel on the pier. I would go down there every morning and take my place beside one of the barrels. The way you do it is to catch the mackerel in your left hand and split him with the right, and then throw him into the tank of water and wash him. The only thing was that the cutting of the mackerel was bad for your hands, because the bones of the fish wear away your flesh.

Both men and women worked there, and the gulls would be flying around all the time. An old veteran would be salting them, and the women were splitting them like any man and packing them into barrels. I think a barrel took about three hundred and fifty fish. A heap of Scottish women from the North of Ireland used to do the gutting and packing. They had a big long tank about eighteen or twenty feet long, and the fish would be dumped down into the tank, and there was also an old smoke house where they smoked the herrings.

I worked with a buyer from Donegal called Byrne who brought down a staff with him for curing the herrings. I'd say about half a dozen girls and a couple of coppers for the barrels. They would come down in September and stay till December. The girls were working class girls from Burtonport in County Donegal. They were dancing in the hall, and they had a great deal of admirers too. But they never got married, although some men got near it.

After splitting the mackerel I went to sea. My uncle had the Kingfisher, and she was a grand boat in her day. She was part of the small fleet of boats that was based at Cappaghglass at that time along with three sailing schooners. My uncle who was captain could be a very stiff man. We had no bloody fun, I can tell you. But one thing I will say for him was that he always consulted the crew when he wanted advice.

Our dress going to sea was big heavy leather boots – sea boots we used to call them, and they were high leather up to the knees. Those bloody heavy sea boots drowned a cousin of mine – he slipped in off the boat and sank like a stone. We had no rubber boots early on. In good weather we wore trousers, a ganzy and a shirt. We made our own oilskins from calico and three layers of linseed oil. We boiled the oil, and just rubbed it in, and spread the pants out in the sun. They were very cheap and worked well. Some men used flour bags. If the oil was too fresh, they stuck together and it was hard to tear them apart.

No one was ever seen wearing a life jacket, and I'll tell you, when it comes to life jackets in our job it's "good morning". No one would be seen in one alive. Very few fishermen knew how to swim. The reason for that, I think was their closeness to the water. They say that if you are going to be drowned, you will never be hanged, and that's only old boloney. If you go down with her, you go down with her, and I wouldn't give myself the trouble of swimming if I was too far from the land.

We were as keen as barnacles in our fishing. In my young days the channel outside of here would be one block of mackerel. If you fell out of a boat you would hardly go down with the mackerel and that's a fact. Now you have to go out fifteen miles for the fish.

Our boat was a sailing yawl, and everything had to be done by hand. There was no wheelhouse, and you just sat down and took the helm in your hands and faced everything. If you had a headwind coming in, all you could do was to sit in the stern and let the water splash on top of you for six or eight hours.

You would be tired all right. It was very hard work, and I was only a young fellow. You might have the pants on you, but nothing above that, or you couldn't work, and if you had on a shirt, it stuck to your back with the sweat. It was all night fishing. The round fish, like mackerel, come up to breathe during the night, but the flat fish stay at the bottom. We had no winches, and hauling in the nets was a hard business. There might be a mile of nets with ropes underneath and what we called the springback – "Bringback" was its right name. You would bend back the ropes under the nets and there was what was called a diamond in every half net. The front man would shout "Stopper gone away!" and you had to be quick. Pulling away with our hearts in our mouths and our arms falling off us with exhaustion. And all that night would be lucky to get a piece of bread to eat.

The usual thing was to start early on Monday and take a course from the far island five miles out, check the clock and go over the course. South by south-west and perhaps an hour or so later we'd throw out a net if there was any sign of gannets. You'd watch the weather. You couldn't be a fool – there were no echo sounders or radar, and no such things as weather forecasts. You would see the wind coming up, and the appearance of the sky, and some people were very good at judging it. You had no business to go out in bad weather.

Drift-net fishing was always heavy work and little reward. Stretching out in your oilskins and clothes, and at the dawn you'd be up again hauling in the nets. The blood of the mackerel would go down into the hull, and the smell would be frightful. We would be throwing water, but it would be no good. I was seasick and doubly seasick. If I had been left in the bunk I wouldn't have cared, but I had to get up and haul in the nets. A mile or so of nets and mountains of fish had to be cleared before we came in. I can tell you to pick twelve thousand or so mackerel from the nets was hard work. The cotton nets weren't so strong, you know, and you had to learn how not to break the mesh.

By the time we got into Cappaghglass we would have cleared the nets and there would be great heaps of mackerel there. The usual thing was to wait for the fish auction, and then go to sea again. But it had been a long night with no sleep, and we would go to the pub for two or three pints that would act as a drug. You would catch some sleep after the pint. Sometimes it didn't work, and although I had a good intent, all the fishermen would be there drinking and talking, but the next moment someone would start to sing. I was young then, and I had two choices to make – to drink with them or go out of my mind.

It was just after the First War that the first French sailing ships came in following the mackerel. They were very large sailing boats with a crew of thirty to thirty-five men, and they would salt the fish on board. They would always come in during March when there was a big bright moon, too bright for drift netting. We used to love to see them coming in on an easterly wind and their gunwales deep in water all the time.

The men on them were poor as church mice and only came ashore when they had something to exchange or sell. They were big swarthy men in dungarees and they would walk around selling tobacco and chocolate for anything they could get. What they really wanted was hens to eat. "Poule, poule," they would call out, and that was the only French word we knew. Sure you wouldn't give them a hen that would lay an egg, but an old dying hen. They would go round to the women on the farm and say, "Chocolate good for little piccaninny." So long as the chocolates were covered with paper the women didn't mind the children taking it. We talked to them nice and friendly, but we couldn't understand what they said. They were mad for the girls, too, and they would have chocolate for them.

They were a very poor class of people and God knows there wasn't much to eat at the time. I remember they used to be after rooks' eggs and they would eat anything. You know the watercress that was in the river – they'd fill bags with that and take it over to France with them. When they got steam drifters they had a big twenty gallon tank in the cabin and they would get everything you could think of into the pot and spoon it out. Even seagulls. I remember seeing a long line of plucked and gutted hanging over the deck. I've seen a gannet cooked for a Frenchman and he said it was beautiful. I drank snail soup with them and didn't know it. Snails there's black ones and white ones that carry their shells on their backs. They found them in old buildings on the walls.

After the war the mackerel fishing went off and there was no market. Boats were scarce then and men were plentiful. We tried our hand with everything. Oh God almighty, boy, there was every kind of fish you could want if you had the brain for it. At one time they were getting plaice in the nets. There was hake and cod and every class of fish on the long line, and the finest of bream. They were made for fishing, the bream. Around Castle Point we used to kill hundreds of them with a line and a hook, using crab as a bait. Then they would be boiled in a pot, 'twas like soup, no bother to them. Gurnet or dabs or whiting or anything. Ling – that was always salted. The island people salted pollack – I'd say, they mostly ate them for dinner. There was no regard for crabs, and as soon as they were brought into the boat if they were found in the trawl net you'd only break them and peg them out. And the same with skate and ray, they would be pegged overboard too. The odd person might pick the periwinkles, but not the mussels. You could get the odd few congers around the pier – but the old lads from the hole in the pier, they turned a sort of bluey-black.

Then the herrings. The boats that were fishing herrings were those yawls. There were four men to them and many of them were under sail until they got Kelvin engines. We would start away in the evening and anchor our nets and haul them away in the morning. We would be back at the pier about nine or ten in the morning. We would spend the night off Dreena Cove and moor our nets with anchors and ropes. Sometimes we would look down at the nets at twelve o'clock at night to see if there was any fish in them. The fish used to be going around in great shoals and you would see them passing under the boat. There was an old fellow and he used to smell the fish when they came upon him, and he would drop the nets on them and get them in half an hour.

We didn't catch salmon here. They were never fished at sea until about twelve years ago, and only in the rivers. We'd see them jumping and everything, but never caught them. We knew no more about catching them than we did about watch-making. We'd be sailing over them and we never knew anything. I used to listen to old men saying – they were well-read men, they were like donkeys and would know everything . . . they'd say, "When you see the salmon jump, whatever way his head is pointing he is going, and he's always going for a river."

We didn't catch salmon and I'll tell you how that came about. In the olden days they had only the cotton and hemp nets and the salmon would slip away. Then this nylon type of netting came out which you could hardly see in the water. That's how drift-netting developed. I tried first with only a 30 inch deep mesh net and we got a good few salmon. Then I got 60 inch deep mesh nets which are illegal now, and them are the most they are fishing now. And they got this other stuff called monofilament which is invisible altogether in the water.

After we had the deeper nets we got as much as a hundred . . . but now they are much more scarce. But there was no great market for them in the old days. The only people who would buy them would be the restaurants and hotels. I'd prefer a whiting to a salmon any day . . . I wouldn't like them at all, they're too strong.

When the market for mackerel went off we used to dump the fish. The queerest of all is the way they are still doing it. This year it was herring – the boys there had caught more then they would get from their EEC quota. They were given reduced prices and they had to spray them and dump them. I consider it a crime – it's like crying out to God for vengeance that good food should be wasted and thrown back into the sea.

There was always problems with the fishing. The basking sharks were there in the winter, and the month of May was a great month for them. I remember one day I was trawling south of Cappaghglass and two sharks swam alongside the boat. They had huge open mouths that must have been five foot across and they were open to swallow the plankton. I wasn't a bit afraid, they were like two policemen each side of us. But once I steered for one and she almost lifted the boat out of the water she was so big. I thought I would give the shark a fright, but she gave me a bigger one. The sharks were a bloody nuisance and often cut the nets. They became so plentiful in June that we had to give up fishing for a time. There were some that were more than a nuisance – the blue shark was a dangerous lad, and there was a kind of electric fish that would give you a shock.

What was worse than the sharks were the seals. The seal would tear the net and eat anything. He'd destroy the whole gear. I hate seals, they're wicked. And I say after shooting them burn their bodies in case they come to life, they're that bad. Burn their bodies – they could do anything, seals.

The Second World War was difficult. We had orders from the barracks not to go outside the three mile limit, but we had to go out miles beyond that to catch the bloody fish. You'd be afraid of everything. Once an aeroplane came down around our boat to see what we were doing and we nearly died of fright. The convoys had no lights, you know, and the German submarines would sink any trawler. Once we were out mackerel fishing, and there was a submarine under us and all the fleet as well. You could hear the vibration in the boat, and our hurricane light wouldn't light. All the other boats from Cappaghglass hauled in their nets, and when we lifted ours they had been cut in two. Our mackerel was going to England, you follow me, and the Jerries knew that, and they would sink you.

Storms, boy. Plenty of those. The worst I remember was with the wind carrying south. By God, it blew a wind and came fast, a bad rain and gale. The man at the stern couldn't see the men at the mast. Force seven or eight anyway, and everyone had a fright in their hearts. We had a couple of nets that night, and were the last boats to come in. We were pressed and I didn't see the danger.

There was a man below in the fo'c's'le and he was more or less in the way all the time. He was on the compass and we'd have drowned if we had only to rely him. There was an awful sea, and at times it was breaking mountains at the back of her . . . and I was giving orders to the two lads, slack the peak and she will come up at the head of you. Cripes it was a bad night. And I was saying to the young fellow who was crying out with the fright, "John Boyne," I said, "don't be afraid she will definitely open it inside ten." That was Peacehaven red light you know. And it didn't happen. I was cursing myself for making a mistake. I was working the sails and the engine, you know, and giving orders. And that fool at the compass wasn't watching. Watch the compass yourself, said he. I took him by the collar and pushed him away with the excitement. "If you don't do what I tell you," I said, "I'll kill you with the hatchet."

We'd be dead if it wasn't for the lighthouse. I could see the flash going up in the air and it was on our stern. I was cursing myself, it meant that we had missed Peacehaven and were going to Faraway Bay, a bad place. We had sail up, even in a sea like that to make her go faster. The sail would lift her while the engine would have pulled her down. And anyway in the end she goes to harbour. It was a frightful night, you know, and it haunted me for there was no need for it. The sea going over her was the very same as you'd see it going over a sunken rock in a strong southerly gale. It must have been the frightfullest night I have ever known. Then up to the harbour and ashore, and blind to the world, drunk.

Next day we went out to sea and one of them was shivering and shaking. "What's wrong with you?" And he never went out afterwards again.

I'm pulled out of fishing, for it's a tough life when you are getting old. I still have a small punt, but my legs aren't as supple as they were, and you can't step off the pier like any young fellow. I tell you, Peter, that I've given more time south of the lighthouse out there than north of it, and I want that for my last address. But I don't want to be drowned. I don't want that.

Sometimes people ask me, "Johnny, aren't you lonesome for the sea?" and they will talk about the grand life and how to appreciate and see nature you must be close to the sea. But that's all boloney. If I had some letters after my name, maybe I would feel like them. But to tell you the truth, the love that I had for the sea was for the few quid I made out of it.'

Jerry O'Shea, Farmer and Fishseller. Aged 67.

Scarlet fuchsia hangs in the hedge, the foxgloves only have a few florets left and the orange montbretia is coming into flower. Jerry lives outside the town by the sea. When he looks out he can see the trawlers coming and going, the quivering light of the lighthouse on the horizon and every mood of the sea. At the back of his house is the tiny farm which in its heyday supported five cows and grew a little corn and potatoes.

To the right and left are lines of new bungalows sharing the same marvellous view. Some are holiday homes lived in for a few weeks in the year. Others belong to people who have retired to this beautiful place. The bungalows are mostly built on bare rocks and are approached by sweeping tarmac drives. Many have multi-coloured brick and wrought iron balconies. They are full of friendly people, Jerry says.

★

'I was born on the 6th of August, 1916 in this very same house I am living in. Farming is a very good business now, but in those days it wouldn't raise cats. You would get no money at all. The bad 'twenties, the worse 'thirties and you were only scraping along. My people were working-class people and a farm of twenty-six acres was different from a bigger one. We had two and a half cows.

In those days everyone was catching fish. A lot of that fish would go to England. A train left Cappaghglass at 4:30 and they'd have a reply from Billingsgate the next evening. If you put that fish on a CIE* lorry now, you'd be lucky to have it in Dublin by tomorrow evening, let alone get a reply back here.

Anyway even though plenty went to London, that still left plenty of fish behind. And the market went off. Mostly the poor fishermen weren't making a bit. Everyone was selling fish and everyone was sick of it. Oh Christ, they sold the fish in Cappaghglass and Curragheen and there were plenty of buyers around. There used to be tanglers, donkeys, ponies and cars, and everyone coming around the country selling them.

On market days the women would be lining the road with baskets, and lobsters were nine shillings a dozen. I remember as a boy walking up the main street of Cappaghglass with a strap of pollack over my shoulder knocking on doors. A dozen other boys were doing the same, hawking the fish around. There was a boy from the island whom they used to call the crab boy and he had the crabs. No one wanted crabs. The best day I can remember was a St Patrick's Day after some local races. I made eight and six pence and I thought I would never be poor again.

Then because of the small living we made from the farm my father began selling fish around the country. He used to buy it down at the pier. A hundred mackerel would cost a couple of bob.

We had a long car, not like an ordinary country butt at all, but with long shafts and a long body. Early in the morning, the night after my father had bought the fish we used to load up and be off. It didn't matter the weather. If there wasn't a glut, wet or fine, rain or sun, the old car rattling away and the heap of fish in the back covered in straw. My father sold them for a shilling a dozen, and maybe you might get thirteen. "Fresh Mackerel" was his slogan all the time, and God knows he fed the country. The country people were mad for spring mackerel because they hadn't anything else to eat. God almighty, they were fine healthy eating with potatoes, and you could get a pint of porter for tuppence to wash them down.

There was no tarmac in those days, just rough roads going about the place, and we travelled over the three parishes so that by the time I

* Coras Iompair Eireann – Irish National Transport Company.

grew up I knew every twist in the road, every boreen and hedge, and every person living there.

I would be sent up to the farmhouse while my father remained sitting in the car.

"Do you want fresh mackerel? Do you want any fresh mackerel?"

Sometimes I might see a woman peering through the window, and the youngster would come out and tell me "Mammy isn't at home." They mightn't have the money, but we would still give them fish. There were big families in those times with six or eight children in each house, and somehow they had to be fed. They would pay you sometime, and we never kept books. All the figures were in my father's head. Perhaps he would hand out a dish of mackerel to an old woman living alone by herself, and sometimes you saw someone who looked hungry.

I remember once seeing a man who was breaking stones for the road, and he was so poor, and with such terrible pants on him that there wasn't a leg that wasn't patched and raggedy.

"Fresh mackerel" I called out, and of course he hadn't a farthing to pay for them. I told him I would pass that way next Friday, for God knows you would want to get something for all the work. He wasn't there on Friday, but two weeks later I passed him and somehow he had scraped the money and I gave him another bag of fish.

The years passed away . . . you won't believe me . . . but I met the same man again. "Don't I know you?" he said looking at me carefully. "Weren't you the man that sold me the fish?"

He had gone to England and made tons of money and now was dressed to the stars. There was nothing else but brandy that night, and later he called up his family and was tearing mad about me and what I had done.

"That's the man who gave us all mackerel when we were hungry," he said, and they thought I was the Lord Mayor or something.

When my father died I continued for a time. When the pony died I had donkeys to pull the car. Donkeys are very awkward things to get trained until they get used to the car. They would run away with it, they would go off the hill, boy, for they are very strong in the mouth you know, and stubborn. I would rather have a pony; he would go head straight. You see a pony is kinder. But a donkey was cheaper.

The tinkers used to bring them round, gangs of them. On fair days they would bring in twenty donkeys and stand them there in the street, and they would be coming to the country houses with them trying to sell them, for they were getting them for nothing but to take them away. They were a bit aged, the donkeys the tinkers had. The country was full of them and they were troublesome. All donkeys have one bad foot, so they say, and they never have all four feet sound. We called them "velvet lugs" after their ears.

Did you know in winter 'tis best to have them in, for donkeys are very cold animals, they shake from the rain and cold. Oh, the house is the best place in the winter for them. They come from hot countries, and the more heat the better for a donkey. They would be delighted with the heat. I fed them a bit of hay and a few spuds and kept them in when it was cold.

I had the wheels of the car shod at the forge. They mostly put on rubber wheels today and the rubber is all right on the road, but if you are on the land the band wheel is the best wheel. There's more of a dead pull on the rubber. The roads are much easier to travel on now with a pony and car – you can go as fast as you like, the road is so smooth. Before it was all rocks and gutters and the water was stopping everywhere, but they are great roads now.

Later on I gave up selling fish and people were saying that there would be hunger in the country since the O'Sheas stopped going round selling fish. It's all a long time ago. Misha, the old crowd are gone and the young crowd turning grey, and we in our turn did the best we could. It was the 'thirties that done it – the economic 'thirties. And they are back again.

I think there is a need for the dole when a man is thrown out of his job but I do think it's bad for younger people who could try to find work. You are throwing away the best years of your life drawing dole. They should get up and try and do something, for there's a lot of things we can do. When they went to America in the old days, they went out in old sailing ships, they had no education, they had no trade, they got the dirtiest job in every country they went to . . . only that they were good workers, they built the railroads in America and Australia. But the strange thing about it they were great to work in any other country only their own. They were too lazy to work their own.

That's what I am talking about, that if the young people grow into this, and think this sort of stuff is going to continue for evermore, where are they going to end up? If you have a young man on the dole for twenty years, what does he know about work? His limbs are practically limp from doing nothing.

He might raid the bank. Now the banks look like something from a western movie with the guards outside. Those bank raids would never happen in the old days. It's gone to the devil altogether now. There was no such thing as that. It wouldn't matter how poor you were, that kind of work wouldn't be around. There was nothing to steal. You might only steal a rope above in your yard. It's all bank work, now, and big things.

They knew right from wrong in the old days. The masters of the schools would have them all warned, and the priests in the parish they wouldn't have it either. The only people were the island people, they would rob a church. They thought it was right to steal. I was walking down the road about twenty years ago thinking about nothing at all, when this fellow from the island jumped out from the back of a ditch to have a crack at me with his fist. From blackguardy.

If I didn't do anything I'd be a nervous wreck. Look at all the foreigners coming down here buying plots and building houses. There's none of the old crowd here, and it's a pity to see the old names gone. My neighbours are grand people, but we were different people altogether when I was young. These newcomers have no friends or anything, and that's a fact. You feel sorry for them and wouldn't like to say anything blackguardy against them, because they are quite innocent people. While they were in the cities they had nothing to do but go into the public library to read books – nothing to do but sit on their backsides, and I'm sure that's very monotonous.

I live surrounded by the English. The first one to come was Howard Wilson who died of cancer. He built the bungalow right beside me, and he was a friend of mine from the start, and a great friend of mine. When he first came down he said he'd like to know his neighbours and I said, "I'm one of them." He said would I mind if he walked on the fields, and I said, it wasn't like that . . . you are free to walk wherever you like. He said, "What about the next man?" "The next man is the same, and you don't have to go any further" . . . He was under the impression that you couldn't walk in the field . . . I was better friends than neighbours if you know what I mean. I mean, he was a right genuine lad.

When he died Commander Hewston bought his place and lives beside me. "How are you, Jerry?" he might say and talk about the garden and weather and make conversation to you. Then there are the Simpsons and Mrs Oldfield and the Rothernburgers in the old Rectory who are Germans. When I had the Stations last year they all came. They are a nice crowd but have nothing to do but kill the time. They might be in the garden and see a blade of grass, and they might pull it.

I never married, I steered clear of all that, and in a sense I think I am lucky. A neighbour of mine whose wife has recently died never had to make a cup of tea for himself in his life, but now he would die of hunger before he would do it. He lost his wife when he needed her most. But I can wash the clothes and cook and keep the house tidy.

I tell you, Peter, the way it is, only for the fish I would be dead. I eat fish three times a day, and I'm lucky in that respect, for I would rather eat fish than meat. Dan Sullivan gave me two pollack last night. Ah, the youth of today wouldn't eat any fish. They have nothing for them but Gateaux cake, pork and biscuits and chips. Sure, Jesus Christ, the youth of today wouldn't eat any fish. They won't live longer, they won't, with the frigging world all drugs.

I read there in the paper that horses sold to the continent are making thirty-four pounds a hundred weight. 'Tis a great price. And they reckon their meat is number one. If I didn't have a fish, I'd eat a horse sure. I'd eat a child if it was boiled. You're frigging right, I'd eat a horse. They say it is grand meat, far better meat then the beef. For why? The horse is getting no chemical stuff, no injections like the cattle.

The food isn't the same now, and you won't get the same potatoes to eat or the same turnips. Once you would get half a bucket of turnips and it wouldn't do you any harm . . . now it would burst you. You see they all grow the bag stuff. You take the chickens. You get a chicken that went around the farmer's place picking around the haggard, and now you get one at the supermarket and put it on the table. You'd know the taste of it in a minute. And the same with the eggs. Sure you would know the egg immediately you cap it – there is all white in it. I wouldn't say the mutton has changed as much as the chicken and eggs or the vegetables. Sure they go along now with a dash of hydrogen, and they have vegetables up in a week and you'd throw them into a pot and you have nothing.

People are healthy when they are living out over the salt sea. When I get out there in the morning and inhale that into my lungs, 'tis as good to me as the breakfast is to another man in New York. It's given down that people near the sea shore live far longer than the people inland – that's given down in history. The salt sea air kills all the germs.

What I don't like is people bothering me and bringing me comforts and food. The nurse asked me the other day, "Would I take the dinner? Would I come?" Look, I'd go down into the grave before I take it. 'Tis the depths of charity. When you get to the stage that you can't look after yourself, it's better to be thrown into the sea than rot in the County Hospital.

Tommy Connolly, Island Man. Aged 82.

'What age am I?' A skeletal face with cutting blue eyes. He is preserved like a fossil.

'Sixty-five?'

'I wish you were right. I'm eighty-two and I don't give you a word of a lie. Oh God, I feel thirty, but still at my age you know you are not young any more.'

He spent most of his life on the island that lies off-shore from Cappaghglass. When he and his wife left twenty years ago they were the last to go. The place had become run down. There was no school, no nurse, no running water or electricity. And no people. They had been cleaned out. His own children had long left, and he and his wife were increasingly lonely. When there was a chance of a Council house in Cappaghglass, they were glad to go.

*

'Living on an island makes a person apart. He has different values from the person on the mainland, where they can lead more independent lives. The dependence of the island people on one another can never be fully appreciated by outsiders. Everyone was the same. There was no lord or master or anyone, and we all paid the same rates and rents to the last.

When we were young there were about a hundred and fifty people living there and every house was occupied. The old houses used to have thatched roofs and were all built to the same model. There was the kitchen and the parlour and two small rooms upstairs.

My father was a fisherman and a small farmer like everyone else that had lived on that island for ever and ever. The farming would produce the food for the winter time. You'd have wheat and take it to the mill, and get flour from that, and you'd have spuds. You'd have a house of spuds for the wintertime. Sometimes there might be a bit of boiling beef or pork, and that might be a real luxury to us because we couldn't buy the meat.

We had our own cattle and pigs. If we wanted to sell them at the fair at Cappaghglass it meant swimming them across. We would put a halter around their horns to keep them up, and there would be a man holding up his head and another rowing. We would swim our cattle over in the evening before the fair to the nearest point of land and then walk them up.

The problem with all of us was money and the lack of it. You'd get three pints for sixpence, you'd get a hundredweight of coal for one and tenpence and you'd get a hundred cigarettes for sixpence, and you would get a load for your money in those days, but you didn't have it. The most we would make fishing in the summertime would be thirteen or fourteen shillings a week. I remember once going into a shop with my mother, where there were thick back rashers at tenpence a pound, and I said, "Lets take some of them," but she said, "We won't because we haven't the money." On Sundays in fine weather we used to sail over to Cappaghglass for Mass, and there was never a penny even to put on the plate. A penny was a big thing then.

The only thing that would buck us up for Christmas was that we would get a fist of currants, or a fist of raisins and an apple or orange, and you would never see these things again until next Christmas. We were never given sweets. The only time that ever happened was when a visitor came to the island and might give us toffees. We would eat the paper and all, we were so eager.

The winter was the worst time and we were badly off. The summer would be a better time to live on the island because there would be full and plenty. We had three cows, and you could never get as much butter from three cows on the mainland, because on the islands the grass was sweeter. Most families would salt a keg of butter and that would come in very useful. The hay would be growing, and the fowl would start laying, and the fish would be coming in. There was a big strand near us and we used to straw the sand and bed the cattle on it. Then it would all go out with a heap of manure for the land.

When the child was growing up he was learning from his father and the daughter from the mother. I could sew and thatch and mend my own shoes and put a sole on it when it was broken. Even now I can make a cake fit for the Queen of England if I had the stuff to do it. The men were very handy and they could do anything in the world. But it wasn't just the men who were good, for the women, too, were real champions. For one thing, we used to bring the turf across to the island by boat, and the women were strong and powerful rowers. They would help in the fields, sowing, or looking after the cattle when the men were away, and after a storm they would go down to the beach to collect wood and other wreckage. There wasn't a job they hadn't done.

But it was mostly in the home that a woman would reign queen. She'd be cooking in the whitewashed kitchen on the old open hearth. I remember the crane and a grand smell of smoke. We had homemade bread, salt fish, salt bacon, boiled eggs and plenty of vegetables.

The life on the island was different, you see, from the world of today. Let me put it one way, that there wasn't a key or lock on the island or any need for them. And there wasn't a doctor or a midwife. When women had their confinement they would take their babies inside and the island women went from one to another and they would lose no babies. When you got sick, we had our own medicines for there were no hospitals to go to. We were given boiled milk with pepper in it if you got a pain, and there was Beecham's pills if you got constipated. Another cure for things like arthritis was the use of sage. They would boil it away and strain it and rub it on the pains of their knees or back. My father would mix it with porter and it would work wonders. A favourite medicine was black tea without any milk, or seal oil which was put in bottles. The doctors condemned it, and said that there was salt in it. But it was good.

The medicines weren't the best, for a lot of people died and they didn't know what it was. I remember a friend out fishing, and he got a pain and he started roaring with the pain, and the next thing he was dead. They didn't know it was an appendix they thought it was just natural pain that killed him. Then there was the Newman family with three little girls, and each one of the three died at different ages from a disease no one could understand.

Island people are different, for they live closer to nature and to God. We think it's a big thing nowadays when we go to Mass, but for them religion was a much deeper thing. For my mother going to church was very important to her, and the people prayed more at home, you know. Perhaps I might be out fishing on a bad night, and she often told me when I came home that only her faith had kept her from despair and crying. Our people were dependent on each other and were hoping and depending on some higher power that they wouldn't get into a disastrous situation.

If someone died they would have a wake with plenty of eats and drinks, and that would last for two nights. They were buried on the mainland and they would have to bring the coffin across on the boat. Every house on the island had a boat, and every boat would be at the funeral with a rope from one to the next. They would row to

Cappaghglass like swans swimming after one another, and there would be a hearse and two fellows at the grave and down they would go.

The best part of my life was spent on the island and there was a mother's love and all that. We had no feelings against anyone, no matter what class or creed, and everyone had a very good relationship. I think the biggest drawback for us was education. We had no school on the island, and because of the bad weather we only averaged forty-five days a year at the school on the mainland. All the books that were necessary for our primary education our father got for us, and the chances were that we had read them three times over when we returned to school in March. We used to read by the light of candles, and my father, who had fished all around the Irish coast, would tell us of his experience and stories. You heard a lot of stories. There was one about a boat that kept vanishing in the night – one moment she was there with her lights blazing and the next she was gone. And there was another tale about the time they saw a stork on some rocks, some old bird, you know. And someone said "Whist!" to frighten it, and the next thing was a naked man ran up the side of the rocks, and that's what happened. Do you know for a fact that none of us lobstermen liked tying up to a pier in case someone or something pulled her in?

I remember when the first radio set was brought to the island, a little battery set, and it was fantastic to the younger people that it could be put up on a table and that it could make a sound and there was nothing feeding it.

My mother used to wash our legs before going to bed in the hot water that had boiled the spuds for our dinner. Red soap and a towel to dry in. No one had shoes or stockings and there were women on the island who had never worn shoes, and could walk over a broken bottle and it wouldn't penetrate the skin.

You might think listening to me it was all suffering, but the reverse was true. We were never lonely. In the wintertime we would be having a dance every night. We would have the 25 card game and we would have tea and poteen and porter, and there were fiddlers and lads playing the mouth organ.

But the most important thing of all was the fishing and the boats. Anyone that fished would never like farming and used it only as a standby. Fishing was nicer and there was something about it all the time. Even through you had a lot of hand hauling and trawling from the bottom and plenty of work to it.

The lobster yawls would be about twenty-two feet – open boats, you know. I remember the St Kieran, the Kathleen Ann, the Island Queen. We creosoted the bottoms and painted them from the water-line up, green or blue or white, or whatever colour you would like. All the men on the island knew how to look after a boat. They could make their own oars and sails and trawls. You would buy the mackerel and herring nets, but for the trawl you would buy twine and make it.

During the summer you would almost live on the boat. One Monday morning myself and my father and brother would set off with the others for the lobstering, and we all returned back at the weekend to help with the farming. We would have hay to cut and scutling and spraying and helping the women. Sometimes we would fish from five or six in the morning and later on in the day get a load of sand.

The yawls had two oars and a lug sail, and we took with us two strings of twenty-five pots. Did you ever see the standard lug and the little mast on her? We used to go everywhere around the headlands as far as you could go, out to the far islands and everywhere out in the deep rocks. Our main propulsion was rowing, for you couldn't haul in the pots by sail. One would be hauling the pots in by hand, and the other two were rowing the boats and keeping up with it. Craw fishing is better in the day and lobstering by night.

We would be hauling until one or two at night and then when we were tired we would anchor the boat and sleep under the sail on a bit of straw. We would carry our own food with us, an egg for breakfast and brown bread, and when we were short we would bake our own bread in an iron pot and light the fire at the entrance to the mast. Any fish you boil in the boat in salt water is nice.

We sold lobsters and craw fish to a man in Cappaghglass who kept ponds. Nine shillings a dozen was the price for them, and it didn't make any difference if they were as small as a mouse or as big as an elephant. The price for lobsters is outrageous. I have sold them at one time for half a crown a dozen, and others can tell you that. The craw fish went to France, for French people would eat any kind of shell fish. What happened to the lobsters and craw fish happened equally to us, and it sometimes seemed to me we were like brothers. The island people were getting thinned out, and so were the lobsters.

I remember going out one day around Keay Head in October just before the weather was breaking, and we caught ten dozen craw fish in thirty pots. In those days you could get four or five inside a single pot. We got thirty shillings a dozen for that lot, and now they would be worth hundreds of pounds. Oh God, they would. We used to get big craw fish, and they were loaded with peas for spawning. But the government was not good and they weren't allowed to remain plentiful. Then the skindivers came. I heard a fellow sing in a pub lately:

> "And the fishing is dead and quite fragile,
> And my spirit was never so low,
> The old craw fish are scarcer than limestone,
> Where did the lobsters go?"

We did all sorts of fishing besides the lobstering. We'd catch pollack – there was plenty of that lad – and rock congers from a hole. Grunets or dab or whiting or anything. Every house had a barrel of salt fish and salt pollack they mostly ate for dinner. We would dry the ling on the roofs of outhouses, or even your own house. Paddy Burke's house was almost slated with ling drying out.

In spring we collected seagulls' eggs from around the rocks. In the month of May we would walk along with our buckets and our baskets and just fill away. The birds wouldn't touch us. I think we got fifty-three or fifty-four dozen in one day, and they were sent to England.

During May you'd see sharks and other big fish with eyes as big as a motor car lamp shining ahead in front of them. And sometimes they struck a boat a few times. Oh Christ they did. Don't be talking about the fish, for you would see the queerest in the world.

Often we had broken and stormy weather, and you wouldn't dare go fishing. He who lives in danger shall perish therein, isn't that an old saying? You always came into calm water when there was a storm and you would always run away from danger. The old people were brilliant about forecasting the weather and we used to learn from them. A circle in the moon would cause wind, and seabirds coming inland or spots on the sun meant we were going to have a gale right away that evening. We would prefer to go hungry than to go out fishing on a bad day. When the white seas are outside the weather is going to be bad. "*Garrai an iascaire*" the fisherman's garden, they used to say.

I can remember a storm in December 1942 when you wouldn't dare go down to the pier in case you were carried away. It wasn't so much the wind as the waves that were lifting the harbour rocks into the air and they must have weighed thirty hundredweight or more.

When I was a boy a ship called the Savannah foundered beyond the west rocks. It seemed like trees had grown up overnight but what they were were masts and spars and the old sails still shaking. The only thing that came off that boat was the cat. Someone had a little rhyme about it:

"When Crowley woke up in the morning, a strange pussy cat leapt on the floor,

And that was the token of wreckage from the Savannah inside the old shore."

The first job after any storm was to collect the seaweed and wreckage. On the morning afterwards the whole world would be there hiking and drawing away the weed. We had no artificial* going then, and what we called the black weed was used on the potatoes, mangles and turnips. Some of the older men chewed it.

We were born to the island life and had to put up with it. The English and American money helped. When I was a young fellow all the money was coming from these places. Every son and daughter that went didn't forget their homes, and sent home a lot of their earnings. When the registered letters came you would know it was money. People might turn around and say, Don't mind England, but it was England that reared half of them and so did America.

There was once a big population, but in the end everyone left. The island was a thriving place up to the First World War and then they went. Once it starts there is nothing to stop it going down. A lot went to America, and others joined the British Navy, for of course, being in the nature of seamen, they were mad for the sea. The youth had gone, no one was getting married, and the old people were left behind. My brothers had gone away, my mother was sick then, and my own family had grown up. My wife said, "Try and leave, you're getting old," and then we had the chance of this house in Cappaghglass. It was good luck in a way, and yet the worst. Island people often die after leaving their houses, it's a well known fact. But here I am over eighty, and as you can see, still going strong.

I can remember the day we left and we had packed up everything except the bare necessities for spending the last night. The next morning when we rowed over, it was one of those calm flat mornings and for the last time we waved goodbye to the familiar shore. I think I'll never see that sort of picture again, it was so peaceful and everything.

I didn't return for about two years, and when I did, I was on the beer

* Fertilizer.

for a week. Everything saddened me. Where we had fine crops and cattle, there was nothing but weeds, and it had all gone very shabby. I missed the people and the old life, and walking there I was remembering the twenty-eight of my class who were confirmed with me and are now all dead and scattered. And I was remembering my parents and the life we had in that old house.

There's no use in thinking of something that's quite dead. A priest once said to me that there would be great material for a book. But I told him it wouldn't be interesting except to a small amount of people. And it wouldn't be very optimistic.'

Captain Slattery, Retired Skipper. Aged 89.

The Captain is a small square man with very blue eyes, and although he is so old his face is startlingly unwrinkled. He speaks in a sing song voice of the Brazils and Antarctica as if they were only a few yards from the window of his small house. His grandfather built it half a mile from the sea and in winter you can hear the waves drumming against the cliffs. After a storm the surrounding fields are scattered with white foam.

The interior is spotless and bare, freshly painted and everything in place. On the sitting-room wall are watercolours of various ships painted by his brother which have a primitive charm. He points out the pilot boat which his father owned, a two-masted schooner caught in gigantic tumbling waves, and a fleet of sailing boats and schooners at anchor beside Cappaghglass pier. There is a heavy frame photograph of his father, fierce and bearded, another of himself, youthful and bearded, and beside the front door stands a figurehead from his father's boat of a generously breasted lady.

In the garden his shirts are drying in the wind. He has hens and fruit trees and tends his patch of vegetables on which he still piles seaweed taken from the shore. Most days he eats fish given to him by his neighbour.

Nearly everyone he knew has died. Only last week he went across Ireland to the funeral of a shipmate with whom he sailed sixty years ago. He doesn't believe in religion, and says travelling has done that for him. Too many creeds, too many people holding up their own particular answer.

After midday the sun suddenly comes through the mist and blazes down on the seapinks cradled on the rocks and the cliffs on which stands a ruined castle. 'Jesus, I have been all over,' the Captain says, gazing out of the window.

★

'I got my ticket in sail just before it finished, and I believe that any man who was lucky enough to do that was worth a dozen who trained in steam. When I was young they had trouble getting the seamen for those sailing ships because the work was so hard. You are pulling and hauling and you could be called out any time on your watch. You took pride in the work, but I wouldn't do that again if I had my time.

In the First World War there was still a lot of sailing ships around. I saw the Pamir and the Passat. The Pamir was lost in the Atlantic in 1954 when the cargo shifted and she turned over. The old skippers would never carry grain in bulk but always in bags. In that way it would never shift. Coal wouldn't shift, but the only thing about it was that it could go on fire. I saw the Patzona, a fine five-masted barque that lifted five thousand tons, and she took fire off the river Plate with the result that an Argentine ship came out and sank her because she was a danger to navigation.

Ireland had only schooners which were busy on the coal trade. My uncle owned what we called a double topsail schooner named the Madcap. It was a nice life on its own, but, still and all, there was hard work attached to it. Training on sail is quite different from steam where you have nothing to do but paint and chip decks. I started off a cook – that was the style in those days. But I also learned how to mend the sails, splice ropes and wires and all the rest of it. You might be an ordinary seaman for twelve months, and then you would go up to AB. From what I remember my wages were £9 every month, and they went up to £12. That was the highest. We would take coal, grain or anything. The loading was a skilled job and you would shoot it into the main hatch. The cargo wouldn't shift at all. The only thing that would shift, as I told you, would be corn or wheat, for even oats usually sticks together.

We used to run down the British Channel and to any port around the south or west of Ireland. We sailed into port and sailed out because there were no engines. Say you were at anchor . . . well, you'd heave short, and you'd get a certain amount of sail on. First you would put up the foresail, then the main sail and then the inner jib – they call it a standing jib – and boom jib. You'd set your topsails and heave up your anchor and start to make some headway, and every man to his position.

Out at sea we would always keep a four hour watch, four hours on and four hours off. At night-time you had your sidelights, the starboard light was green and the port light red. The steamers then had a mast headlight so you would know what course they were steering. The important thing was always the weather. Every man learnt the stars and the wind and the look of the sea. There was no other form of weather forecasting. When the stars twinkled at night they said you were in for bad weather, and if they didn't, it would be fining up. You watched the wind and the clouds and anything at all. One moment there might be a strong south-westerly wind and the next when the pressure moved to the east, the wind would fly into the north-west. Anything could change it.

If a storm did come and you were caught out at sea, the first thing was shortening sail. The only sail you could do from the deck was the topsail, and to reach it meant climbing up the rigging and out onto the yard on the foot ropes. We would roll the topsail on top of the yard and put ties around it and then reef up the other sails including the flying and outer jib. That was the form.

In the First World War I had a brother lost when his ship was blown up by a mine. During those years we also sailed to the continent and northern France as well as England. The reason we went to France was to take pit props over for the trenches. I have a good knowledge of harbours. When we got to a port the discharging was always the worst part of the journey. Usually we winched up the coal tubs in a dolly winch, and the mate who was always standing on the gangway would push it ashore into the cart. Then after we had cleaned up we would be out again to sea.

Sometimes we were towed from places like Milford Haven right across to the South coast of Ireland with a naval escort because of the danger of submarines. The Admiralty used to send a tug out and it would take a string of five or six sailing ships. We would kick off from Milford Haven before noon and get across to the Irish coast by next morning and just drop the tow line.

When you have served a number of years in sail you are sorry to have to stop, because you are in a different life in the steamship. Most of the sail vanished around 1920 in a couple of years, and suddenly there were only a few square riggers left that the Germans had built for the guano trade to South America. Some of the boats were sold, some of them were run for a year or two and then broken up, others were just thrown on the beach. I can tell you it wasn't a nice sight to see them go; it was like having your own heart pulled out of you. The last time I saw some of the old schooners they were being used for balloon barges in the Second World War.

After 1920 things weren't easy for anyone. The coal trade went down and there were no cargoes. Here in Ireland people were shooting each other during the Civil War. I think that was crazy. By then I had what they called a fore-and-aft ticket and in 1927 I got my mate's ticket in steam because the square rigged tickets had died out.

I took a job with a yachtsman who didn't want any greenhorns on the boat with him, and visited South America. I have been to the Falklands and Port Stanley and in the Antarctic marking whales. I have been to Borneo in one of WR Carpenter's boats and went in the Blue Funnel Line from Singapore to Freemantle. In my job you kick off as second mate, then you become mate and finally master. I emigrated to Australia when there were a lot of small boats around the coast, but that's finished with now. I have been through two World Wars and the Spanish war. I remember going into Tangiers, or was it Algiers, and the Spanish fleet was in there and they had shot all their officers. That was about 1936 I think.

My grandfather built this house, but I could have settled anywhere else. If I had my time over, the Brazils would be my country. In those days it was a young country growing up and the opportunity was there for anyone with drive. I have a good knowledge of the Portuguese language and if I started again I'd have half a dozen or even a dozen languages because in that way you are then worth twelve men.

I have mixed with every race and religion and it made no difference. Black men, white men, Chinese or Indians, they are all the same. They talk about the Roman Catholic Church and the Protestants, but you know, all this religion came from the past and I wouldn't pay any attention to it. When you are around the world for a few trips, you know what life is like, and I gave up religion years ago. Sure it's just a natural thing that you come into this world, and you cast out when your time is up . . . unless you meet with an accident or a thing like that.

I think if I was going to have my life again I'd become an anthropologist. I remember I was in Dublin once during the 'twenties and came upon a book written by a man named Stevenson who discovered a new race of Eskimos. I can still remember parts of it. "My first day among the Dolphin and Union Strait Eskimos" – that was a strait between Northern Canada and Victoria Island . . . "was the day of all my life to which I have looked back with vivid memories. It introduced me as a student of mankind and of primitive man, especially of a people of a byegone age."

Now when I go into a pub in Cappaghglass when the tourists are here I can pick out the different races. The fair whites and the blondes, those having red or yellow hair. Blue eyes and fresh complexions. That's really a fascinating subject, you know.

I think the reason why I have stayed healthy is that I still care for what I eat. Good teeth are important to you and I eat a raw potato every day, for there is an acid in it that cleans your teeth. A doctor told me that in the daytime the germs won't do any damage when you are breathing fresh air, but when you are asleep and there is any food left in the gums, that's the worst time of all. Before I go to bed I always take a few drops of Jeyes Fluid in a tumbler of water.

My people have been here for six generations and when I die that will be the end. In the old days there was plenty of company and you had a big crowd of sailing ships. All the men around Cappaghglass travelled the world. But that generation has gone, and in fact the man who was buried yesterday – I was sailing with him in the First World War. We were brought up together. When you're dead, you're dead, and my idea is that when you pass out of the world, that's the end of you.'

Danny Sullivan, Farmer and Seine Fisherman. Aged 71.

Danny is a strong, friendly jaunty man and a good farmer. His house is just about the last in the area to be built in the traditional style of mortar and stone. It stands on a little peak of rock, and around it a series of small green fields fall down to a pier and reach the water. On a hot summer's day, bright with colour, the scent of seaweed mixes with freshly cut hay. The slender shape of two old black seine boats lie rotting on the beach, their days long spent.

★

'The sea is in my blood and in my bones, you see. We are what you may call fishermen-farmers, for the people round here have had to mix the two together to make a living. Farming was a terrible struggle around here because there wasn't much land anyway. Do you know what I'm going to tell you, my dear man, that no matter which way you turned you couldn't make a pound out of the land. I was brought up in a small little farm, and I am used to the hard grind.

I was thirteen years old when I first went seine fishing with my father. There was a net called the seine and we would have two row-boats and seventeen able bodied men, all rowing. I was at the end of a seventeen foot oar, you know, and I was thirteen years . . . rowing with a seventeen foot oar. There were ten men in one boat and seven in the other boat. One of them was a bigger one that carried the net. It was always the oars in my time, although in the end there were a couple of seines that got engine boats.

We went out at night. Sometimes all night from eight o'clock in the evening until the stars would leave the sky in the morning. You'd get used to the night, for you were not very far from the land. If you had any luck, you could bring in enough in one haul if you shot the net right. And you'd come in then. Sometimes you would get back at ten or twelve in the night and the first of the night.

At one time I was steering with a rudder and a bit of stick, and I gave a number of years to that. But then I went up to the bow. There was supposed to be a man at the bow of the seine boat to keep an eye on the fish. I would sit up there, and God be just to me, I'd see a shoal of mackerel that might go from here to the top of the mountain. If there was a bright moon they would be easy, but if there wasn't it would be difficult.

Once we saw them we rowed out to them, each man pulling hard on the oars like a racehorse trying to hit the mark. You would shoot the seine around the shoal and then you put a rope underneath, for the seine was as long as here to my house, maybe longer. And there was a rope underneath it then, and there were rings on the seine and the rope running through the rings, and they would haul one end of the rope into the seine boat, and the other end to the other boat, and the two ropes were hauled up into the same boat. At times you would get a lot of mackerel and when the net was coming out of the water it would look like a great hamper. The fish would be put on one boat and the nets in the other, and when we had a heap of mackerel we would try to sell them.

There were buyers then, English buyers from Liverpool, and Irish and Norwegian buyers. The buyer brought the barrels and salt, and he'd put them on the strands and he'd give you commission. That was five shillings in every barrel. He'd pay for the fish and put you in charge of the salting and curing of it, and give yourself five shillings in every barrel. The women and the girls did the splitting and salting. All the strands which you now see deserted were full of women salting fish. There would be seven or eight stations at some of them.

The season would start at about the 15th of August and it would go on until the first of November. As they sold the fish they got a docket for the amount of fish, and when the season was finished they produced the dockets to the buyer and he would pay the money. Then there was one night appointed and they divided the money – the seventeen of the crew. And there would be a bit of celebration that night, you know – a few barrels of porter in some house and dancing and singing.

Some seines did better than others. In those days the money was better value. If a father of a family had fifty pounds for the start of the winter he'd be a happy man. He'd be well off and saved. You had your own potatoes and your own eggs. Oh, no, no, not mackerel. You'd get sick of it. You couldn't look at them when you were fishing, Oh, no, no.

Of course sometimes we couldn't sell them. There might be a glut or no salt for curing. And then we were like lads on a raft rowing from place to place trying to sell them. Sometimes we dumped them overboard. You couldn't look another fish in the eye. Sometimes we might row eight or nine miles and with only a crust of bread to keep the hunger off.

The fish are all gone to hell. In the old days you just went out in a little boat and you would be out for about an hour and come back with a boatload of fish. Now if you went out for a day you wouldn't get two fish. As for the mackerel they are sucking them up. The harbour down there – every year the shoals of mackerel used to come in. You could see them if you stood outside there. You could see the mackerel shoaling in the harbour. You'd go out then. But today you wouldn't see anything. It's like a fresh water lake. There's no mackerel coming in at all, and I miss that a lot, because I used to love to look down and see the shoals of mackerel, and you know, they would put water in the sky. They would break up, and break the water, and would put a spray of water up.'

Martin Harty, Trawlerman and Fisherman. Aged 25.

Martin's father, who married late in life, is seventy-eight, so in a way Martin has skipped a generation. He is well content with the old style in which he was brought up. Like his father, he uses the word 'blackguardism' to describe the sexual revolution of the young.

While many of his contemporaries had farms or small businesses to fall back on after they left school, he had nothing. His father, who had been a fisherman, a journeyman, and at one time or another had turned his hand to almost everything, now has his pension. Martin has been as resourceful as his old man. The pier has always been a pivot of their activities.

Martin's first job was as a 'decky' on a small seventy foot trawler. He has done trawling all over the coast, changing jobs and ships as the mood took him. In intervals between ships he stayed at home. In the country, unemployment takes on a different perspective from unemployment in the city. For one thing, even in a time of recession, you can often find a temporary job, particularly in the summer. Martin's part-time employment is connected with boats. If fishing is bad on the big trawlers, there is salmon fishing on a friend's small boat, scalloping or even taking out tourists for a look at the sea and the islands.

And there is always the dole. Martin disagrees with his father, who regards its acceptance as a fall from grace. To him and his contemporaries it is a necessary evil that allows them to live in Cappaghglass without the thought of emigration.

He is a careful young man, who daydreams about the possibility of marrying a farmer's only daughter. He would like to be quite secure, with a nice modern house and plenty of food. He might have to look after a few cattle, but there would always be the association with the sea.

★

'In between jobs my father had a small converted boat and I used to go out with him in the summer holidays from school. We caught crab and plaice and sometimes did a little trawling for mackerel or herring. My father packed it up about ten years ago when people were getting bigger boats which cleaned up the small men. The fish were also getting scarcer.

The boys at school with me were mostly sons of farmers – small farms, what we call croft or fringe farms. Nowadays with one of those there's little opportunity to make a living all your life – to marry and then support a growing family. Many of my friends trained as inspectors and milk recorders . . . things like that. But I chose the sea. There is great excitement about fishing and a lot of the feeling of the hunter about it. You see them on the sounder, and then you are hunting, chasing after the damn things, and there is nothing so nice as a netful of fresh fish.

My father decided to send me first to a fishery school run by the government. Rather the devil you know, he said to me. It was only a short course learning about things like mending nets and splicing, with a little navigation thrown in for good measure. Then I was on my own. Getting a job on a trawler is unlike anything else. There are no contracts like in England and everything is casual. You might meet a fellow in a pub or on the town, and it would depend on hearsay. The most successful fishermen are always on the move like tinkers.

My first boat was a seventy foot stern trawler. A fish will rot in a net, but a trawl is a different thing because when it comes over the side, everything comes loose. I think its a better system than netting. I started as a "decky" with only half a share in the boat. How it worked was like this. The skipper would get a share and each of the four men in the crew would also get a share. And I got my half share. And then there would be five more shares for the skipper who had to pay for everything. It was a scratch living, and most of the boxes of fish we caught went on paying for the day's fuel and other overheads. Some skippers who have bought expensive boats on a mortgage have to pay off twenty or thirty thousand before they have a penny in their pockets. If the fishing was good and each share was making two hundred quid, I would get a hundred. But that didn't happen often. Mostly I couldn't buy a bloody stamp.

I wouldn't call fishing a hard life compared to, say, a man working on a building site. The worst thing is the cold and the sickness. You could be up all night and never dry, and that was part of it. Sickness was something else. When I started off you would have "the green" coming out of you all the time. What they called the flu from the pancreas and stomach below. At first the others would be laughing at you as they had their eggs and sausages. The only thing was to suffer on and make an effort to eat. You could try some oatmeal and hot water and that might settle you a bit. It took me six weeks to get over it, and now I don't feel anything any more. Only after a fair weekend, and if you have had a booze-up or if you go ashore for a week or two. But I think it's quite natural to get sick.

The work on a fishing boat is always varied. If you are fishing the herrings that means spending the whole night out fishing with only a couple of hours sleep before bringing them to port. And then you're off again. Another type of fishing is netting fish. You go out about five on, say, Friday evening, and shoot sixty or seventy nets that carry about two miles along the bottom, and leave them there till maybe Monday. Even if they are thirty miles out, the Decca will always find them.

Catching fish is a team effort, but still and all, a bad skipper won't last long. Much of the success of a boat will depend on his judgement and skill. Generally the skipper won't believe in a close relationship with the men. They won't even speak or drink with you. Fishermen are great boozers when they have a few bob, but the older skippers will never join the crew. We often talked about it, but never found the reason. They just won't speak.

There is always this little bit of secrecy about fishing. On most boats a sort of mate is appointed and the skipper will have a chat with the mate . . . a little whisper . . . and they will decide where we are to go. But although they are always trying to keep things quiet, the others will soon find out. I remember one evening we caught a hundred and twenty boxes of pollack twenty miles east of Cappaghglass, and next day there were sixty boats in the one area. The boats have radio telephones and can monitor each other, and they learn where there's good fishing.

When I first started, the local boats worked from their own ports, but now there isn't the fish even to pay their fuel bills. For things like herring and white fishing they have to go to other ports. The funny thing about fishing is that while no one will praise it, they wouldn't leave it either for another job. It's a game of chance and I couldn't put my mind on anything else. Often we get disappointed and are just about to pack it in, when we catch something, and then it doesn't matter. It's hard to explain. Often you are very wet and miserable, and then a group of men living in cramped conditions will get on each other's nerves. Once a man who had had too much high stool in the bar, you know, ripped my oilskins with a knife from top to bottom. The next day I left that boat.

The trouble about fishing today is that its getting very expensive. I think the seventy foot trawlers are a thing of the past, and now we're talking of a hundred and twenty footers for mackerel. I would say only five per cent of the big boats are making money, and unless something is done to preserve the shoals of fish it will soon be all gone. For the moment it's cheaper and more profitable to fish out in the small local boats, and in that way we save on the diesel. That's what I am doing now. I share with a friend. We have a fifteen foot boat with a fifteen horse power engine, and that way there's no upkeep.

My father says that if every man, woman and child went out fishing, they could never catch one third of the salmon he used to see when he was young. When we started last year we caught one salmon, and we thought we were in clover, but it was a couple of weeks before we caught the next. Shrimp is the new thing, and that only started five years ago. In the old days they shovelled the prawn over the side, for there was no market for them. Then scampi became popular in England, and now things like crab and prawn are the biggest sellers of all. And they are beginning on the little octopuses they catch at night. Then there's the dumping. If the EEC decides to give intervention to fish, that's what people will do. Last year they were dumping hundreds of cran of small herrings because there was no market for them. I think it's the same thing for farmers.

We don't get many difficulties in the small boat. In May we get basking sharks and they get tangled in the nets and tow them all over the place. At two hundred pounds each this can lose us a lot of money. The only thing to do is to tow the sharks to a beach and kill them. Remove the tail for a start. But we never touch the porpoises or seals, even when they cause us a lot of damage.

I suppose I am in fishing for the money like the next fellow. I might go abroad for a year to Scotland or some other place and make a heap of money and have a great life with no one watching you. Then I'd like to come back here and do fishing in a small way. Nothing too big. I wouldn't like to get into debt. The present generation is getting into debt too much. My father is a man who paid for everything and didn't bother with it at all. The modern trend with young fellows is debt. They are going into debt for their homes and for new cars. All hire purchase. No problems at all. They are inclined to get CB radios – talking to girls and boys and different people on the radio, you know.

I'm doing one thing even when I'm not working. I'm putting in money on a bank payment I'm making towards putting out mussels. That's a new thing now, and it's going to be a world-wide thing when the waters have been fished out. We all know it's happening. You can tell me anything you like, but I know for a fact that there is less herring and less mackerel in the water and no if's and but's. And they are going to have to start cultivating the fish. You can put out ten rafts and you're going to be a rich man if you can sell those every year. I think the whole thing could balloon. It's very hard for two months of the year, and the rest of the year you are watching your money grow. About the start of April or the middle of March you have to go to the rocks at low tides and start scraping them off the rocks . . . then you transfer them from the rock to a boat and pack them, and take them to the rafts. There are people in this town who are putting out huge outlays and think they will be millionaires. I don't think that, but it's a good thing to be involved in all the same. But I tell you Peter, I'll stick to the trawling while I can.

I would never live in the city. If you lived in a city it would break you, and you would spend every pound that you had. In the country you can get a potato or a turnip and you can hold your money. I love eating; a good feed of turnips, a roast leg of lamb, and best of all a lump of bacon and cabbage. Fish is fine as well. Did you know that the last man on a boat often acts as cook? Being on the coast, of course, we had the pick of the fish. Fine yellow sole, and sometimes there would be salted ling for a treat. Ling is the same round shape as a conger, and half the size. Sometimes the skipper, when he was blackguardy, would say, "Conger and cabbage for dinner today." Ling is the grandest thing with a good sauce. Steep it for the night, take it out in the morning and boil it for half an hour, and everyone would go mad for it.

The city . . . in a city a young girl is getting her hair done one day, dresses the next day and lots of people become destitute and leave nothing behind. Now we are getting the city people coming to Cappaghglass, and to tell you the truth, Peter, I don't like them. The British person and the foreigner are inclined to be better. There is money to be made from them. The city people build their bungalows and act the big man around here, all right. Maybe his father or mother has a yacht, or he had one himself, and he'll do nothing for me and I'll do nothing for him. They own houses here and think they are in a big position, and they are trying to impress people with what they have, like. My father won't have anything to do with them. If he knew I was going around with people like that, he wouldn't have anything to do with me. He has a more old-fashioned system, but I think it's better too.

There's another thing, Peter. The youngsters today know more than I ever knew. They are acquainted with things like divorce and abortion, and that's the truth. So you can imagine where this country will be in ten years more. Cripes, they are blackguarding about it, and they have gone to the devil altogether. I'm rural, and it's the difference of the way you are reared.'

Catherine Kearney, Fisherman's Wife. Aged 25.

'A fisherman is a good man to be married to because he is great in the home. I think fishermen are like that, they can cook and housekeep because they have had to learn. On board a ship you have to be tidy, so they make wonderful husbands; Dan is wonderful about housework, and his father is too. When I first married I stayed with his parents, and I never cooked a meal, and nor did his mother. It's supposed to be a modern thing, to get the liberated husband rushing around with the dish cloth, and it's been that way with fishermen for a good time, I'd say.

Dan will help with the baby, getting up in the middle of the night and feeding and changing him. And a lot of young married fishermen are doing that. They are even boasting about it in the pubs. That is something new, I must say. Dan has this story about his father, who is great in every way around the house except for the nappies. And his mother came home from shopping in the pony and trap one day to find him staring helplessly in the kitchen with this bare-bottomed child and the coal shovel, scraping at his behind. And that was his first and only experience.'

Jack Jobson, Retired Shopkeeper and Story-teller. Aged 65.

From his sitting-room Jack looks down towards the harbour and the lines of anchored yachts. Little escapes his attention. A man walks on the pier with a sack on his back. 'There's Joe Sullivan with a load of crabs.' A boat is setting out and some Frenchies are hoisting their Blue Peter for customs clearance. There's the familiar sight of Dermot Doyle who has been bending his arm at Jerry's Bar wobbling along the main street.

Around Jack's home are photographs of Cappaghglass in the old days, showing plenty of carts and donkeys, barefoot people and women in shawls. Names of ships are decipherable over the doors. Here's a picture of his father's shop when he was selling pigs' heads from a barrel. He has sailed small boats all his life. His first boat was a sawn-down barrel. 'It didn't mean to go to sea!' He dislikes intolerance, cant, dogmatic religious views. He likes talking to people, and he likes the winter when the tourists have gone and Cappaghglass is left in peace.

★

'You've heard about the Latvian cargo boat? Did no one tell you about that? Really? It was during the Second World War. Let me think back a bit. It must have been just after Dunkirk when France fell. This was a cargo boat trading in the Baltic, about three or four hundred tons. She had already been expelled from up there in Latvia, and she had come down. The people on board here were evacuated Latvians, do you see, and she arrived in Le Havre just at the time when the Germans were advancing into France. It appears that the harbour authorities opened up all the bonded warehouses in Le Havre, and they told any boat to take away anything it wanted. Grab the stuff before the Germans get it, do you follow?

So these Latvians took the French harbour people at their word, of course, and they loaded her from the keel to the main deck with everything you could think of. Anything you mention she had it. To give you an idea now, she had religious insignia – chalices, crosses and all that kind of stuff on one side. She had all kinds of musical instruments on the other, trumpets, drums, fiddles and 'cellos, all kinds. She had furs. She had engines, motorbikes, everything. I've never seen such a cargo. She had tons of scent and brandy and champagne. That's when I got Gretta's fur.

But I missed out badly, because, you see, this happened very suddenly. I was inside Curragheen and some fellow came up to me and said, "Good God, did you hear about this boat that's in Cappaghglass?" She had come in the night before, and was unloading about three hundredweight of coal for Jack Good who was a merchant here at the time. It appeared she had gone from France to England, where she had loaded up a part cargo of coal in England for Ireland – part for Jack, and part for somewhere else up the coast. And they had this other stuff on board they had picked up in France.

When she came in, the word got round they were willing to flog it. The lads went down and went on board, and the customs went on board. He was Denis Murphy – he's dead now. He was fond of bending the elbow, you know, a nice fellow. So he went on board and they proceeded in making him blind drunk. So that marked him. So the next thing was some of the locals got too much booze in them and there was a fight started – this was in the night-time about eight or nine. And someone got hurt, and they got a local doctor fellow by the name of Paddy Burke – they rang him up. Do you remember Paddy? Paddy was tight and the Customs man was lying on the ground. And then the Guard came down, and he was also fond of bending the arm, and he got blind drunk as well.

The Latvian captain was making sure that they were all drunk men. They did a few transactions that evening. But only one or two of them could speak English.

Eventually the lads got off, the Guard got off, the doctor got off and the Customs man got off. The following morning they started unloading the coal. The coal heavers were local fellows who used to bring down a couple of slices of bread and jam for their lunch, the Latvian mate said, we'll give you some of these big things of champagne. Not a magnum, what do you call the other one? The big one, anyway. So they had some of those, and filled up their billycans with champagne. And these fellows got blind drunk, and there was no more coal shifting that day. There was another couple of fights, and next thing they got the army down. This is a fact now. They got the local defence force fellows, do you follow? The coast defence force. They were all local men keeping the people off the boat, parading up and down the pier.

Word was getting round by now. I put twenty quid in my pocket, which was a lot of money at the time. It should have been two hundred quid, but I didn't know it was as good as it was. I put on a pair of plus fours, twenty quid in the pocket and hopped into a van. I came down and when I got to the top of the town there was a westerly wind that day – and there was this terrible smell of perfume. They were firing bottles of perfume off the boat to the people on the pier who were buying it. You could smell the bottles that got broken right over the road there. It was a damm shame, you know. Oh, dear, dear, dear.

I got to the pier and I met one of these fellows guarding. I knew him very well. I said, "What are the chances of getting on board?" He said, "Very little." But then he said, "Do you see that man up that way?" A wink is as good as a nod to a blind horse. So he walked up and I jumped aboard and made myself scarce. And lo and behold, I was amazed, for half the town was on board buying stuff.

I found the first mate who took me into his cabin, and we sat down inside, and he poured out for me a big dollop of brandy. Well I knew bloody well that if I drank the brandy I'd be like the rest of them. So I was chatting away to him – he had a drink himself – and I poured all the brandy down under the bunk, you see. I bought off him, I think, twenty bottles of Chanel. They worked out at ninepence each. Now I didn't know anything about Chanel more than bog water, but I thought the bottles looked damm nice, and I realized it was bloody good stuff. When I went home they told me it *was* bloody good stuff. If I had known I would have got another couple of dozen. Then I came along, and I got some gloves, the knitted black lace gloves for the evening. Feminine things all over the bloody cabin. Every member of the crew had his own cache, and it was stuck under bunks in lockers. I made an awful mistake. There were these big bales up on deck. I only learned later that there were fur coats inside them, made up fur coats. Worth hundreds of quid, do you follow me? They weren't cheap stuff at all. I should have got a knife and slit them and got a couple of fur coats for myself.

What happened then? Oh yes. I went down to the cabin and I saw some fellow coming up with some nice little squares of fur. Cured and all, and ready to be made up. "God," I said, "where did you get that?" "Down in the cabin, they're flogging them." I went down to the saloon, and the first thing I saw was the local priest, Father McCarthy. Did you ever hear of Father McCarthy? He was a character, a hell of a character I do know. He had come out in a boat. He went down below, and he bought quite a lot of stuff. He had the boat alongside, do you follow, and of course he got a lot free with the old collar on him. If I had a collar too, I'd have got a lot more stuff. He got a damm nice engine for his boat out of it. Afterwards his bishop thought he was having too good a time with the fishing and all that, and banished him to a city parish.

Anyway, everywhere you went there was a crowd trying to make a deal. When I saw Father McCarthy I said, "I'm rather stuck, Father, in trying to buy something of their stuff." "I'll sort you out," he said, and he made the bargain for me. So I bought twenty of these skins at four bob a piece. They were baby seal, and although I hadn't enough to make a fur coat, they made a nice sealskin wrap for Gretta. And I got four suit lengths, beautiful stuff. At that time you couldn't get suit lengths. I think they cost me ten bob each. I can't remember half the stuff I got. Some of it I got from a couple of lassies. I don't know what they were doing on board, but they were flogging stuff too. Everyone had his own little stock, you see.

The garda kept well away. They were afraid to go on board because they might be beaten up, man. Sure they were all like mad dogs on board and they would shoot them. As a matter of fact both guards were blind drunk too.

I never got stuck into the Captain, but apparently he had some very good stuff, do you follow. I saw Sammy Kingston, the fish merchant and he was getting a lot of chalices from the Captain. If I had only known I would have brought more money.

When I was coming out I rammed the stuff down my plus fours, you see, and they were fairly baggy. That was my idea. I had about three or four magnums of champagne, and I think they gave me them for nothing. There was a guard who came along, and he was half shot, and he said, "Look, this is contraband, you can't have this stuff at all." "Jesus," I said, "Go away out of that. Don't be annoying me, go to Regans and have a couple of drinks and tell them I'll pay for it." "Oh thanks, Sir,' he said, and went away to Regans . . . and cost me the price of about four drinks.

When the boat left next day she still took an amount of stuff with her. What she sold here was only chicken feed. She was loaded, I'm telling you. Wait a minute, now, I believe she was torpedoed or bombed after that. She was too small to be torpedoed, she must have been bombed, and that was the last I heard of her anyway. It was a bloody shame.'

CRAFTSMEN

MICHAEL FITZGERALD   Blacksmith, *Aged 83*
TIMMY MAHON   Harness Maker, *Aged 65*
TOMMY GEARY   Cobbler, *Aged 78*
JIMMY SLATTERY   Tailor, *Aged 62*
THADY HICKEY   Carpenter and Musician, *Aged 75*

The crafts of arable farming, of animal husbandry have done more to shape our thoughts and instincts than the trampling of armies.

Irish Folk Ways, E. Estyn Evans.

All I know is a door into the dark.
Outside, old axles and iron hoops rusting;
Inside, the hammered anvil's short-pitched ring,
The unpredictable fantail of sparks
Or hiss when a new shoe toughens in water.

The Forge, Seamus Heaney.

Michael Fitzgerald, Blacksmith. Aged 83.

In spite of their age, the brothers still put in work every day at the forge, bending farm machinery and making ornamental gateways. They seem to have been here always, and, indeed, the lane where they work is called Jacky's Blue Boreen after their grandfather. On a clear winter's evening you can see the rain of sparks they make rising up against the sky.

'Come in out of the cold' say Michael and John and a tumbler of whiskey is put in my hand. They talk of the past – the usual things, crossroad dancing, threshing parties, their small farm, the happy days. Like so many old people they make you forget the hardships they endured. The brothers witnessed the revolution in country life which came with machinery. While other farriers went out of business they adapted. Even in the 'twenties they could see the changes coming, and although horses didn't fade away until the nineteen fifties, Michael had already prepared himself for different times by taking a course in metal working. Today the forge is filled with scrolled gateways for new bungalows and pieces of decorative iron work. Instead of the old shoeing irons Michael works with an electric welder, using books of new designs.

★

'I suppose the blacksmith must be the oldest of all crafts. It goes back to Vulcan and the Dark Ages before Christ. I remember reading that in England the blacksmith used to be the constable of the town, and if you hit one you were six months in jail. Of course that was England, and all I know here is that he was regarded as next to the P.P., which is saying a lot. He was also a craftsman and made the tools for all the other crafts, and when I look at some of the old metalwork done in the past, it makes you very humble about what you can do yourself.

I was born in 1901 and at that time there was a very good trade and all the forges were busy. It was all horses then and donkeys, and the main street would be full of side cars, traps and carts. The gentry, who were still around, had phaetons, landaus and other different sorts of coaches.

My father never did any other work but shoeing horses. He used to tell us that he was thirteenth in his line, and sometimes I wonder if that was an unlucky number, for John and I are definitely the last. Even my mother's people were blacksmiths, and I have three or four generations from that side as well. My father was a farrier – that's the real term, and the vets would call them that, you see. But the ordinary people called them blacksmiths quite wrongly, because blacksmiths were a separate trade altogether. A farrier's work was mainly in shoeing horses – making shoes and dressing the feet and correcting faults and that sort of thing. That's what my father did. But he was also more versatile, mending things like farm machinery and making socks and collars for the ploughs and shoeing wheels and making axles for cars.

I used to make harrow pins for my father, who also made the nails. That was a craft too, and there was a special man for making nails. I still have the old tools he used. First of all you had the hearth and bellows. And then they had the double blasted ones shaped like a drum and operated from the top. We also had a pear-shaped one which you pulled by the handle up and down, and that was very effective. And then you had the anvil. It's a wonderful piece of evolution, if you like, still being used by the highest class of smiths for all kinds of iron work. Most smiths make their own hammers, and we had about ten or twelve in a whole variety of weights and shapes – perhaps a very light one for a light job or a sledge. Then you had the tongs for holding the iron.

At the First World War I was thirteen years old and just walked into it. If you like there was no option for my father needed me, as it's always a two man job. Being a blacksmith is a sort of closed job, and we didn't take on apprentices. John followed me almost ten years later. I remember that my father had a certificate made from vellum to say that he had done some tests before he was accepted as a member of the Guild. It was a very colourful thing, done in beautiful Celtic scroll, and beautiful handwriting. A certificate of merit, if you like.

My work at first was mainly sweeping the floor and keeping the place tidy. Bringing in the coal . . . we used black coal . . . lighting the fire, and helping to form and make the shoe. There was always a lot of work to be done, with a line of horses waiting at the door. Fair days were especially busy, and it was all sweat and smoke and everything. The average day's work was to shoe four horses with complete shoes and that would mean dressing the feet, making the new shoes and nailing them on. Once, after I got good, I did five horses one summer's day, and I went for no dinner or supper until night-time. At that time there was no electric drill or bellows. My father used to shoe horses at night time by candle, but of course there was always plenty of light from the fire.

I think we had ten other smiths in Cappaghglass and they were all hardy men. I only heard of one who became a consumptive, and that was through working in an open place and getting a cold which he neglected. My father had a theory that by inhaling the smoke from the hoof it made you sort of resistant to all diseases and always healthy.

When I started work we got three or four bob a set and when I finished it was around nine pounds. That will show you the way prices took off. In those days there were no cold shoes which you just fit on, but everything took time and skill to produce. Before the hard roads came in a farmer's horse would kick out at least three or four months from a new set of shoes.

I have a funny attitude to work in that I never enjoy anything until it is finished, for there is always some urgency or a bit of worry. Things mightn't go well, you see, and that kind of thing, and you know the old saying that for want of a nail a shoe was lost, and for want of a shoe the horse was lost, and from that it was the battle. They also said "No foot, no horse" and that means if a horse doesn't have a healthy foot you would lose him.

Working with horses you have to be a bit of a psychologist to understand their different temperaments. Over the years I got to know most of the horses in this area and their little foibles and peculiarities. Even the size of their feet. In shoeing it's very easy for something to go wrong, and you must always be very careful, for you are dealing with a living limb and an animal that wants help. In that sense I have always found it a most satisfying craft.

Some people have a mistaken idea that they would want to fondle them, but to tell you the truth they just like being spoken to and nothing more. It's dangerous sometimes. You could always be kicked by a horse and maimed for life. I know one poor fellow that happened to, and he spent a lot of time trying to get some redress from the person he was working for. He got nothing, of course. The easiest animals to deal with are, strange to say, the highly bred ones. The reason for this is that they have been well-handled since they were foals and they have built up a relationship with their grooms. Unfortunately we didn't have many of those in these parts.

It wasn't only the grooms that were important, for the forge was a sort of assembly point for the men of the village and there was always a bit of story-telling and skullduggery going on. All the farmers would be looking for news, and talking to each other over the latest thing, and there would be fellows hanging over the fire heating themselves till we closed down. It was always good crack.

The First War brought a great trade in horses to these parts, but of course when it finished everything had changed. The machinery was coming, and we had the Rising and the Civil War and we had a curfew in the town. People were shooting at each other and you could see the end of the old order. But what I remember most about those days was the great flu. The doctors hadn't the serum, and there was no such thing as injections, and the only thing they could recommend was whiskey and to keep warm. I remember getting a headache and going to bed and hovering between freezing and heat, and all the rest. The neighbours were wonderful and kept us alive with soup and drinks. But there were thirty funerals a day and the nicest people were being knocked off like flies.

After all that the blacksmiths and the other crafts began petering out one by one. Of course the horses were still there, and the repair work for the farmers, but it didn't take much sense to realize that the writing was on the wall. I would have to look for a new business. It started almost accidentally, for I had noticed when things quietened down, they were building new houses that needed gates. One day a man brought us a damaged one with an "S" shaped tang out of it which he wanted repaired. Today it would be a simple enough job, but at that time I hadn't the foggiest idea, and it took two weeks to make the new part. Anyway the outcome of it all was that I told my father that I wanted to learn about metalwork. But of course he didn't approve, for he was one of those men who never said "that's a good job" or gave you any encouragement. He more or less cut you down.

I've been inquisitive all my life, and thank God, I have this sense of purpose and wasn't disappointed or deterred. I went off and took a job with one of my mother's people who had a forge outside Dublin. I went to evening classes, and there was a terrible rush to learn welding at this time. We had overcrowded classes so that on many nights you wouldn't get hold of a torch. But I kept going somehow, and began to get interested in decorative ironwork and anything that I could see. Some scroll or pattern, a bracket arm and the old lampholders down on the pier. People didn't know anything about it then. I started making things in the traditional blacksmith's way, heating the iron and beating it out in shapes and fusing it in the fire. Now they have a machine called an "Ironworker" that twists bars, and rollers that can bruise them into shape. But I find them very standard and repetitive and not like what you can do by hand.

I only gave up shoeing horses a few years back. It was not that I didn't like doing it – haven't I been doing it all my life? – but I objected to the new crowd of people. Most of the farmers have gone, and horse riding has become a prestigious sport. There is something very patronizing in their attitudes. Compared to the old people to whom it didn't matter who you were or what you were, they are only beggars on horseback. I couldn't tell you half the trouble I had, and how they had the cheek to come along and tell you how to do your own job.

It was a woman that finally finished me. She was always cribbing about this and that, and she had brought along this horse with what we call "shelly" feet which takes a lot to get the shoe on. You have to have this excess of horn over the margin of the shoe, so that when they stroke themselves the edge is rounded off and there is no sharpness. And this woman told me as blunt as I'm speaking to you now that it was done wrong, there was too much shoe on it. I told her then that she would have to take my apron and tool if she thought she knew more than me. "Oh," she said, "I shouldn't have said anything." "You should not," I said, "for I expect a little more from a lady of your standing." It was ignorant criticism and hurtful too. I said that you won't go to a doctor and tell him how to give a diagnosis, and you won't go to a cobbler and tell him how to make a pair of shoes and you won't come here and tell me my business. And that was the end of the horses for me, and anyway I suppose that my time was done, if you like.'

Timmy Mahon, Harness Maker. Aged 65.

As the Fitzgerald brothers are the last blacksmiths, Timmy is the last harness maker in Cappaghglass. When he goes there won't be any to follow because no one is doing the apprenticeship any more. His small shop backs off the main street, and in spite of the changed times, there always seems to be a pile of old harness bundled in the corner waiting to be repaired. Most of his business is mending – shoes, bridles, anything leather.

He is a small greyhaired man who wears glasses and looks down at you like an absent-minded professor. All the time his hands are busy sewing at the leather. He isn't altogether sad at the harness maker's demise – stitching eight hours a day wore your arms down. A lot of people talk about old crafts, but you can be sure of one thing, Timmy will say, that they never put an hour's work into them. If they had, most likely they would be talking differently.

★

'The horse gave employment to everybody, and everyone had a horse because there were no tractors. And I'm not talking about prehistoric times, but the last years of the war. And it lasted like that almost to the late 'fifties.

When I started my apprenticeship with my father, there were four other harness makers in Cappaghglass, and we all made everything that goes with the horse. There were the collars, bridles, saddles, britching, the winkers and all the harness for the cars and traps. There wasn't a farmer in the whole area I didn't know, and make or repair his saddling. There were a lot more people anyway, and sometimes on fair days they would break the harness maybe at your front door, and you had to fix it. Otherwise they couldn't get the cart home.

Collars were the most difficult thing to make, for it all came out of your head, and there were no patterns or anything. Sometimes a man would specialize in this one thing. In the old days we had to make about half a dozen collars a month, and the work was very hard on the hands as well as on the eyesight. You didn't need many tools, but it was always very laborious stitching away in the shop until the bad light made you give it up.

All we had was a mallet, a stitching machine and a kind of teaser, and for a week's hard work you got four or five pounds. When people see a bit of saddlery or harness, they don't understand all the work that's gone into the making. For something like a britching there might be twenty feet of stitching six to eight stitches in every inch. There would be at least four hours work in that.

The end didn't happen all of a sudden. The progressive farmers got their tractors, but the smaller man still kept using the horse. I made my last collar at least a dozen years ago, and by that time the material was getting very expensive and worked out against you. The last customer

I had wanted to buy a collar as a souvenir to hang on his wall as a bit of a novelty, and I suppose I could be hung there as well.'

Tommy Geary, Cobbler. Aged 78.

Tommy is still repairing shoes in the small wooden shed that he and his brother built up one of the steep lanes of the town. The sharp tap of a hammer, the smell of leather, and inside you can see all the familiar objects of a lifetime's use.

Where did the cobblers go? The last war finished them off. Before that boots and shoes were always a bit of a luxury around here, something to be looked after and treasured.

A cobbler's life was always a poor struggling existence. Tommy picked up the craft by working with his brother, and it was a hell of a life. You hadn't a penny. Most of his life has been spent within the confines of Cappaghglass. He has never owned a car or taken a ride in a plane. How many shoes and boots has he made? Quite a few. Every morning he leaves his terraced house and comes up here to the shed. Filling in time, his neighbours say.

★

'You could make five pairs of boots at your ease in a single week. But you wouldn't make much money from them. You would make a pair of boots in a day, and if they cost twenty-four shillings, you would be lucky to get five shillings.

When I was a boy growing up we only wore boots in winter. Your feet got hardy walking the roads to school and there was no tar or anything. When you came in after wearing boots, the first thing was to wash them in a bucket of cold water. In those days the ordinary working man had only one pair, like, say, for Sunday and Monday, and the cleaning and oiling of them was very important. I remember well how my father used to wash and polish them on Saturday night, so on Sunday they were shining like two stars.

If boots and shoes were scarce in my childhood, cobblers weren't. There were six of them in the town and you could smell the leather walking down the street and hear the banging. There was Jerry Magnier, Phil Dwyer and a man we called The Whiskers from his long red beard. There were also the itinerant cobblers who travelled from place to place. They would come in as free as the air, for they carried no tools, and say, "Have you a stand for the day?" and you'd give them a couple of bob and they would be gone, and they spent every penny they made on drink. They were a thirsty type of man. I can also remember a nailer who was called Jimmy Punch and the nails he made were exemplary. Wire or hob or big iron nails, and I can still find them around the shop.

If you ask me why I became a cobbler I don't know. Perhaps it was the scarcity of shoes as a boy and not having them always on my feet. Again it was a sort of skill, and even today I'm never happier than working away making a piece of thread or soling. I joined my brother and it became a way of life.

What we made then were what are called working boots, and then were all the rage. Heavy brown leather that never dried or cracked and often as good in ten years as when the farmer first put them on his feet. The first performance in making them was to get the belly of the cow, what they call the inside leather, and cut it out to whatever size you want.

I still have all the tools here. You see that old Singer patcher – I bought that in 1932 and it's still working. I have the sewing awls and the different sizes of lasts, sewing needles, pegs and tacks and God knows what else. I still make the thread with fifteen different strands at a run. I won't bore you with the details and anyway, all that skill has gone and no one wants it. There was hammering, tacking, petting, sewing and at the end of the day you had a fine pair of boots.

I'm at it still, but only as a sort of sideline in repairs. The last boots I made was in 1948, and to tell you the truth I haven't made a single pair since then. And that's a big gap of time. When someone wants a shoe mended I do a bit of repairing. Of course the modern shoe today is only an expensive joke. There is nothing in them and they are only stuck together with glue solution. They are just compressed paper, if you know what I mean, and they won't take a stitch or a tack. That's what happened to our craft.'

Jimmy Slattery, Tailor. Aged 62.

Mrs Simpson told me about Jimmy Slattery who has made a couple of suits for her husband. Her first visit: 'We went up the hill expecting to find Mrs Tiggywinkle or whoever it is, and here is this charming man with my idea of a dream house. It opens onto a sunny white wall, and there are chickens and ducks and dogs and everything, and there he is with his wife making coats and we talked for a while. He was trained in Savile Row, and he pointed to a rack and said, "Those six jackets are going to the Attorney General in Chicago who comes every year, and this is going to the head of the Supreme Court in Washington."'

When I went along I found him among his bolts of cloth, needles, scissors, hand irons and piles of half-finished clothes. His current commissions included an Irish General's uniform with gold tabs, and a lawyer's robe. The radio was playing full blast.

When he started you could buy a tweed suit for thirty shillings. Now his clients are rich enough to afford the basic one hundred and fifty pounds that a new suit will cost. Although his skills were learnt in London, in the end he chose to come back and work from home. From the window of the shop you can see the sea and at the back the small wood is thick in bluebells.

*

'A good tailor is a dedicated artist, for he has to have everything dead right in his head, lines, material, cutting, everything has to be perfect. I think that unless a tailor has both a sensitivity and some artistic skill he will never be any good, even after working a lifetime.

I'll tell you why I regard it as an art. A painter will paint something, but the picture won't talk back to him or move like a suit. You are a decorator of the human frame, and in that way you are artistic. When you put a suit on a fellow for a fitting and they look at themselves in the mirror, you are always wondering what is in their mind and what they see. You know the suit is good, but perhaps there is something wrong, and each person sees it in a different way. If I could figure out what he has in his mind I would be halfway.

In making a suit, each individual has his own design. If you lay the width of the lapel to go with the times, and the width of the trousers, the rest is something he has created himself. Compared to this the factory mass-produced clothes are all done on the conveyor belt. One man is taught to do a small job like a pocket, another the collar, and that's all they know.

My father was a tailor and his father before him. The grandfather was living around the time of the famine, and that brings you back a bit. He used to tell me that they were evicted south of Cappaghglass before the famine. They had a small farm, and when you were evicted you were forced to leave your farm and go to the mountains and build some sort of shack there. We have been here ever since. Without the farm, the grandfather took to the needle.

I can remember the old-fashioned tailors who used to work around. This type of man would be living in the country and instead of people coming to him, he would go to the people and work in their house. He would make the frieze trousers, make the clothes for the kids and do a week's work in the house before moving on. All he carried was a pair of scissors, a needle, thimble and a tape measure.

Then there were the journeymen tailors and I could tell stories about them fellows that would curl your hair. A journeyman would be a tailor working from an established tailor, but travelling around. There was the small job maker whose skill was only in making waistcoats and the more qualified fellow who could finish a jacket. During the winter they would take a job in a town and they would go to someone's workshop and say "Give me something to keep me going," and all they wanted was money to buy beer. Some of them were clever all right. I heard of this man who cut up the blankets of the digs he was staying in, and sold them to his landlady as longjohns for her husband to wear. After that she would never take in a tailor.

They would stay for the winter months and at the first turn of the sod, when they could put their foot on three daisies they would head off into the country. And it was all over Ireland and in every town and village you would see them. And if they didn't like the man they were working for, they would get the hell out of it quickly enough.

There were a few apprentices, but most of them packed it up because it was very tough work. A lot of the fellows were pretty intelligent and they could see that the standard of tailoring was not good at all. And you are supplying a badly-paid service. When I started in 1941, a suit would cost about two pound ten, and a tweed suit only one pound fifteen, and by the end of the war they had gone to ten quid. An average suit would take three days to do. The sort of thing a farmer wore then was a Dugdale navy blue serge, although sometimes they chose a dark grey, and very rarely a brown. The farmers in those days liked a certain style of their own. They liked their trousers made a certain way and their jackets nice and comfortable. And a suit had to last and last.

By the time I left my father I had picked up a bit. I could make a waistcoat and trousers and only part of a jacket. A jacket is much the most difficult thing, for the cutting is very important and the fitting is also very important. You can be a genius and the thing is wrong anyway.

I left home at sixteen and got a job on my own. How much I was getting paid at that time I'll tell you. We got four shillings for making a waistcoat and five and sixpence for trousers, making nine and sixpence a day. We worked six days in the week. I paid thirty bob for my digs in the 'forties, and that was a lot of money. I was a rich man, for there were fellows around working for only ten shillings a week.

That was in England. Mind you, it took time to work up to that. One of the things that sent me to England was that fact that in Ireland the standard of tailoring was not good at all. When I arrived in London I got the sack about six times because I wasn't good enough. And that's a simple fact. The first thing I had to say to myself was "What am I going to do now?" I got a job as what they call an improver. Now you take two years as an improver and you tend to come out as a fairly good tailor.

At the time I'm talking about at least 80 per cent of the tailors in London were Irish. I remember one man from Aran was little short of a genius who could do almost anything with a piece of cloth. The trouble was that the Irish were all boozers and they didn't come to work on Mondays and Tuesdays and you couldn't rely on them. So what happened was that the Jews and Greeks took over. It was sad.

I enjoyed English people and particularly the Cockneys and their sense of humour. I remember one man coming into the shop where I worked who wanted to be the best dressed man at some particular gathering or show, and the tailor, who was Jewish, said to him, "I don't know about you having the best suit, but you will have the most expensive anyway."

Styles were changing. There was the long Burton jacket, and when you took it off the poor man had no shoulders anyway because it was all padding. Then there was the short jacket they called the bum freezer, and that was a terrible dirty style of suit. When I came back to

Ireland the Ready Mades had taken over. The tailors I remembered were all old men, and their sons hadn't stuck it and left the country. No one knew how to make suits any more, and some of those I've had to alter would make you weep they are so badly made. They are produced on a conveyor belt system, and you can teach anyone to do a small job like that. Make a pocket, make a sleeve or collar. They'd be all cut by a machine with no seams, guaranteed to be badly fitting. The Ready Made is only a covering anyway, and they are cheap rubbish. It's just like a cheap make of car compared to something like a Rolls Royce. I could tell a Ready Made from ten yards away. But thank God there was still a percentage of the population that respected their body and used something decent to cover it.

There is no way you can put good workmanship into a suit and deliver it in one day, for good tailoring always takes time. A two-piece suit costs a hundred and forty pounds upwards. Look at it this way. The price of material is high. Three yards of good quality stuff can set you back sixty-five pounds, and you haven't started yet or paid the postage. If you make two pounds an hour you are lucky. Most of the people who come to me now are rich foreigners. But I still get some of the older local men who want a tailor-made suit. They are used to a fairly decent job and nothing else would do. I remember one old man getting a suit made and saying "This one will bury me." Then a few years on he came back and said – "I didn't mean that . . . this will bury me." Four more times he came back, and he only died at ninety-two. I lost all those people to the undertaker.

I can still get work. I never liked the city and it was like living in a cage. Here you can go up to the mountain for a breath of fresh air or take a boat or do a bit of pony racing.

I'm weak enough to enjoy a good compliment. I made a suit for a writer some years ago and I got this letter back from America. It said . . . "I wish to God my books were as much admired as the two suits you made for me."'

Thady Hickey, Carpenter and Musician. Aged 75.

His house stands on a lonely stretch of road deep in the hills. The grey cement walls are surrounded by a yard and a little circle of fields that quickly turns to bog. Near the house are the ruins of a copper mine, stone buildings and an abandoned shaft covered with briar which is a danger, not only to livestock. A couple of years back, Thady says, a young man fell down it and died.

His faded mauve curtains are never drawn. Inside, the furniture is rudimentary, a couple of chairs, a table and a trestle bed against the wall. An iron range is stuck in the hearth, but nowadays he uses a little bottled gas stove. The floor is uncarpeted stone, and the room is chilly. Thady is a tall angular arthritic old man with piercing eyes and a reputation that if he doesn't like you, you'd better watch out. In fact, he is mild-mannered. As he talks he smokes incessantly and a large biscuit tin holds extra packets of cigarettes.

★

'My first impression of my father was the noise of him banging away. My father and grandfather were coopers, but when I was growing up, that sort of work was dying out. There were no machines to help you, and you had to work away with the old saw. I had no formal training, and the first job I was given was to take an old plane and go planing away as best I could. I didn't do much coopering. I made a barrel once, but only to see if I could do it, and I can remember splitting the oak staves. We made the "kilos", the small little oak tubs for bringing butter to the market. A barrel would take a week to make, and it cost about thirty shillings.

The wood was a lot better than with the white deal and pitch pine and the grand yellow pine that never rotted. I wouldn't say a lot for the present stuff which they take fresh from the forest. We did a bit of everything, doors, windows, chairs, beds, roofs, stairs and anything else you could care to name. I was always mad for the wood, and it's the same way even today. I'm much happier when I'm making something and inside the workshop door. I'd live and die for a good piece of wood.

My workshop today has little enough in it, but thirty years ago it was quite a different thing. The whole place was so full of shavings that you could hardly walk. A big part of the business was making carts and wheels. I could make the whole thing, cart, wheel and all for about fourteen pounds. But it was a pile of hard work, and it would take the best part of two weeks to finish. I gave that up soon after the war.

I used to work a lot in people's houses. In those days things were a lot more homely, and they would treat you as one of themselves. Maybe I should have been a journeyman, but I was too young. Did you ever hear of the journeyman? He was just before my time. He was the man who was always on the road, and he took his few tools around with him in a bit of a sack. Perhaps an old plane and saw and screw driver and hammer.

The best journeyman I ever heard of had no tools at all. My father said, one time, he knew this old carpenter, and he was from Kerry and he could do anything. But he wouldn't stay anywhere. He was down at Cappaghglass one day, and they gave him a job of fitting a roof which had proved difficult. So he got the timber and roofed the whole thing, and there was no trouble about it. And he was just a journey-man with borrowed tools.

I think I was about sixteen when I made my first fiddle. I just drew it out on a piece of paper, and it was no bother. That fiddle did me for many years, and I would be walloping away all the night. I used to cycle around from Cappaghglass to all the local dances. There might be an old accordion and the fiddle and a bit of crack. At the crossroad you might have one of your pals playing with you, and we would tune up together. Some people could learn by note, but I never bothered, for I would have hundreds of tunes in my head. At that time people could remember a song, and even if it was twenty verses, there wasn't a bit of it wrong.

Do you know Ladd's Cove? Well I have a song about Ladd's Cove. At the time it was built, it was built for a penny a day – that's what the builders were getting. I can't hardly sing it now.

> "Tis in Ladd's Cove there is a fine building
> It is fit for a duke or a lord,
> It was built by the noble great Richard
> Called Ladd, and his name is on record.

Well if you want to view this fine mansion
There's a charming fine prospect to see
From Finnegan's Cove to Kilcullen
And up to sweet Ballykee.

Where the lobster and crab are in order
And in coursing the harbour they meet.
Where the scallop and oyster most charming
And the young birds are warbling so sweet."

I was good at every class of dancing. I could dance the reel and jig,
the hornpipe and the Walls of Limerick and the Bridge of Athlone and
all these dances, and the sets, all of them. The whole lot. I was a good
singer in my day. Did you ever hear of Roger Casement? He was
caught at Bannow Strand. Do you know the place? Well they made a
song about that at that time. Do you remember that? The Lonely
Bannow Strand, that's what they called it. Here's just a verse:

"It was on Good Friday morning at the early dawn of day,
A German ship was signalling outside upon the bay,
She had twenty thousand rifles all ready for to land,
But she could never get a signal from the lonely Bannow
    Strand."

I often used to stand up and recite that and a lot of others too. Here's
another verse:

"No answering signal from the shore, Sir Roger sadly said,
No comrades here to welcome me, alas they must be dead,
But I must do my duty and at once I am to land
So it was in a boat that he pushed away to the lonely Bannow
Strand."

I'm the last of the old carpenters, and the rest are buried; you have to
go to the graveyard for them. There aren't any carpenters now, only
what you might call handy fellows, and they haven't a bit of skill in the
world. All he can do is to have a planing or moulding machine or
something like that . . . that's all he can do. Most of the furniture you
get in houses now is factory stuff. People today can't even sharpen
their own tools, and the best saw in the country is no good to them.
The saw wouldn't even cut your finger, and you couldn't throw it at a
dog. They can hardly polish their own shoes, and that's a fact.'

EDUCATION AND THE YOUNG

MARY DONOVAN	Retired schoolteacher, *Aged 75*
PEADAR O'MURCHU	Irish Speaker and Teacher, *Aged 55*
MICHAEL MORAN	School Leaver, *Aged 18*
CHRISTY O'DONOVAN	Shop Assistant, *Aged 21*
PAT HICKEY	Trainee Carpenter, *Aged 19*

When parents were asked why they favoured secondary education the reason most frequently given was, 'Without a good education you can only get a labouring job' and 'People have more respect for you.'

Limerick Rural Survey, 1956
Edited J. Newman.

Like as the arrows in the hand of the giant; even so are the young children.

Psalm 127

Mary Donovan, Retired National School Teacher. Aged 75.

Although she retired many years ago, Miss Donovan is still very active in the town, working on a number of local committees like the ICA, Meals on Wheels and the Public Library Service. Her career as a teacher began in 1926 in a small national school outside Cappaghglass which has now been demolished.

★

'Before 1922 there was no Irish history taught here, only English. I remember learning about the South Sea Bubble. Wasn't it ridiculous to teach small children about that, which meant nothing to them? I remember hearing about Silken Thomas, and I think that was the only bit of Irish history I learnt. I remember the Inspector coming in one day and examining us on Napoleon and St Helena. When we were being taught poetry, Master Miley used to say, "Would you like any other story?" and I would say something like "The Bridge of Athlone, Sir", for we were quite tired of "Horatius and the Bridge", although I suppose it was a majestic sort of poem.

My mother was a teacher before she married. In her time they were great on English literature, and the books were passed down, and they knew them off by heart. We had the same subjects, except that she wasn't teaching Irish, and I was. She taught me to read before I went to school. My first lesson in reading was at the railway station. I knew how to spell every advertisement before I went to school at four years old. I could spell Bovril and I could also spell Edwards's Dessicated Soup, and that's how I was taught the ABC.

When I went to school as a child, the teacher was always known as the Master. Master Miley taught us, and later his son, who was John, the Master. We had no secondary schooling like they have today, when the bus collects the children. If you wanted secondary education your parents would have to afford to send you to a boarding school. When I was a child we did a full range of subjects like arithmetic and drawing, and we had nature study. All the boys knew about the birds, and girls like myself knew the names of flowers, which youngsters today seem to be ignorant of. Most of the other children came from farming stock like ourselves. There were a few Church of Ireland children. One of my greatest friends was a girl named Ruth Love, and I remember the delight we had in discovering that our religion shared the same twelve apostles.

I started off teaching in the same little school where my mother had taught, and it had hardly changed since her day. You would come to the door, and there was just the one room and very tiny windows and the beautiful view. The children were lovely you didn't have any discipline problems. The only consistent misdemeanour was smoking, and you just couldn't stop them. They would get crab's legs down on the strand and fill them with I don't know what, and smoke the crabs. Most of them were still barefoot as they had been when I was a child. I remember as a girl I wasn't allowed to go barefoot because I had bronchitis, and I envied the others. I didn't realize for a long time that they were too poor for shoes.

In winter my first job was always to light the fire. The government gave us a certain allowance, but it wouldn't be enough at all, even though there was only one small firegrate at the end of the room. Wet days were always the worst, for there was no way to dry clothes, and the children would all arrive wringing wet. We used to stick newspapers up around their clothes and dry their coats around the fire. They would take turns to come up and sit by the fire and get warm before going back to their desks.

In the old days the classroom was bare enough with big long benches which were very rough, and desks in front. The school had no running water, and only a dry lavatory. For washing there was a slab out in the hall, and the children would bring in bowls of water from the stream.

Most of them had to walk several miles to school, and they brought their own lunches and milk, which we used to heat for them. I don't think anyone was hungry – they had lovely brown bread, a really dark brown, although in those days they had no use for butter. In later times before I retired, it used to break my heart to see children throw away their lunches because they had so much to eat. If you only saw the beautiful lunches thrown around to the birds, sandwiches, cheese, ham and everything, and then they would go down to the shop for chocolate and fizzy orange.

When I started teaching we had English, Irish, arithmetic and geography, and you could do anything you liked on Friday afternoon. There were about thirty in the school, which was a good number. I think forty is the very most you can take in a class, and it's very hard to teach a big crowd all different things. They were very quiet mostly; even the boys were nice. Only when they were bold, I'd give them a slap on their hands. The parents always took the part of the teacher, and if they got corrected at school, they got the same at home. I don't think that's done at all now.

They are all literate now, but they weren't then, and they were sort of shy about writing. By 1928 most of the subjects were taught through Irish, and the Inspector expected you to teach it as best you can. Of course a lot of the teachers hadn't enough knowledge of the language. I think it was a sin crying to heaven for vengeance, the methods we were expected to use. Imagine young children of about seven or eight trying to write a composition in Irish with the grammar and everything perfect. Wasn't it Padraig Pearse who said that everyone in Ireland spoke Irish but the people?

I remember one day I put some old pictures on the wall, and the Inspector came along and asked questions about them in Irish; and I hadn't done the present tense, only the past tense, and you'd be blamed then. All the conversations had to be in Irish, and we'd talk about ploughing, harrowing and horses, and everything old-fashioned and it was very slow-going. The Irish never worked out, and about twenty years ago they changed it. Most of the children I taught dropped it once they left school. I remember meeting one of my pupils who told me how he got a job in the Post Office by learning all the names of the towns in Irish, but when he got into the Post Office he had to learn them in English. It was a waste of time.

The farmer's children always had plenty of farm work to do apart from their schooling. Sometimes you could get careless parents who kept the children at home for no excuse at all, and the Guards would frighten them and make them pay a small fine. They all got jobs like minding the cows, and in summer the whole family would go off to the bog to cut the turf. There were plenty of days when the children didn't bother to come to school for one reason or another.

They left school at around fourteen. At the end of my days there, they did a primary Certificate which meant they had reached a certain standard. It didn't mean very much because there were no jobs for them anyway. Those that had money got married, and those that hadn't emigrated or stayed at home or got a job working as a domestic servant. And there were the old bachelor farmers whom no one wanted. Their parents wouldn't give them the farm because they were afraid they would marry and the new daughter-in-law would throw them out.

If you ask me did the education I taught train people for life, I suppose it really didn't. They could read, and write and do simple arithmetic, and that really was about all. And we had cooking when I first started teaching, plain simple cooking. After that the cooking was dropped, and there was no cooking for years and years, and the girls didn't know how to do anything. I remember one time we had a girl, and she had a dish of hot water with a fish in it. I asked her what she was doing with that, and she said, "Steeping the fish." You see, they wouldn't know.'

Peadar O'Murchu, Irish Speaker and Teacher. Aged 55.

An April day plays havoc with your emotions. The changes made by gusts of wind and cloud and filtering light on the sea and mountains constantly assail you. One moment there is a blast of hail and rain, and then sun and wind. The sky is blue, the waves are tossing and dancing, and the silhouette of a distant boat is squeezed like a drop of paint on the horizon.

Peadar lives in a farmhouse near the sea a few miles from the National School where he teaches. He is an attractive outgoing man, and people who know him say that he is a born teacher. His three children speak fluent Irish. There is no television in his house.

He has strong opinions and fairly fixed views. As a child he heard what could have been the last words of Irish being spoken in these parts – an old woman mumbling the traditional greetings of the day, a vestige of a tradition destroyed by the famine. Now he feels that a knowledge of Irish could be a bridge between the North and the South, between Catholic and Protestant. Speaking it would be forging a bond that would bring people together.

I am scornful. 'What about my family? I am sure all the time they lived here they never spoke more than half a dozen words of Irish.'

'Almost certainly you are wrong,' he says. 'They would have had to speak it out of necessity in order to make themselves understood to the people on their land. And in the North of Ireland you'll find most Unionists originally came from Gaelic-speaking areas of Scotland.'

His family takes its annual holiday in one of the Gaeltacht areas. Although Irish dominates his life, he is utterly against compulsion, and the bureaucratic process that has killed all incentive to learn. The old rural roots are vanishing, and for a man like Peadar, there is something inexpressably sad in the decline. The tradition of teaching has been poisoned by nepotism, and what he thinks is downright hypocrisy. Take the Dail. Who speaks Irish there, and for that matter, anywhere else? Why is it that the best Irish-speaking school is in Dublin? Never mind, all his joy comes from learning, and undergoing the enriching experience of communicating in Irish. It is a better way of expressing yourself, and you can put more meaning into it. Telling a joke in Irish sounds much better. If someone asks you, 'Is your wife good in bed?' in Irish, it wouldn't be offensive at all.

★

'I notice that you can get away with a lot more in Irish than in English, because it is a rustically rooted language. For example, the translation of the Midnight Court: people hide in corners to read it, because you don't use the same terminology, and you don't speak about the same things in English as openly as you do in Irish. This is the point, you see, for Merriman wrote it in total openness and total innocence. The difficulty is that in the English-speaking cultural level you can't openly express the same thoughts as freely.

If you take an example again: The Islandman mentions being at his mother's breast, and while that's awkward in English, there's no problem saying that in Irish. Now he said a lot of other things in that book, and the Department of Education cut them out of the school versions. Things like going for a dip in the nip on the Blaskets, but the tourists coming in were shocked.

Did you ever hear of Raftery? I am Raftery, the poet, and so on, and in the last verse of the government translation is written: Look at me, now, with my back to the wall. But that's not what Raftery wrote. What he said is, Look at me, now, with my arse to the wall. Now "tóin" is a very acceptable word in Irish for ordinary conversation. So there is a difficulty there.

I feel very proud of my Irish culture, and of being able to speak it, really, for it's a lovely language to either speak or read. The old people had a powerful knowledge of Irish. They had numerous words for speech terms which are dying with them, and they will never be heard again. The man speaking Irish in Dublin doesn't speak Irish at all. It's book or Civil Service Irish, and put through a sort of sieve. But a Donegal man will understand a man speaking Scot's Gaelic, and a Scot's Gaelic man will understand a Donegal man. The Dublin man stumbles along and misses everything out.

My father, who was born in 1896, told me he learnt to bless himself in Irish before he went to school. But that was the last of the language so far as he was concerned. I remember an old couple who were a brother and a sister, and they had some Irish, and they would have been older than my father. Their mother was an Irish speaker, and probably their father was too, because the old woman always told me that she spoke Irish as a child. When I knew her she would throw out a few phrases and a couple of prayers, but she hadn't a lot.

At school I was supposed to learn Latin through Irish which was mad. It was bad enough learning something like Latin through English, but through Irish it was crazy like learning Icelandic through Northern Chinese. I think the basic mistake was to think that the schools could make people speak the language, and of course they couldn't. It was too late. For a century before, the shops in the towns, the landlord and his agents, the police and people like that, were all using English. Then the Catholic church through Maynooth put its weight behind the English language.

You need state support, and the support of the church, but you need them in a helpful situation, and not just saying, "you have to have Irish for an examination," but saying, "Irish is the language that is needed, and the language of the future." I think people would have made the effort. In Wales you had a very strong support from the Methodist Church, and that was a very crucial support. In fact, there is the same situation in the Western Isles of Scotland, and the Northern Isles, where the Presbyterian Church was always very supportive and very strong. Both Catholic and Presbyterian churches support Gaelic there, but the churches didn't here at all.

I made up my mind very early to speak Irish, and after school I went on reading. I remember cycling down a particular stretch of road near Cappaghglass, with a friend, and we would speak to each other. We always put a limit on it, and it never became a competition, and that was also helpful. I found being bilingual in English and Irish no great problem. Where I think there would have been problems was if I had been kept away from English.

As a teacher myself I know that learning any launguage depends partly on personal motivation, and also help from school and home.

When I started Irish, it was just another subject, and a painful subject, and I had no interest in it at all. Then I had a teacher who gave us a love for it. He brought us down to Kerry, and we went and stayed with the people there, and we played poker when it was raining, and we played outside with the locals when it wasn't and we had a good time.

That's one of the reasons I am not keen on sending my pupils to the Irish colleges, for the idea is that they would stay in the houses of the people, and at the same time attend classes. But in many cases they cram them in, and there is no Irish anyway. The whole thing is a farce. The government assumes that the people living in the Gaeltacht areas have a love for it, but that's a fallacy. Nobody can make the people speak Irish if they don't want to, and they have helped these people in an unenlightened way. They gave those grants for greenhouses, which was mad, keeping hens inside them, and it was totally mad. There were the other grants for buildings, and God knows what else. Then there were the insulting grants which the department gave to every child that spoke Irish. It was £10 a year, and that class of thing should be rubbed out immediately.

I think we have an advantage in this area, for we pronounce English with Irish sounds, and we don't use the sounds of standard English. In fact, the sounds we use are basically the sounds of the Irish language. I can give you numerous examples of what I mean, and how people think they are speaking English words, but with an Irish formation, you know. For instance, I heard a local man saying long ago that he saw a ship going out of Cappaghglass, out to sea, and he said she was "true fire". But what he was saying was coming from the Irish "tri thine" meaning "on fire". In fact he had no Irish consciously but had derived it from Irish and made it his language.

And the way people ask questions is translated literally from Gaelic to English. It has coloured their English, and it is a colourful type of English they speak, but gramatically, I suppose, it's poor English they have, for the still say "he have" and "he do." That must go back to when people were first learning English all of three generations ago. Everyone here has three or four hundred Gaelic words in their vocabulary which they use in normal everyday life. The names of cattle and different kinds of sheep – the word wether is not used here for a sheep, but the Gaelic word, "moltchán" and the word hogget is never used, but "foïscïn", or little ewe.

I believe Irish teaches people to have a more independent way of thinking. For instance, you know yourself how most Irish people today think in terms of England and America, and "what are the

English doing?" and "what are the Americans doing?" I don't think that would happen if we were Irish-speaking, and I think that attitude is the result of the loss of language. I also feel very strongly that if we had held onto Gaelic, the Northern Protestants, or a great number of them, would feel themselves more Irish, and they wouldn't have this problem of deciding who they were.

I see little hope for a living language, although there are more people learning it. At one time Irish was very much pushed at us, and the teachers at school were tormented totally by the inspectors.

But nowadays the same stress is not on Irish and the Inspector comes in now and says, "How are you?" in English.

There's a new development plan for Irish now, and I was talking to a friend about it. I asked him, "Have you read the plan?" and he said, "Why should I? I'll let it lie on the shelf." He's right, for the plan tells all the things that are wrong, and you know damn well that nobody is going to do anything about them.

What is happening is that the people who are really the store houses for beautiful Irish are dying, you know, in the traditional Gaeltacht areas. And the old people had a powerful knowledge of Irish, and they had numerous words for speech terms which are dying with them, and will never be heard again, really.

I'll tell you the way it is with me. Last year I went on a short holiday to Spain, and I sat down in a restaurant, and there were these two Germans gabbling away. And I made up my mind that all the time I was there I would speak Irish . . . and that's the truth.'

Michael Moran, School Leaver. Aged 18.

This is Michael's last term at school before he goes on to a university. A tall good-looking boy, who finds his subjects and examinations easy, he goes to a school run by the Christian Brothers.

*

'Making up your mind starts with Leaving Cert, when the subjects you choose influence your whole career. You would be about fifteen or sixteen when you make your decision. Basically, if you tend towards the Arts you would take languages, and you would leave the scientific subjects out. I did English and history, and I was advised to do a scientific subject as well, and did biology. Then you simply do these subjects for the next two years.

I take the bus to school everyday, which means two hours of travelling. I think most of the kids like this, because you get to know everyone, and it's sort of yours before the school takes over. I know every twist and turn in the road. There must be half a dozen schools in Curragheen, most of which are free. The one I go to is run by the Christian Brothers, and it is the biggest. Most of the students belong to what you might call the middle-class or farmers and shopkeepers and people from the urban areas. But in a place like this there are no real divisions, since most people who live in the towns have relatives in the country. Of course you get the usual jokes about farmers who have Swiss bank accounts, and things like that, and farmers tend to complain the whole time. We sort of pounce on them, but its more good-natured than anything else.

Although the school is co-educational you will still find the boys mixing with boys and the girls with girls; I don't know if this isn't an Irish thing. You will get mixing at discos and things like that, but basically there is no intermixing even when the classes are combined. The girls sit in certain areas and the boys in others.

I was talking to a fellow who had been a couple of years at a school in England, and we were discussing the difference between here and there. We came to the conclusion that in countries like England and on the Continent you are basically taught how to think, while here you are still taught how to learn and read. So far as the teachers are concerned, they don't order you to memorize anything except for a few passages from Shakespeare and things like that. But if you wish to get the best grades, you will have to memorize an awful lot still.

Subjects like Irish, history, religion and art are called "doss" subjects, because most students feel they aren't much use. They are all scrambling to take science because they feel there's more future in it. Our science classes are bursting because there are too many people. In Honours History we have only a dozen pupils, while in chemistry they have something like forty.

If you get into Honours Irish, it's not so much because you have a love of the language, but because it will be useful to you later on. If you want to become a teacher or apply for any Civil Service job you have to have Irish, and do the bare minimum to get through – that's also an accepted way of doing things. They do oral for Leaving Cert, but all it consists of is about five minutes answering questions. If they are doing Honours, it means going off to the Gaeltacht for a few weeks and brushing it up, and that's the sole extent of their desire. The Gaeltacht areas are artificial areas where you are encouraged to speak Irish, and money is pumped into them. But if you are going to succeed in Ireland you also have to speak English, and speak it well. I suppose Irish has always signified being Irish, and it's a shame to lose it or let it die. But at school there's no desire to learn it. Take myself – I might have liked to learn it in the proper way, but not the way they teach it.

In our school we have Brothers and lay teachers as well, and very often their qualifications seem to be based more on the academic side than the teaching side. Most of them either can't teach or there simply isn't any respect for them. I enjoy studying, but certain teachers can drive it out of you. It means boredom, it means you don't learn anything. We do the normal subjects, and sports, of course. Most people I know are wild about soccer. We also do hurley, but there isn't anything like the same enthusiasm for it.

There's a sort of pessimism in school with the recession and the unemployment – a feeling that things can only get worse. It's beaten into us that we must do well in Leaving Cert in order to get jobs. Apart from Leaving Cert we have exams at Christmas, Easter and summer, when you cram everything into a week or so. We once took a poll, and most students said they could find jobs if they went out and looked for them. But when we looked into it, these were summer jobs, not a career.

So most people feel cynical about politicians rabbiting on about the economic climate. Most of us feel that after doing five years at school there should be something for us to do. In the last year at school everyone gets worried about the problems of getting a job, so you are put under a great deal of pressure. It affects everyone. The majority of boys tend towards Civil Service jobs, even though it's fairly hopeless. We have all the posters up with information about the various Civil Service jobs, but we are charged about ten quid to apply for any post, even if we don't get it. This puts a lot of people off, because you know damn well that unless you are a genius there isn't a hope in hell.

Quite a lot intend to get third level education, and we talk about "grades" as if it was a normal routine. We have to get four honours to get a grant at the Regional College, and the basic minimum is two C's. Most of the farmers' sons, though, and there are a lot in the junior classes, seem to drift off to jobs after Inter, and I suppose they have no impetus to go any further. Then there is something like ANCO, where they train you for something, and keep you occupied for about a year, and then you are back where you started, and draw the dole. Its about twenty-seven pounds a week and its absolutely accepted. Nobody looks down on anyone else because they get the dole, and also you never know if you won't be joining them in a little while.

I like living here, but sometimes people drive me up the wall. It's apathy and even ignorance, and of course, this is a rural area. All the farmers ever talk about is cattle, the price of land, and of course the weather is everything. You could almost live by talking about the weather. If you were somewhere else, the newspapers would give you something about world affairs, but here, even if it is something spectacular like what's going on in the Lebanon or the Middle East, its only given a few headlines.

We have a good library at school, with Kant and Engels and people like that on the shelves, but nobody uses it. Even someone like James Joyce is hardly read. I am one of the exceptions – there's a small clique of boys who enjoy reading. In many subjects you feel that the teachers are putting across their own particular viewpoint. Take something like history, where there is a lot of emphasis on things like the War of Independence, on Dev and Collins and all the rest of them. I know you can't change history or the facts, but it seems to me much of what we read is more devoted to the nationalistic point of view that takes in violence, and that's still going on today. There are a few jokers at school who say they will join the IRA, and during the Hunger Strike we were all making black flags to hang in the main square, and we felt real resentment against the English presence. But when you discuss the whole issue with people, you also realize that it's a sort of dream thing. While everyone would like the North back, they wouldn't like all the violence and unemployment that would go with it. I often think it's a sort of love-hate relationship. While there is an awareness of the problems to do with the North, there's no actual desire to go up there and get yourself shot at. If you joined something like the IRA you would be very close to it.

Religion is another subject which people at school don't agree about. In every class there are a certain number of boys who have become estranged from the church. They look at it and see an old-fashioned system that is more repressive than progressive, and they tend to pick away at this façade to see if there is anything underneath. And usually there isn't. Religion for the senior students is based more on discussion than anything else and we sort of tear the church apart. There is some mention during the year about Hindus and Moslems, and other religions, but you find the teachers know very little. I have heard one teacher make such a blatant falsehood as saying that Mohammed was the God of the Moslems, which is absolute rubbish. That sort of thing tends to drive you away. You don't expect a teacher to be all knowing or infallible, but you do expect him to correct his mistakes. If they don't show any enthusiasm in their quest for knowledge, how are they supposed to instil that in the very students they are teaching? What I want to find out basically is the truth.

The sort of thing that annoyed all of us was the abortion amendment. We felt that this was just another backward step, with the older generation trying to block us before we could do anything about it. Most people are against abortion, right? But there is also the feeling that it isn't right to tell a woman what she should do with her body, neither is it right to close the issue. That's what happened when the amendment went through. The whole issue of women going to England for abortions was swept under the carpet, and you won't hear anything about it for years. That's one of the reasons why there is all this cynicism about the church and its policy. In a modern society you can't have rules against contraception as well as abortion, and divorce also comes into it.

Most of my contemporaries feel this way, but our teachers are completely against it. I have always felt I have been lucky not to have a Brother teaching our class religion, because they can be very conservative. But we have a woman instead for the final year for religion, and she's as bad, totally against any discussion about contraception and divorce. I am eighteen myself, and she is only about twelve years older, but there is a whole generation gap between us. I find that very sad.'

Christy O'Donovan, Shop Assistant. Aged 21.

Christy is a tall good-looking young man, at present working in his father's shop. He's there on a temporary basis until he thinks of something else. Not for him the permanent routine of serving customers behind a counter for the rest of his life. He equally abhors the dole which so many of his contemporaries are forced to take. He is also fiercely critical of his father's generation, although his own attitudes are surprisingly conservative – he believes strongly in a man working his way, and he believes in marriage. But he is a product of the age of affluence which his father never encountered, and was never able to enjoy. He has dreams of travelling and finding success, and is fond of saying where there's a will there's a way. His essentially rebellious spirit is not yet quenched.

★

'I left school three years ago in fifth year, and I should have done sixth to get my Leaving, but I thought, "What a load." I mean, education isn't just schooling, and some people think that just because a guy has been to college he is educated. But I know people with degrees behind them that are the most conceited guys in the world. I know that I'm pontificating to you, but that's how I felt. My father made me do a short course in Management, and I got these two small pieces of paper to say that I was a qualified jackass.

I've tried a few things. In an area like this there is fishing and farming. Our family doesn't have any land, and I never saw farming like some of those hippies do, as something that comes out of a Ladybird book. You know, the idea of a man walking behind the plough in wellies. I thought of fishing. You work on the trawlers for ten years, then you go away and get a small boat, and then you get a bigger one. You need money and you need push, and must be prepared to put in a lot of donkey work. But then the waters have been fished out. I know for a fact that there is less herring and mackerel in the water than there was twenty years ago, and no if's and but's. So there isn't much future in fishing.

I took lots of jobs at one time or another. One which suited my temperament if you are curious about people – and what Irishman isn't? – was barman. You meet all types in a bar, and you see every situation that's possible in the human mind. I've seen men walking into the bar perfectly dressed in a suit, shirt and tie, and you look at their hands, and they are wearing a gold sovereign, and something says "flashy" and they are also wearing high-heeled shoes, and that gives it all away. People here are a science. This is a human and psychological game business, and you pack a lot of life into a few years. Education isn't losing your top at people easily, and if a guy hawks and spits in my face, am I going to hit him or not? I know he would knock the daylight out of me; on the other hand I know that I am lowering myself to his level, and number two, I just couldn't waste my time on him. In Ireland everyone is a potential hero and stands out, except the drunk who is a benevolent drunk. Everyone appreciates character far more than in somewhere like the States, where he is a blob.

The only thing I am really conscious about in Irish history is that America and a lot of other countries around the world got the cream of the Irish generations. They got the very best, and skinned this country out of a lot. In my father's time America was the God, and now it has become the scapegoat of the world. I went there myself for a short time after leaving school. I found the States quite exhilarating in places, and the weather was great. But again, I am a dark climatic person, and my personality was different from theirs. You talk to people who live in somewhere like California, and when they get rain like we had today, they close for half a day – everything. I was there when it rained for two hours, and it was fairly heavy rain, and Jesus, everything closed down. The whole place stopped and came to a standstill, and you couldn't believe it.

People were very friendly on the basis of friendship, but if you go to a friend in the States and ask him for help in getting a job, you meet a blank wall. Another thing I noticed was that in America a person of my own age might ring up and say, "OK, we are going bowling tonight" and it's cut and dried. We pay ten dollars each, and come home, and that's it. But here anything can happen. A friend of mine rang up on Sunday in a great flap because his boat blew a plank and I spent all my Sunday bursting my breath fixing it.

Very few people actually starve in this country, but to get ahead is very hard. In somewhere like the States it is also very hard, but you will get ahead in the end. A lot of my friends who were at school with me picked up jobs and went into a comfortable rut with nice rounded edges, and they go out drinking at night with the boys, and they play it by ear one day to the next. But of course they were the lucky ones . . . now things for young people are very tough indeed, and if money is your God, you have to leave the country, or alternatively come up with a damn good idea.

I haven't the mentality for saying, "I'll work hard, and that's it for life." Although I like security and three meals a day, I also know that the monotony of serving in a bar or in a shop like this would just drive me potty. I would like to cut loose for a year or two to find out where I am going, and if I want to pull in with my dad or not.

I'm conscious of being Irish and I use Irish words in my vocabulary that come through often. "I'm going to beat the tasty out of that guy". Apart from things like accent and words, I feel that most Irish people can winkle into most people's minds and soften them up with a couple of drinks. This doesn't mean that I am not critical of many things around here, like the dole, which I abhor. I mean, a lot of my friends take it, good looking guys of twenty-three and four, who have everything going for them, and they lost their jobs and went on the dole and wouldn't work any more. How did the other half from the famine survive? If it got to the point that I had to live on the dole, I would start frantically looking around for jobs in other countries.

Even in my lifetime there have been a lot of changes that I have seen happening. There is less of the old gentility and of taking it easy. People go into business and go right ahead, and don't care about you. No house is without a television set, and they all have things like spin dryers. Put it this way: in my father's time you drank soup at every meal and the chair was made of leather, now you dispense with soup and the chair is made from synthetic.

Even something like religion is changing, although I caught the tail end of it. When I was very young I was still prepared to talk to a priest or a nun. They weren't regarded as people at all. I can remember the time when the priest would go up to the dancing, and wait around all night, and if he caught a couple necking, there would be hell to pay. Sex and sin. The priest never thought about sex, and it just didn't enter his head. They were pious saints . . . what a load!

I wasn't brought up thinking about Protestants as having black tongues. Although some of my friends would still hesitate to go out with a Protestant girl, that sort of thing, who you are, what you believe, makes no difference to me. I find it quite unbelievable to hear the nuns who are well-educated talking about someone and saying "Oh, she's a Protestant". I suppose that sort of thing is bred into your genes and goes from one generation to the next. The famine tested our religion to the utmost, and now you get these old-fashioned priests and missionaries going to somewhere like Africa and driving their religion into other people. That's what happened to the Irish, and it doesn't work.

I'll be honest with you, that at the moment we are going through war in the house about me not going to Mass. For young people religion is always going to be the pawing ground and they are going to be fighting about it. It's not always the case. Take something like divorce; if you are divorced in another country and come back to Ireland you are still counted as being married. But I still feel that if I'm going to shack up with a woman and sleep with her, I'd prefer to be married to her and have the security of thinking that she is also thinking of me.

There's a new style all over the world to be married for a couple of years, and live it up, and then they are off again and of course if they have any children they get hurt. And you can't live with just one parent, that doesn't work either. I mean, if I get married and come home and put the money in the till, I'll keep a tenner myself that she doesn't know about, but we'll both work at it. I would happily go to church myself, but this formal thing of going up to church every Sunday morning with your parents, I think it's a load.

All right, there's a God up there, and I'd like to say "Our Father" if I was going to die. I suppose religion is a good invention if it stabilizes the people. If that sounds like what Karl Marx said, there's also no doubt that religion in Ireland is also blamed for a lot of things for which it isn't responsible. Like Northern Ireland, where it's not the religion that keeps them apart, but different sets of people who can't get on with each other.

I think Ireland is a tangling country, and every man has two or three different jobs. At the moment I am happy here working with my father, but the idea of spending the rest of my life in the shop would grind me down. I like working by myself. My friends think I am nuts when I say I would like to see the upper Himalayas, and I also want to see Afghanistan and all the border countries of Russia like the Ukraine. The world is a place that is down to the size of your fist, now. What I'm interested in is world movements. When I saw Russia trampling into Afghanistan, I didn't like it in the least, for tolerance is something the Irish have, and that's why you will find them in every corner of the world. A lot of people say the Irish are a fierce aggressive race, but we're not.

Most of the older people around here thought of just England and America, but now education has come, and also television, and people like me look at Australia or Arabia and they say "I'll take a chance on one of them". I'm young, you see, and unmarried, and have already seen a bit of the world. I know that I can walk out of the door now this very minute with what money I have in my pocket.

All right, I'll take some heavy clothing, and I'll get a coat because it rains, and if I need to I'll flog my watch and boots and buy a pair of cheap runners. I can walk out of the door like a hippy and take the ferry to Le Havre and start looking for a job. My friends don't know this, because they haven't done the travel.'

Pat Hickey, Trainee Carpenter. Aged 19.

After leaving his vocational school Pat got a job with a local builder as a trainee carpenter. He has a box of tools, a small motorbike and takes the work as it comes. Fitting a new floor, sanding or working on one of the many bungalows that are being put up all the time. He doesn't ask much from life apart from earning a little money at his trade and meeting his many friends. He has no wish to leave Ireland. The home hearth and a few miles around his house are the perimeter of his world.

★

'I did woodwork at school, and when I was about fourteen I knew I wanted to be a carpenter, for I always enjoyed working with my hands. After leaving school the first thing is to get taken on by someone, which I've done. You spend four years with them doing your training, and then there is the ANCO. You go on an ANCO course for the first twelve months, and after that you are meant to go once a year. When I leave here I would like to start on my own in a small way. I wouldn't be a furniture maker, but I would like to concentrate on things like roofs and doors.

I have two brothers and two sisters, and we were brought up on the farm. Farming is a good life, for you are your own boss and everything, but the only thing is that it's a seven day week. There are four of us staying at home, and if there are things to do, I always help. We have about fifty acres, but the land isn't good and my family just carries on the best way they can.

I used to go out with my father every day for the water, and you might have to bring maybe twenty buckets to wash things like churns, and you had all this carrying. Now we have electricity and washing machines. We put in a stove about twelve years ago where they used to have an open fire, and each year we cut our own turf. I did it this past year, and at the end of April and the beginning of May, and it's hard work cutting turf, for you could be down ten feet and throwing it over your head. We could be drawing it away to dry, carrying it a couple of yards at times and putting it on a rock to dry. You have to cock it then, and stand it up to dry, and then you bag it and bring it home.

I am living here, and none of us ever thought of going. The brother went to America and came back. England is no better than this country now, and most of my friends seem to have jobs. Mostly the people around here try everything for a bit. They might work on the farm and do a bit of fishing, and that's the good life, although I wouldn't care for the water myself. Sometimes you go to the city for the ANCO course and I might have a bit of crack there, but mostly I can't see any pleasure in city life.

In the old days they went around to the various houses, but now the pub and the dance go hand in hand. I go to Cappaghglass on Sunday night when there is a dance, and I would think that I spend about thirty per cent of my income on drinking. You meet the girls in the pubs, and all that.

I wouldn't live in the city for the world, and I suppose that's the way we were brought up. I would like to own a small farm, the same as my father, but I wouldn't worry about it. If I have a job like carpentry, I have always enough to do and that keeps me busy. Now a lot of outsiders are coming in, and I am delighted to see them, for they would bring money and they buy sites and give us jobs. I don't see any fear of the landscape being spoilt.'

BLOW-INS

MARY DALY	Farmer's Wife, *Aged Mid-fifties*
JOHN SIMPSON	Retired Businessman, *Aged 72*
PATRICIA LEE	Settler, *Aged 32*
GUNTHER ROTHENBURGER	Businessman, *Aged 48*
MAURA O'TOOLE	Guesthouse Owner, *Aged 34*
KEVIN O'HALLORAN	Smallholder, *Aged 36*
JOHN SCULLY	Sheep Farmer, *Aged 28*

Mary Daly, Farmer's Wife. Aged Mid-fifties.

'I find the English the easiest and most pleasant race to get along with, and there's no comparison to any other country. Now that we have the continentals coming down here, people who in one sense mightn't like the English, say "We didn't realize when we were well off." In the first place they are more mannerly and easier to deal with, and although we were dominated by them, I still think that this was the luckiest thing in the world. I mean, if it had been a continental country, we might have been fried in some concentration camp long ago . . . you can be sure of that.

But what I could never understand is how an English person could retire at sixty-five and come down here into a strange place, build a house and settle down. There was only one set of people here, and they hadn't a friend in the world, although they tried their best to make friends. They would be very nice for the first few days, and then start giving out, and it would be all over in no time. They never integrated at all. I felt awfully sorry for them. God almighty, whatever about living in the town, but living out in the country!

They came here in the summer time before the gales came from the south-east, and they would build a house with a view, and if they became sick there was no one visiting them, and five years before they had the telephone. They hadn't the same background or anything, and most of them have gone, and I could have predicted that. And it's the same with the city person, whether they come from London or Dublin, they will still be city people except for a very odd one.'

'It's natural, I suppose. I mean, we have been here almost twenty years, and now that we are older we want to go home.' Many of their English friends have already left, and their place has been taken by Germans, Dutch and the occasional Dublin businessman.

John and Margaret live in a farmhouse converted by an architect which could be in the Home Counties. It is furnished with good oak furniture, chintz-covered sofas, prints and some eighteenth century pictures. On a hunting table in the drawing room copies of Country Life lie in neat rows like bridge tricks. Outside on the slate terrace elaborate wicker chairs overlook the garden.

Much of their lives has been spent in the tropics. 'We open the bar at six o'clock.' It is Margaret who really wants to go – she dreams of a sanctuary within reasonable train distance of London. She wants to be near old friends and go to theatres. The problem is the recession. A few years ago the house would have sold easily enough, but it has been on the market for eighteen months without a worthwile offer.

★

'It was very simple really, because I was retiring, and we had to decide where we were going to live. First we thought of the south of France, and this proved too expensive, and then we thought of Ireland. We came during the summer, and it never rained at all. That's a fact. We stayed in a guest house, during one of those warm summers that make you feel part of the Mediterranean. I have never seen seas quite so blue, or such brilliant skies. We came back the following year and bought this house.

Everything about Ireland and Cappaghglass in particular delighted us. The town had those Victorian village shops that reminded me of my youth, with things like leather laces and bulls eyes all jumbled up in the windows. At that time the selection of things just didn't exist, and if some oranges came in, it was a terrific treat, and the women would rush around saying that oranges were in today. I also enjoyed walking around the countryside. If English villages are perhaps prettier, they are also a lot more urbanized, and the greatest thing in Ireland is this sense of space. We can sit here on the terrace without another house in sight, and in England that would cost a lot of money. There's a particular beauty about this place.

When we arrived here first, nothing was spoilt, and it was just a rural community. I remember talking to Margaret and saying I heard a tractor go by in the night, and wondering if someone had been taken ill. There were carts and horses then, and our neighbours were all countrymen and small farmers. At first we tried to make friends with them and hoped they would drop in. We don't do that now.

Just as you are asking us questions now, we had hoped to ask them questions and learn about their lives. The problem of course was that we were different, and in fact they reminded me in some ways of the people I had met in India. There's no word in the Irish language for "no", and people will always tell you what you want to know. That's a fact. You take a man who is going to do some small job on the house and ask him, will he be there next week, and he will say, "Yes, definitely." But he knows he won't, and you know that he won't, and he doesn't want to say it. I wonder is it the result of the country being occupied so long?

We wanted very much to know our neighbours, and probably we tried too hard. They are very kind to us, and always made us feel welcome, but if we got them into the house and gave them a drink, you couldn't get rid of them. Often they stayed all evening until one in the morning. In England it works the other way; if you are asked for half-past six, it would be regarded as a pre-dinner drink, and you would leave at half-past seven on the dot. It started that we couldn't get them in, and when we did, we couldn't get them out . . . and then we didn't care, and the whole desire of doing that faded. It was easier to get to know our own folk if you like.

I blame myself for ever thinking that it was an extension of England – John Bull's other island. It took me about a year to realize that it wasn't. Later I found that it was completely foreign, and I still think it is. The language is the same, and this hides up all the other things that are different.

We were bound to get somewhere into Irish life after twenty years. What made me feel that we had arrived was when I started to sum up people by thinking, "He's a Proddy" or "He's a Catholic." I didn't jump to this change in me for ages. Suddenly I realized one day that's what I am doing. I think the Protestant farmers are more conservative than the Catholic farmers, and more inclined to sit on the fence. As a community I find the Protestants much more introverted and more watchful, and the Catholics seem more open and gregarious.

We didn't have too many problems from the repercussions of the political situation in the North. The burning of the British Embassy and Mountbatten's murder were appalling, but we only felt them as distant shock waves. We lived through the Arms Trial, H-Block and the rest, and the only things that ever happened was that once a person spat at me, and the car was smothered in manure. All right, there was the Brits Out signs scrawled on every public wall, but in spite of them, we were always regarded as welcome. I remember coming back from a holiday after Bloody Sunday and wondering what sort of reception we would get, but it was like a royal procession, and everyone came out and shook our hands and said, "How are you?"

No, it wasn't the politics that changed our minds about staying. It was a combination of other things. We are both getting old and most of our friends have gone. There is also the sad fact that the area around Cappaghglass is almost doubled in size, and when the tourists come in July and August you can't even park your car, it's as bad as that. And everywhere you see the new bungalows going up. It's scandalous the way anyone can get plans for fifteen pounds and destroy the country-side. I think a lot are built by farmers for themselves, and they sell off their old houses to the Germans and French who are looking for something picturesque. The EEC, of course, has done a lot of harm to Ireland. I don't think it was a good thing because it brought in so much money at the wrong time. And the small chaps didn't get a chance. One person I was talking to said this country has exchanged one set of colonels for another, and he meant the nouveau riche.

I have no regrets about coming to Ireland. It's so beautiful, for one thing. Margaret says the Highlands of Scotland are masculine, while Ireland is feminine – soft and green and sad. I have enjoyed the free and easy way things are in this country. I mean, you keep a car on the road here under the most appalling conditions and no one worries. I know the Sergeant in Cappaghglass has no handbrake on the car, and all the other cars are the same. If they ever had MOT tests over here, seventy-five per cent of the cars would be off the road including mine.

Even though we've got a good deal out of the last twenty years, if we are lucky enough to sell the house, we won't regret leaving, I'm sure of that. Of course there will be many things that I will miss, but I also know that I can put lots of things in their place. Margaret complains about the lack of stimulation, and going to cinemas and art galleries. Her eyes lust after beautiful things. We'd also like to be near our son. We are lucky to see the grandchildren once a year during the summer, and we are very keen to see more of them. We'd like to be near London – not in it, but on a good train route. A complete contrast to this place. I want to be able to take a train when I like, and be able to say to Margaret, who is very self-sufficient and doesn't miss me at all, "Look darling, I want to go to London next Monday and stay until Friday," and she'll say, "Of course, but the week after, it's my turn."'

Patricia Lee, Settler. Aged 32.

A tall blousy intelligent English woman, she gives the impression that she is losing the impetuous quality of dissent that made her break away from her family. She has a heavily-bearded boyfriend named Adrian and two small fair children. They arrived here ten years ago from the English midlands when Irish life appeared to them to retain the zest and mystery of a South Pacific island. Instead of palm trees there was heather and hawthorn and instead of sun the grey months of winter drizzle.

They acquired a remote cottage in the mountains behind the town where they grew their own vegetables and obtained the dole. There were plenty of others like them planted in the furthest and most desolate valleys in the mountains seeking the alternative lifestyle. For Patricia and Adrian smallholding in Ireland lasted four full years before they returned to England.

When I met them they were paying their first visit back to the area. In England he's managed to qualify as a social worker, while she is absorbed with motherhood and involved in left-wing politics.

★

'Before we decided to come to Ireland everyone said, "You'll get shot . . . You'll starve!" and I heard my father say in the background, "What are they going to do and how are they going to earn their bread?" and all the time like a chorus, "They will be shot by the IRA." That was the image of Ireland in my parents' home. But when we got here we heard far less about the troubles in the North than we did in England.

Coming here was absolutely lunatic and we knew nothing. But I had some links. I had an Irish grandmother, and I suppose that's where the Catholicism comes in. Being a Catholic in England you are a bit of an outsider and meet lots of Irish people. Then I went to an Irish nun's School. When we arrived Adrian said, "Be careful," for it's a very old country and there is something strange about Ireland. You walk along those lanes for a couple of hours and there are the hills and the sky and a different sort of consciousness. I think the thing is this very long memory. It's the island behind the island, if you know what I mean, and while people here contemplate their history, the rest of the world is getting on with things like electronics.

As I mentioned to you, Peter, we had nowhere to live, and we put everything into a thirty hundredweight van and arrived. At that time the settler community came out here with two things in mind. One was to see and experience traditional life, and the other was the attraction of arriving in what seemed a virgin country where they could create their own Utopia. Behind them were their homes – our homes too – in industrial suburbanized England. I still think we came out a bit like the first white man stepping into a place like America. Although we spoke the same language we didn't know anyone or anything about tradition and custom. It was a foreign place.

What amazed me was the amount of other outsiders. There were lots of younger or middle-aged Irish people who had lived in England most or all of their lives, and were coming back to buy up farms. Like John and Brigid who were our neighbours, if you can call it neighbours five miles over the mountain. John was born here and had gone over to England when he was nineteen or so, and got married to Brigid whose parents were Irish but had lived all her life in England. They had three children and didn't want to bring them up in a place where there was the threat of racial violence. They came from Derby.

Then there were all the others escaping from the rat race or from the nuclear holocaust. The Germans felt the end of the world a bit more acutely. Another lot of neighbours were a couple from Berlin and perhaps they felt it more than most. They really believed that the Russians were going to take over Berlin at any moment, and that's why they came over here. Of course in the 'seventies there was this tremendous sense of doom, and some Dutch scientists actually worked out that if there was a nuclear war in Europe this part of Ireland would survive. That sent property prices up.

We had very little money and the place we found had no running water or flush lavatory. We stayed four years. I'll tell you it was hard work, and it's very time-consuming when you are forced back on your own resources. You get your own water, make your own bread, dig your own vegetables and make a little money from handicrafts. We made jewellery both of us. Neither of us is artistic, but it's amazing what you can do when you are driven to it. We worked twelve to fourteen hours a day. We had sold our van and we had to hitch everywhere and we were flat broke from day to day. If we wanted to go to Cappaghglass to buy food or even get a library book we would have to put aside the whole day. At times we were living on £11 a week, and when we got the Irish dole our income came to around £27.

There were lots of things that we liked. People around here will talk to you, not like England. If you go into an English rural pub there will be this dead silence. All the domino games will stop and they will look at you and hope you won't stay and think the sooner you are gone the better.

In England class dominates everything, and I think class is even more important than race. Here it is quite different. In England the upper class took the Arts over and there is this tremendous snobbery. If you write or paint it is assumed that you belong to a certain class, and you don't have this in Ireland. I've sat with a friend who makes pottery and the farmers talk about her work in an unpretentious way. I love that. In Ireland there used to be this marvellous sense of freedom and space, while at home your mind's cluttered and overworked. The TV's going and everyone is talking and you get fed with wads of information ranging from the most trivial like Princess Di's hairstyle to what is happening in South America.

If I ask someone here what they think of all these English and other foreigners coming in, I honestly think they are as puzzled as the settlers are themselves. I think they mean it, when they say it's bringing in money and opening up the country. They don't see the problems that have developed. When we first arrived people were kind of interested in where you came from and somehow it relieved the boredom of their lives. You were something different. That of course is gone, and their main purpose now is to squeeze as much money as they can out of tourists. Once you get tourism into a place the tourists are just money-making objects and a nuisance in any other context. But when we first arrived things were completely different and you could make friends.

The settlers had all the advantages because they were able to draw on the best of society – the freedom, the peace and the beauty – while at the same time they didn't have this rigid social code forced on them. They hadn't the same pressures to conform. It's no wonder that we liked it here so much because we had the goodies without paying the dues. If you are an outsider you are not being hammered into the same mould as the local people, and you have the best of both worlds.

We had a friend called Ann who was Irish and a widow, and she was watched by everyone. But it didn't matter what I did. I was a foreigner and a blow-in as well. I could sleep with every man in Cappaghglass and no one would give a damm. But let a local girl like Ann step out of line and she would be talked about and ostracized.

I found that in some ways Catholicism meant a more caring attitude towards society than there was in England. Before we came over here the two great concerns in England were abortion and homosexuality, and law reform in these areas. Everyone jumped on the bandwagon without thinking about it, "Oh yes, we must have abortion . . . Yes, we have homosexuality . . ." But there was never any serious discussion about these profoundly moral issues. While in Ireland we found that people wanted to discuss these things seriously.

One reason why settlers never break in here is because they are not Catholics, and so much of the social life revolves around the church and its ceremonies. Most settlers tend to be anti-religious and the Irish cut them off. I used to hide my Catholic origins, or at least not broadcast them – life was complicated enough. They say the Church opens her legs to anyone who comes along, which is crude. But there's some truth in it. You are never a non-Catholic, but a lapsed Catholic, which is awful, and you can never escape it. I have a love-hate relationship with it. After all those years I still have the sense on Sunday morning of wishing that I was a Catholic again and going to Mass and belonging to the place. The one thing I felt coming here was that Mother Church was going to get me back again. My mother used to say on the 'phone, maybe you'll get your faith back again and I really had the feeling that the Church would suck me in again.

I can only give a very personal feeling about being a woman and a Catholic and that is I don't think I could ever have an abortion. But, my God, I would never condemn someone else for doing it. I have seen people in terrible situations with terrible choices. What I hate in England is how abortion is practically used as a contraceptive measure. But I also get very angry the way Irish women have to go to England, not only to have their abortions, but very often to have their babies. What sort of society is it which drives its women away?

Coming from England we thought first of all that a mixed marriage had to do with race, and not with religion. So much on that side seems crazy. I have a Belfast friend, and she told me that once she was walking past a Protestant church and there were children running across the graves. When she tried to stop them they turned on her and said, "What does it matter, they are only Protestant graves?" What fascinates me about the Irish is that they are generally a gentle courteous people and this is hard to square with what is going on. I mean, only the other night I was talking to a man who said that most of the violence in the North came from the Protestants "with their anger, their folly and their shooting" – that's how he put it. Although I thought this was a marvellous way of summing it all up, I also thought that he could only see one side. It was always the Orange people, never the IRA or Republicans. The funny thing was that Protestants around here used to assume that because I was English I was a Protestant, and that used to kind of draw me in a bit.

It's so hard to get the feel of local custom. Of course it's harder still for Europeans. There was this German couple, the Berliners I told you about – God, when I think of the way we used to walk ten miles to see them. They had bought their house here and came over every summer to work on it, and one of the things they spoke about was how they hadn't got to know any local people. They still didn't understand that it takes a very long time.

Anyway one day when I was there a farmer's wife called in with some milk, and Klaus tried to get her to stay, but she wouldn't, and stood in the doorway a bit awkward and everything, and Klaus pulled some money out of his pocket and said, "Let me pay you for the milk," and she was immediately embarrassed to be paid in that way in front of strangers. To her it was something crass. As you know, Peter, if you are going to pay for milk here, you go up after two or three weeks and you talk about everything else and slip the money under the teacloth. But Klaus was being very Germanic, and for him this was the right way to behave, while to her it was brutal. So she said, "No I couldn't take the money," meaning I can't take the money standing in your doorway, and finally she left. And Klaus turned to me and said, "You see how wonderful these people are, they won't let us pay for the milk." And I thought, O God, in a month's time she will be going around the village saying those awful German people, they don't pay for their milk. And this typified the whole culture clash. Not so much a clash, since they missed each other by light years.

Coming back after such a gap what we notice are the changes in other people and also in ourselves. Everyone talks about the creation of the new bourgeoisie in Ireland, and my God, you can see it. Estate agents, solicitors, the new rich businessmen – they all want the good life. And the local people have changed and their attitudes towards us are much more ambivalent. They talk about the hippies and the people who are playing poor.

What has happened basically is that the city person has come down and bought the local culture and Micky Moused the whole area. It used to be a nice place in the early 'seventies. You remember the horses and carts, the old characters at every turn of the street, and how even the local regattas were local boats before the fibre glass yachts came in and took over.

The other day I was giving a lift to a farmer whom we used to live beside. Normally he was a quiet sort of man and perhaps this time he had a bit too much to drink. He kept muttering in the back, "Oh you are all down here looking for big mansions" and "You'll never get my green fields, and you'll never have them." I had been trying to ingratiate myself by saying how great it was to be back, but it kept rolling off him, and I couldn't take any more. So I stopped the car and said "Michael, what the hell would I do with your land even if I got it. You sound to me as if you're jealous of all those new houses going up." I haven't heard from him since.

I never had that feeling of alienation when we were down here before. Only once – and that was crude nationalism. We were in a pub and there was this argument about the Jews and the Palestinians, and one of the men said Hitler was right and they should all be killed. When I tried to argue with him he turned on me and said, "You've done enough damage to this country, and you've no right to say anything." The whole bar went absolutely silent and he finished his drink and walked out. It was the only thing of this line that had ever happened to me, and one of the women said, "I'm awfully sorry – don't listen to him . . . it doesn't mean anything." And everybody was very nice to me for the rest of the evening.

Nowadays you don't even have to be English to get the flak. Yesterday we were all in the chip shop with the kids and this Dublin friend. And the man behind the counter said in a resentful voice, "Where are ye from?" And my friend said that the ladies came from different places and mostly England and she came from Dublin. And he said, "That's the same as being English, isn't it . . . there's no difference."

That sort of thing tires you after a bit. I suppose I've changed too. Someone once said to me about an African that once he puts his foot down on the tarmac he can't go back to the village. I feel a bit like that. To be honest I can't sit in a country kitchen any more and talk and listen to them. It's boring to me.'

Gunther Rothenburger, Businessman. Aged 48.

The Rothenburgers came here ten years ago. They bought the old rectory which stands on three acres outside Cappaghglass. The reedy fields have been drained, the rough avenue is tarmacadamed and the old stables which housed the Rector's Morris Minor have been refurbished to contain the Mercedes and the BMW. The house has been re-roofed, the ceilings lowered and the old windows gouged out and replaced by double-glazed plate glass. The symmetrical arrangement of flower beds and the stone troughs filled with off-colour geraniums herald an interior very different from the old Church of Ireland shabbiness. Black leather-covered arm chairs have been placed in position by a master plan, the tiled terrazzo floor, sprinkled with Persian carpets, smells highly of polish and the glass topped tables are covered with huge ashtrays and toys for nervous executives made out of chrome and silver wire. Some pieces of antique furniture are a bit heavy for non-Continental tastes, and the old picture in its gilt frame looks as if it came out of a medieval church.

Gunther started a small industry in Ireland, an experience he would never repeat. In a decade Gunther and Lise's enthusiasm has dimmed. They have enough money to maintain a spectacularly pleasant life style, but they don't have much to do. One suspects that Lise is the more edgy about their enforced idleness and their isolation. Their neighbours are friendly, but conversation has seldom developed beyond pleasantries about the weather. Their nearest German friends, whom they see often, live twenty-five miles away. They insist they still enjoy life here. The sea is around them and Ireland is a place where you can be happy escaping the forces of bureaucracy.

*

'In my opinion the Irish are as different from the English as the Germans are from the French. They have their own special way of doing things. The mistake which so many foreigners make is to try and change them, and that's always fatal. We start talking about the stupid Irish, and it's wrong, because, as I say, they have their own way of life.

We came here to be in a country where we would feel more free. In Germany officialdom reigns supreme, and there is nothing you can do apart from breathing without the state interfering. For instance, if you want to make a little change inside your house, it means putting in a special drawing.

You will laugh at me, but I arrived here by accident. A flight from New York to Dusseldorf was delayed at Shannon, and once I saw the country I knew it was what I had been looking for all these years. It looked so green and peaceful. I mean, there were no industries, and the people seemed to be living the life we used to lead in Europe but now we have forgotten. All those small farms and empty mountains. Most Irish people I have talked to don't realize that the majority of Europeans live in flats, and your next door neighbour won't even know you. Here it is quite the other way.

What we didn't like or understand was all that junk thrown around like the Middle East. When a washing machine doesn't work, they throw the old one out and leave it there. Or if there is a worn tyre on a car they just throw it in the nearest ditch. And of course they don't have gardens. Their music seems almost oriental too, and their way of going about any business.

Take something simple like buying a house, or perhaps the word "simple" is not the one I should be using. If someone has a property for sale they say, "What would you like to offer?" I think that's wrong, and the man who holds the property should know how much he wants for it. But he starts going the other way around. I offer, say, fifty thousand, and then he goes to someone else with my offer, and they go around and around and never come to an end. That's why I think it's oriental.

I went to an estate agent because I knew he had a particular house. I said, "What's the price?" and he said, "The price is so much." I said, "If I say yes, do I have it?" and he said "Yes." I said "OK" and put down my money, and then he telephoned the owners and they wouldn't sell it any more. Then I tried to buy it from the people themselves, but I couldn't. I agreed on the price, but it fell through three or four times. That would never happen in Germany.

I suppose it is because the Irish have a more tolerant and easy attitude to life than we have on the Continent. In Germany if you make an appointment, you have to be on time, but here they don't seem to mind. In my opinion the Irish attitude is not good for business.

I had a small business exporting Irish goods to the Continent, and in the end it defeated me. For one thing costs for basic things like the telephone and electricity are twice as much here as in Germany. If I send a letter to another business in Ireland, I know I won't get an answer, and I won't get the right man on the telephone, because he is running away from me. If he's done something wrong he isn't there. So many times you pick up a 'phone and try to get through to, shall we say, County Mayo. Nothing! Perhaps one should open the window and shout, and then perhaps they will hear you. In 1984 you can't get through on the 'phone system. I say this to you, Peter, because I know that you are Irish. You can't communicate, for God's sake, and this is 1984! Then there was the Telex. I waited for two years for the Telex and the company I was dealing with in Germany did not take me seriously. I like it here, but I also know that if I had to start another business in Ireland I would have a heart attack.

If I had to work hard for a living again, it is better to go back to Germany where I can make the money. In Germany people specialize in one thing, but here everyone has four or five different jobs. A man who sells me a newspaper might also have a small farm. And they are all subsidized by the EEC. In Germany the farmer makes a profit, and has to build the shed out of the profit, but here everybody is borrowing and nobody is paying. I still don't understand how it works. How can the supermarket be more expensive than the small store? How can this happen when they buy in bulk? In Germany the big supermarkets always drop their prices.

I have learnt a lot about simple life here, and I think the Irish have a natural source of wisdom that we have lost in Germany. They live much closer to nature. I find them very friendly, but it's not easy to get to know them and they won't let you into their circle. I enjoy our garden, but when I think of all the time and money that is being thrown into it, I think it is madness. Every winter we are talking of doing something or going on a holiday, but always we do nothing.

If I seem to complain too much, we are also contented and are learning a little. I think, too, that people are learning from us as we are learning from them. We have brought in carpets on the floor, and now our neighbours have carpets as well. They start cleaning their yard and clearing their rubbish, and I think how nice it looks. They have even put in some flowers.'

Maura O'Toole, Guesthouse Owner. Aged 34.

Maura works in her daffodil-filled garden in early March. Around the house the fields are chocolate furrows of earth, while at the farm up the lane a woman is white-washing a wall. A pheasant clucks in the fuchsia hedge, which is still a brittle brown, although the bank below is already studded with primroses.

Maura and her husband, Stephen, an accountant, came down here seven years ago with their two children; since then they have had a third. The idea was that Maura should run the house as a B and B, while Stephen did accounts for the local shopkeepers and farmers. They were young and enthusiastic and Cappaghglass was still enjoying the tourist boom. But things weren't so easy. Stephen had a struggle to get work, and in order to have the house approved by Bord Failte, the Irish Tourist Board, they had to spend a lot of money. It took time to get used to country living, and Maura still has mixed feelings about the visitors she entertains during the summer. But she has no regrets and says Stephen has none either.

*

'The other morning I had to drive to Cappaghglass, and it was a morning just like this. I am not really a religious person, but I just said, "Thank God I'm alive, and although we haven't much money, I am in reasonably good health." It was just beautiful. I felt that if I still lived in the city I would have hopped out of my suburban house into a car, and gone to the supermarket in a state of tension. Here wherever you go you arrive relaxed.

When we came to Cappaghglass in 1977 it was like coming to another world. I had been brought up in a middle-class city way, and was reared to believe that things like nursing, guards, doctors and all the other professions were pensionable and desirable and what one should aim at. It was a big decision for both Stephen and me to abandon that mentality. But I couldn't go back. Now I couldn't go back to the city, and even when I go on a visit, after a day I'm longing to return home. On Wednesday, for instance, I am driving to town, and I'm visiting a beautician, and doing some shopping and so forth, and I'm going to enjoy my day, but I will be just dying to come back here. I hate the city. I hate traffic. I hate driving in traffic. I find that people living in the city are much more pressurized. They live at a much harder pace. Stephen and I wanted to escape the malaise and the meaningless standards imposed on city people. We wanted to get out of the rat race, and this place offered itself.

It seemed to us that living in a place like this offered a great deal more in the way of quality of life than Dublin did. We both felt suddenly that you have one short life and have to make the most of it. Dublin was becoming more and more commercialized with everyone looking over the next person's shoulder to see if they had a bigger television set and that kind of thing, and that was never our style. And one gathers that with all the crime and drug-related problems, Dublin has got to be a pretty terrible place since we left.

It didn't happen quite overnight. I was a child of suburbia, and I never visualized myself living here, nor did Stephen. We had these obstacles to commitment. Coming down for holidays was one thing, but from the start I was terrified of the prospect of the long winters. The winters are bleak, all right, and you can't go out so much becaue of the rain. It's all around you, on the mountains and everywhere. But I've accepted it, and now I feel that nothing is so depressing as orange sodium lights in puddles – that really depresses me.

I enjoy the seasons – I've no desire to walk around Dublin in spring under those cherry blossoms. Here there's gorse and the birds and everything. I love being near the water. The beach in winter is just as dramatic as it is in summer. And then there is the general feeling that country people aren't in such a hurry and have time to talk to you and things have modernized a bit so that most country houses are just as comfortable as those in any town. I've never felt lonely here, and neither has Stephen.

We first thought we'd take a house in Cappaghglass itself – there was one for sale down near the harbour which would have been very suitable for B and B. Thank God nothing came of that, and we finally decided to come out here. The town itself was a nice little fishing port when we first came here, but now it's getting messed up. All those bungalows along the coast are becoming just a dreary suburb. Stephen says the coast road is like the Clonkeen road in Dublin. And of course if we'd settled in Cappaghglass, we'd have missed all the country bit.

I dread driving to the city, even to see my mother. Even my children complain of feeling cramped when they stay a few days with her.

When I see the kids in flats in Dublin I get upset for them. Brought up in a concrete jungle and all they have to play with are those swings with concrete underneath. Here there's always something to do. They can go to a football match, or fish in the river, or sometimes a friend will take them out in his boat. Even if they are idle, there's not so much mischief to get into – they are coming to the age when if they lived in the city there would be temptations like drugs and drink.

I remember how when we were here as visitors Mrs Kavanagh made us a beautiful crab salad, and we were typically pompous tourists – how would she know how to make a crab salad, an old woman like her? But after we came here, and as the years passed, I began to have respect for the country people and their ways, although – yes you won't believe me – at first I found it difficult to understand what they were saying. Even the simplest greeting could have been Chinese or Russian, and we were on two different wavelengths. The other thing that I found embarrassing, when I could interpret the words, was the bad language country people used. You meet a nice old man, and he will suddenly bring in a couple of blistering words into his conversation. It's just part of the way they talk. Now I have to control myself that I am not as bad as them.

Again, I come from a very conservative society, and everybody was Mr this and Miss that, and it was all very formal. Here everyone is on first names, and if you aren't on first names, it means that you aren't friends. Then, it takes time to know people, and you must remember that the tourists are only here for three months in the year, and for the rest of the year you are living with your neighbours. And to many of them a city person is worse than a foreigner.

The children will hop into anyone's house and say hello, but I still find it difficult. I love people coming to see me, but being a city person, I find it difficult to walk into someone's house because I think it's an intrusion on their privacy. Here they just drop in, and when it first happened to me, I'd say, "Do you want something?" and they would say, "Oh no, I just came to say Hello." Then there was the business of country funerals. When I was a child in the city you only went to funerals of people who mattered, like close relatives, but around here, if someone dies, everyone is meant to turn up. There is a great deal of jollification, and everyone meets each other to discuss the farming, children and so on.

When we started we had a little money to buy the house, but in order to take in B and B's we had to borrow. And we are still working for the bank. I hadn't realized what this sort of work entailed – making breakfasts and beds seemed too easy. But of course it isn't like that. Tourists can be incredibly demanding, and I don't particularly like them. You get very tired and exhausted and are looking forward to when it ends. 'I wish it was the end of August" you keep saying after a bad day, even though you know you're cutting your throat by saying it.

I think you get two types of tourists: the genuine people, who don't mind living in the wilds, and the others who come here and say, I love Cappaghglass, it's so unspoilt, and at the same time are yelling for ice and lemon in all their drinks and they want hot water and showers and heating and everything you have in the city. And their young are just the same, wanting colour television and discos every night. We had to get colour television just to keep the little darlings quiet.

We have eight bedrooms, although when we started there were only three. Stephen is good with his hands, and apart from dividing up some of the rooms, he did most of the work when it came to building the extension. Then we had to put in heating. I was reared when there was no heating in the house, and you went to bed with a hot jar, but now they are frozen if the heating is not on right into June. We have a solid fuel thing with radiators as well as an open fire in the sitting-room. When you are doing B and B, the season begins about Easter, then you get a bit of slack, and by Whit weekend at the end of May things are in full spate, until the schools open at the beginning of September.

During the season our routine, if you can call it that, is to get up at about half-past seven and begin the work of preparing breakfast. What I dread is some of the English people who ask, "Could we have an early morning cup of tea?" just for the time when you are beginning to get everything ready. The breakfast in any B and B is a carnival of sorts. For lots of tourists it's the main meal of the day. It's a way of saving money so they won't have to eat again until dinner-time.

Even if they are dying in the morning, and have drunk themselves silly the night before, they still want a big breakfast. They will have fruit juice, cereals, a colossal fry, and anything else you can give them. I keep saying to myself, "How can they eat so much?" when some of them would be the colour of putty, and at the same time trying to get their money's worth of breakfast.

After breakfast the work goes on for most of the day. Sheets into the washing machine – without that and the dryer, no guesthouse would function. Nylon sheets, of course, so they don't have to be ironed. Some people don't like nylon sheets, but that's too bad. And they make a fuss about foam pillows. A neighbour helps me to make the beds and clean the rooms. She might find a sock in a funny place, or a pair of panties at the end of a bed, or the odd time something that I won't mention, and she comes down and says, "I don't know what sort of people were staying last night." Sometimes they bring drink up to their rooms, and she will be muttering about that.

I think the Irish way of B and B is going to change. If I go on a continental holiday, I don't expect breakfast. You rent a room and perhaps if they are feeling generous they'll give you half a cup of cold coffee in the morning. I wouldn't be surprised if that didn't start happening here. As it is, the foreigners who come to Ireland just can't believe their good luck.'

Kevin O'Halloran, Smallholder. Aged 36.

He is tall, heavily-bearded and what you can see of his face is bronzed by the sun and wind. He speaks with a strong Dublin accent. All round him is the farm and the four cows, the big black bull, the pig, four calves, ducks, chickens, six cats, two dogs, not to mention his wife, Catherine and their three children. Before they came here from the city ten years ago they hardly knew the difference between a fork and a spade, but in spite of that, their creed was already self-sufficiency. They still feel that they made the right decision throwing up city security for their eight acres, but they admit it has been very hard work.

They have their own milk and butter, their own vegetables grown without chemicals or fertilizer, and all that livestock. Even their neighbours give them grudging admiration, while their friends from the city who come down to stay during the summer (paying for their board and lodging) ask in wonder, 'How do they do it?'

Today Catherine is doing what they call the dairying. A neighbour has brought along a cow in a trailer to be served by their bull. The children stand around and watch; they know that it only works if the bull has his two front legs off the ground.

★

'When we came here we knew nothing about country life except for going on holiday. My parents were city people, and if you showed them a cow and asked them to milk it, they wouldn't have known where to start. I was brought up with the idea of entering some business, and when I left school I got a job in an insurance office. It was the usual nine to five thing. Already one could see that the old security of that sort of life had gone. We knew a number of people with apparently permanent jobs who found themselves out in the cold because of the recession which was just beginning then, or because their company had been taken over by a larger company or any other reason you can think up. But I was still reasonably complacent until my father died suddenly. He wasn't insured properly and he hadn't covered his social welfare contributions and he had lived all his life working for other people. It wasn't even a very long life, he was in his mid-fifties. That woke me up. It was a time when we were beginning to see the deterioration of the city, and what with one thing and another, we opted for a different lifestyle.

We didn't choose Cappaghglass, and we like to think that Cappaghglass chose us. Call it kismet or fate or whatever. One day I happened to see in the *Irish Times* a freak advertisement put in by some local auctioneer. "Be self-sufficient . . . do your own thing", along with details of a small farm someone wished to sell. We were interested, and talked about it, and one day Catherine stood up and went to the telephone, and the next thing I knew what that she had rung the guy up and he would send up details.

That farm was no use; there was no electricity or water, and what they flatteringly described as a picturesque cottage of undressed stone was virtually a ruin. But we had more luck with the next one, and that's what we eventually bought. The eight acres were what we were looking for, and it had the added advantage of a primary school less than a mile away where we could send the kids. Although the money to pay for it seemed small enough, it meant selling our city house, frightening our friends and bank manager, and saying goodbye to that job. Everyone thought we were crazy, and I think deep within ourselves we also had a few doubts.

I am still amazed at our ignorance and blind stupidity in rushing into something we knew nothing about. We took it on faith completely, and didn't even get the fields examined by an inspector to see if they were any good. The sale of our house in Dublin gave us enough money to get some stock and to see us through the first twelve months, because, let's face it, you couldn't come into a place like this and harvest, because there was nothing to harvest. The previous owner had died years before, and the land, which was marginal, needed a hell of a lot of work.

Before coming down here, I went to a good library and read everything in the agricultural section – anything to do with smallholding and crofting. At that time the vogue for the self-sufficiency thing was in full spate, and these books became our bibles. They would tell you, for instance, how many oats you should plant to the acre, and about the use of natural manures, free range hens and everything. I think we bought poultry before the cattle, twenty-one hens. We had this idea that we wanted fertile eggs, and then we would have young chicks which would give us fowl to eat. The food production was a sort of cycle. I had a one-year plan, and a five-year plan, but they didn't work out exactly the way we wanted.

People who work in offices have no idea just how much hard work a small farm like this requires. If they did the same amount of office work they would all be millionaires. You are constantly making decisions. Like getting your cow into calf at the right time, when to get a vet, or when to do a thing yourself. When even a little thing goes wrong, it can be a major blow and set you back for months.

But from the first we realized the advantages of living here. In Dublin I got my pay cheque every month, and never saw the money. I had credit cards and bank cards, and wrote cheques, and every once in a while my bank manager wrote to me informing me that perhaps I had better stop writing cheques for just a while until we caught up. You walked around the shops and saw things, and said, "Oh, I'd like this or that" and you had a decent car that had to be maintained, and your children also had big eyes for all the things in the shops.

Down here it's not so much the money that you make from a smallholding, but it's the money we don't spend. It isn't a consumer society, it simply isn't, and I don't think of it as being a sacrifice. I am aware of the fact that I am probably a trifle impecunious and essentially this means cutting out luxuries. If we find ourselves with a surplus, we can talk about holidays, or something special like a colour TV set, or new tapes, but in practice this hardly ever happens, and we just survive.

I take any jobs that I can get, like doing the post if the postman is sick, mending the roads, and doing bits and pieces. Catherine does some of B and B during the summer, and although the place is far from

being up to tourist board standards, visitors seem to like the picturesque bits. To be technically fair, I am unemployed for much of the year.
That means that I get unemployment benefit, and I must emphasize it
is benefit, not assistance. I wouldn't like to have to live on it pure and
simply. A lot of people call it "farmer's dole", and to be quite honest
with you, I would say that any person who wants to live in a
reasonable fashion could do with it. But I still don't know if it's a good
thing. I would rather see the people in an area like this taking
responsibility for keeping their own roads and hedges.

We feel very strongly that while we may control this land at the
moment, it's an onus to leave it in good condition and to pass it on in
good heart to the next person, whether it's one of our children or
somebody else. We may own it in one sense, but something like land
cannot be owned by people. I sympathize with the American Indian in
terms of settlers on his land. "Yes, if you want to come here, that's
OK." But it never occurred to the Indians that the Europeans envisaged ownership because that was outside their conception.

Our idea is hopefully to run a sound ecological system rather than
just an agricultural one. It's based on the mixed farms of the eighteenth
and nineteenth centuries. For instance, those ducks which are a bloody
nuisance sometimes, causing havoc in the vegetable garden, also keep
the land totally fluke free. That's good for the cattle. If you feed a small
quantity of whole grain to the cows, they only digest a small percentage, and then the hens must come along and scratch through the
cowpats, spreading them out over the surface of the ground like lots of
miniature harrows.

In so far as it is possible, we practise our own self-sufficiency. We
have four cows, and we have enough milk for sixteen people a day,
and also we have lots of meat. In the old days the pig was the
gentleman who paid the rent, and they put him in a barrel and cured
him. Now he goes in the deep freeze. As well as that, he is a fabulous
compost machine. I mean, to make compost outside, you have to have
a bin, put the compost in nice layers, and then put in an activator. With
a pig you simply fire the food in at one end, and the pig fires it out at
the other, ready for the land; it's absolute magic. We haven't reached
the end of the possibilities on our few acres. I noticed the other day that
around every cowpat there is a tuft of grass which the cattle won't eat,
but this could be used for feeding sheep.

I think it's very important to say that "there's nothing special about
us", and I mean that without any exclamation mark. There have been
problems, and, let's face it, in any small community there are one or

two people who don't want you there, whatever happens. If I enjoy farming, the fact of even living here is something I still never take for granted. It's like being stoned all the time.

I'm not fearful for my children's safety in the street, I'm not fearful of my own safety, and I'm not going to get mugged either going to or coming from the pub. The only thing that comes in through our front door is the wind, and not guys with sledge hammers and balaclava helmets. We are not living in a plastic world, and the values are more real. Ever since we have made friends with people down here, we have evolved away from our former friends in the city, and I suppose that's regrettable in some ways. I could never have envisaged that I would spend the night talking to an old farmer like my neighbour, who wanted company, and it would be a privilege.

Catherine said to me the other day, and I thought it was very true, that a great deal of children are being educated for a career of idleness. Even with a very good education, they won't be able to get jobs. I think the beauty of this place is a very important thing, and the children have benefitted enormously from living here.

We survive by a combination of extremely hard work, and an ability to live on very little, and I mean, we do have a choice, and are not prisoners here. I don't see us leaving now, and the only likelihood with our land, is that at the end of it they might dig a little hole and put me into it. There was a man I read about who died, and his body was cremated and in accordance with his last wishes, his ashes were returned home and mixed with the compost in his compost heap. I thought that was a nice idea.'

John Scully, Sheep Farmer. Aged 28.

You are always being told that half the 'hippies' in the west are PhD's. I don't know if John is or not, but his farmhouse outside a village west of Cappaghglass is crammed with books whose high sounding titles suggest that he has advanced fairly far in third level education. He's given up learning for sheep farming and has been living here for five years. From the windows of his house you can see the sea, and in front of it the fields he has reclaimed all velvet green. From the kitchen you can see the mountains where his sheep graze. Sometimes in the evening he finds time to write poetry.

★

'Chaucer talks about silly sheep and so on, but what he really means is simple, because they are dead stupid. But they are very clever in their own way. I'll tell you a story. A year ago I bought ten ewes from somebody near Bellevue, and they were fine young ewes, and I put them in a place that was wired in. But they managed to break out and escape. I spent three days wandering the hills up here and around there looking for them. Then I got a 'phone call from the Post Office, and they had arrived back in the field where they were born. They have this extraordinary sense of where they belong.

There is an old fellow in the village who talks about driving sheep all the way from Curragheen and putting them up on the mountain, and then spending a week on the mountain minding them until he was fairly certain they would stay there. One day he came down for a few days' rest, and when he returned they were gone – all gone back to Curragheen.

I was bone ignorant when I started. I inherited this house and I was fed up with the University. In some ways I was lucky, but I will say there was some canniness as well. Most of the land around here has been let go. I mean, look out of the window and you can see what I am talking about. Today is a beautiful calm day, but on a winter's day there are forty foot waves breaking down on the strand, and the wind comes raging over the place. Cattle could never do well here, horses can live, but they need extra feeding and care, but sheep will do well, and that's why I got them. The beasts are extraordinarily independent and are also hardy, and able to thrive in these sort of conditions. They are also wild animals, not domestic animals the way that cattle are.

I started off with ten ewes which I bought for £16 apiece, and then I bought this prize-winning Suffolk ram and bred him with my sheep and had great success. The idea was to cross-breed lowland sheep with mountain sheep – they get the meat qualities with the father and the hardiness of the mother, and the ability to thrive on bare rock.

It was a gradual thing, and I had a lot to learn. I'll tell you, Peter, I learned a good deal of it in the pub. That's where the people who know gather in the winter, and if I had a sheep behaving in a peculiar manner I would hare down there and seek out somebody. The pubs around here are a bit like an open university, and I would say, now, Peter, that I could walk into anyone from here to the far side of Cappaghglass, and the barman or woman would say, "Hello, Johnny." An outsider who doesn't do farming couldn't talk about the kind of things that people consider important. It's a matter of sitting over three pints in the course of three hours. I tell you it took me three years to kind of like that, and now I enjoy it. You turn over your left shoulder and have a joke with the fellow there, and you turn to your right shoulder and have a joke with him. During the winter I could be down there three nights a week.

Another thing that took me about three years, and that was how to tell one sheep from the next. It's my party trick, now, and I amaze old friends who can't see any difference. I'll do it for you tomorrow – I have some sheep in a pen and I'll be marking them. I know which lamb belongs to which ewe, and which animal I bought in Cappaghglass that had mastitis. There's a slight difference in their movements and their faces and shapes and things, and shepherds all over the world can tell this and their lambs as well.

To look after sheep you want to be young and have the ability to go without sleep for three or four days. You also need a good dog, that's most important. I bought Jack as a tiny pup at the stage when I only had the ten sheep, and by running round a lot I could manage them on my own. I used to carry him around in the pocket of my coat. I did make some mistakes in training him. Some of the most amusing books I've ever read were dog training books which all seemed to be written by retired English colonels. And some of them gave very bad clues. I remember one on how to teach a dog to walk to heel, and it said, always have a handful of pebbles in your hand, and when he starts trotting ahead, throw them at him. So I threw them, and Jack turned round and gave me a look that said, "You bastard, what are you doing that for?" and I never did it again.

The most important time is lambing. Usually I let them lamb on the mountains, because it is quite dangerous to move them when they are heavy with lamb. I more or less camp there for about six weeks from March 14th to the middle of April. I only come down from my tent for meals. I remember very well the first night there was lambing, and I did it sitting up there with a book in the middle of the night, and reading the book by torchlight and saying, "What's happening?" and "Oh, God, what do I do now?"

There is one lamb I can show you, and her mother had a peculiar thing which is called Twin Lamb Disease, and it's a kind of diabetes. Basically the only treatment is to fill them with enormous amounts of glucose every two hours. I would get up to inject her, and finally the disease got worse, if you like, and she was dying, and I could also feel by putting my hand on her belly that she was very close to lambing. As she was obviously dying, I hit her on the head with a hammer and delivered the lamb by Caesarian operation. I just cut her open and pulled the lamb out. But I had to take a very deep breath before I made the incision.

Another tale, if you like. I brought this sheep down from the mountain, and she started lambing about midnight in the house, but obviously she was in difficulties. She was having twins and I thought they were tangled up inside her. I reached inside her and pulled one of them backwards into the world, and it was the biggest lamb I have ever seen in my life. It was huge; no wonder she was in trouble. The second came naturally, which was a little chap, but born alive, and she was still in difficulties. So again I reached inside her, and brought out a little freak, if you like, a kind of dwarf lamb. But I did manage to rear it, believe it or not, with an eyedrop for the first week. When you save one of their lives it gives you a tremendous feeling of achievement. Also it's great when you see new life bounding on the hillside – when they stand up and walk on their first staggering legs with such courage and such determination to survive. It's always a kind of miracle, and a thing that is puzzling – how they know where to find the milk.

I was one of the first around here to start sheep farming more intensively. Last year my lambing rate was a hundred and ten per cent – in other words, one out of ten of them had twins. My trouble is that I can't be cold and calculating about sheep farming. I get too involved. You make pets of them, and last year I had six being reared in the kitchen. I had one lamb that was savaged by a dog, and I nursed her for six weeks. I had to treat her twice a day with antiseptics, and so on, and she had great affection and would always run over to me. Then one day she escaped through some wire, and a couple of dogs chased her and she landed halfway down a cliff. I was so fond of that sheep that I got a rope and crowbar and was just about to grab her horns when she jumped and went over. I was passionately fond of that animal, and I would rather have lost a thousand pounds than that sheep.

I tried to rationalize my feelings, this getting fond of individual animals. They do have a great kind of spirit in an odd way, you know. I don't even know if fondness is the right word, for its not the same fondness you have for a dog, even though you have handled the sheep and petted it. But it's more a matter of pride that you have managed to bring it into being, and kept it alive. I think the attitude towards farming in general is pride; pride that your land is in good heart, that your fields are greener than your neighbours and that your hay and your sheep are the best around.

I felt I couldn't allow myself to get that sentimental. I accept that something like vegetarianism is a person's right of choice, but there would be no sheep in this world if we were all vegetarians. I thought about it a lot. Unless you are going to be hypocritical, you couldn't combine all that feeling with just shoving them into the back of a lorry and letting them go off to the slaughter yard. So what I actually did was to kill a sheep. If you are prepared to raise animals for meat, then you must be prepared to kill one. Around here they use a spike and hammer, and I didn't enjoy it.

The fairs were another thing I had to learn about. The cattle fairs are gone, but they still sell sheep by the old method. It's the sort of day that everyone enjoys, and there are plenty of jokes and japes flying around. For the Fair animal there is the fair price, and you have to be canny or clever to get the few extra quid. I enjoy matching my wits against the next man's. But of course there are certain things you must look out for. Something like a sheep's teeth are very important, for unlike cattle they will eat more or less to ground level. Another simple test is to put your hand on the back, because you can actually feel the fat. And then there's the ribs and the meat on the hindquarters, and the length of the back is also important.

Last September they sold something like two thousand sheep in Curragheen, and I sold mine for £47, £45 and £37, depending on their quality. Mine are better than most. For Scotch mountain sheep the fair price would have been £32 to £37. You want to get there early, and I usually leave about five in the morning in my truck, and expect to arrive about seven. It takes a long time to load and unload them. It's not desolate, but bustling at seven o'clock in the morning, which is unbelievable in Ireland.

The first thing is to pen your sheep in the street, and they actually put up hurdles. There are usually lots of small boys around, and I might give one of them fifty pence, and say "mind the sheep" and then have a look around. You see some wonderful sheep, too, and tour up and down and find out about prices. You say, "These are nice ewes . . . or nice lambs, and what price would you be looking for them?" And if they take you for a fool and give you some ridiculous kind of answer, you say, "My God, are you a mental defective?"

The buyers are usually recognizable because they have dockets and markers, and I know many of them now by sight. They can be bold jackeens, and step right into the middle of a pen, and I've seen them pick an animal up and say, "Ugh, no good" and shout out a number. Then there is the maker, a sort of wild wandering Tom who will try and clap your hands together with the buyers' while you keep them tightly in your pocket. There is an awful lot of walking away from each other, and saying "You can do better than that" and you start haggling from there.

It always takes a while to get your price. Last year I had ten beautiful lambs and they weighed about ten stone, and a buyer offered me £43 which wasn't enough at all. About eight o'clock we all went off for a walk, and then about ten the buyer called around with £45 and still it wasn't enough, for I had hopes of getting fifty. Then the price maker came, and as I said, I was trying for fifty, and he was trying for forty-five, and the maker said, "Look, you'll split the difference" or something like that, and then we clapped hands and sold for forty-seven. Later we all went to a pub and I gave him a few pounds luck money. Buyers must have the most terrible livers in the world.

Of course you can be cheated. It would be cleaner, quicker and fairer to sell them on some automatic scale, but there would be no crack. I think that's also important these days when so many other things have vanished. I still expect to make a good profit on the kind of sheep that I am breeding, and that's not counting the wool. You get the wool as a bonus, and last year I got £3 a fleece.

One of the most hilarious days of my life was when I tried to shear a sheep for the first time. Unfortunately I picked the wrong one. Young sheep are much easier to shear than old sheep, because old sheep know what is going to happen to them, and they don't like it at all. And their wool tends to be tougher and thicker. So I picked this old sheep of mine, and I tied her hind legs with a rope to make it easier, and started shearing according to the book. I had this book with a kind of diagram of how you did it, and you started at the neck and went to the belly and cleared the two sides away – so I had the principles. Anyway the sheep and I, we ended up about half a mile from where I started – she was kicking, and we were rolling over on the ground and everything, and we were both bleeding from many wounds. I still have the scars.'

THE BIG HOUSE

JOHN LACEY	Lord Cappaghglass, *Aged 65*
THE HON MARGARET LACEY	Gentlewoman, *Aged 83*
MAURICE NOLAN	Butler, *Aged 68*
JOE McCARTHY	Retired Farmworker, *Aged 76*
MARGARET HANLY	Dairy Maid, *Aged 84*

The Anglo Irish ascendancy class, which dominated the whole colonial period, answers best to the description 'upper class'. As well as its political and economic supremacy, it possessed a culture, a set of manners, a life-style which constituted the measure of social status.

Contemporary Irish Society,
Michel Peillon.

I came on a great house in the middle of the night,
Its open lighted doorway and its windows all alight,
And all my friends were there and made me welcome too;
But I woke in an old ruin that the winds howled through;
And when I pay attention I must out and walk
Among the dogs and horses that understand my talk.
      O what of that, O what of that,
      What is there left to say?

The Curse of Cromwell,
W. B. Yeats.

John Lacey, Lord Cappaghglass. Aged 65.

In a countryside of small farms and rugged mountains, the great belt of trees is as unexpected as the moving wood of Dunsinane. Part of it is conifer plantations, but the heart of the estate consists of oaks and beeches planted by John's ancestors. The mile long drive winds through this forest, which opens out into parkland where the trees are scattered and vast – specimen oaks and sycamores. Then you catch your breath as you see the eighteenth century mansion. It appears to be surviving in good trim, together with the formal garden, the walled gardens and the complex of the yard.

'We can't heat the hall.' John hurries you through the pillared drawing room. He is a small neat man who seems to be the quintessence of an English country gentleman. The speckled shabby tweed suit is worn even when he is driving the tractor, or shifting muck. The voice is upper class English. 'I remember when I first went to school in England and lost my "middling" Irish accent, my father was very upset.'

Bellevue is ten miles from Cappaghglass. In the old days the Laceys were the main landlords in the area, and it was said you could walk on their land all the way to Curraheen, a twenty mile journey. In the library John has a black box full of family papers. 'I've never looked through them properly. I believe there's some sort of scroll which says Charles II gave us this place.'

When he took over twenty years ago at his father's death most people thought he would sell up. He had spent most of his life in London where he had a job in the city. But to everyone's surprise, including his own, he enjoys living in the big house and trying to keep together what remains of the estate. It isn't easy, as much of the good farming land has long gone, and the house is daunting. In the old days the family hardly knew where the kitchen was; now they eat in it. Instead of the butler, footmen and maids, they have a relay of cleaning women. John is chairman of the agricultural show, a pillar of the Church of Ireland, and an outsider, or so he feels, even though his family has been in Ireland for hundreds of years.

'I was brought up with people who were awfully nice and had a good boyhood around the place. I remember all the cottages around here and the people with those natural good manners you associate with the Irish countryside. I was let loose with a gun when I was ten, and I could always get someone to show me where there was a woodcock or a snipe. And they also used to row us about.

I went to a prep school in England. I remember so well the joy of coming home and throwing off that stupid straw boater we were forced to wear and meeting all the familiar faces again. There was Jack O'Shea who lived with his sister in the back lodge. A wonderful man with black hair and blue eyes – I always thought there must be foreign blood somewhere – and his sister walked barefoot and you could hardly see across the house for the smoke. When he died they found buckets of money hidden up the chimney. My mother was very intimate with all the families on the tenant farms and knew everything about them and their children. At harvesting there would be a whale of a party, I remember.

The house was a super place to grow up in, and it's become part of me now. But you go through that middle period when you don't want to know about it, and you wish you hadn't got it. I had a decent life in London, and my family were all at school, and so on. When my father died in 1962 I was in two minds about the prospect of coming home.

When my grandfather was alive this was the big house, and he was the big noise, the JP and all that sort of thing, he served on the Grand Jury and owned more than five thousand acres. But he was still always liked, and in all the time I have lived here I have never detected any sharp remark about him. The house survived the troubles – I suppose that proves something. My father was brought up in the old tradition, although by his time much of the outlying land had been pruned off by the various Land Acts. I have an old photo somewhere showing the inside and outside staff which was taken on his twenty-first birthday, and it resembles an army or at least a good battalion. That was just before the First World War, but up until the second war the family lived in style. I needn't tell you how numbers have been reduced since that photo was taken.

As I have said, I am not aware of any act by my forebears which may have been considered unsuitable in this part of the world. But some people still think of me as the landlord, and I wish they wouldn't. Of course, it's no longer true if you go along with the definition of somebody who gets his income by taking rents. The other day I had a funny feeling when someone said "you're an improving landlord", after we put a bathroom into one of the lodges. It hadn't occured to me that I was doing any more than improving the assets that we have and keeping the place looking as reasonable as possible.

I have the misfortune to possess this big house and fifteen hundred acres and the kind of assets that are beyond most people's ken. Anyone can see the snags. If I show a visitor the hall, their first comment is nearly always, "Gorgeous place, but it must cost a bit to keep." It's true, a house like this couldn't run itself and was hardly built for the owner-driver.

Doing everything yourself you get – what's the phrase? – work-aholic. There's always something to do, and you find it difficult to relax. It's hard to appreciate, to stop for a moment and think, Gosh, it's beautiful. When I look out of the window I see a lovely view, but what I see first is the crack in the pane which needs repairing. You feel the burden inevitably. Its almost a cliché, the knowledge that you are just a tenant. All the stuff is technically your property, but you don't get over the feeling that you are just looking after it for thirty years. You hate selling anything. Last year we had to get part of the roof repaired, and if I had sold off one of the paintings, that would have paid the bill almost exactly. The money was raised out of securities instead. You think about all the generations that have looked after it before, and worry about what's going to happen. From time to time you get the temptation to flee. Plenty of people with houses like this – especially in Ireland – have done so. You call in Christies, make a bob or two out of selling the furniture, and go off to live happily ever after somewhere that's properly centrally-heated.

I'm cynical about something being part of a national heritage that most Irish people don't want. There's no National Trust in Ireland or grant-in-aids. It wouldn't be politically feasible for someone to stand up in the Dail and pass legislation to protect houses which they regard as being built by the hated invader. Bellevue is a Georgian Palladian house designed by an English architect, and in the present political climate that doesn't help. I think it may be a matter of luck that I want to live here in such an ostentatious house. Perhaps I suffer from *folie de grandeur*. When we walk up the avenue, Daisy always says it's the place she loves, and the house is ridiculous. But I like the space. In spite of the problems there's nothing self-sacrificing or angelic about my living here just because I have a notion of preserving it.

If I was an efficient farmer, the first thing I would do would be to knock the house down, then rip out the trees, and I'd have no truck with the walled gardens. In fact I've already turned three acres of one into a paddock. But as a sentimentalist, preservationist, whatever you want to call me, I struggle to preserve the status quo. I can remember my mother saying that it should be kept looking well, and I certainly inherit that view. The place imposes its own discipline. I do much of the work myself. For instance, today I've been scuffling the avenue with an old chain harrow which I tow behind the car.

I don't know how long these sort of places can survive the capital transfer tax and so on. The only way Bellevue has escaped so far is because my father turned it into a limited company. When he died he had twenty men working on the place and a little over fifteen hundred acres. Now we are down to about a dozen men. There are problems about employment which my father never had. In his time sons and fathers and grandfathers all worked on the place, and as soon as a son was born he would be marked out for a job eventually. The whole place was regarded as a community and everyone was involved. Now if a machine breaks down and a man is idle for an hour, I'm throwing a five pound note on the fire.

The two main sources of income for this estate are forestry and farming, and they are both becoming a problem. The private wood-lands don't get much of a look nationally, since the forestry depart-ment is selling timber at a very cheap rate. For a time I thought of opening the place to the public at a nominal charge of twenty pence, but both Daisy and I hated the experience. The litter was terrible and people would bring down carloads of children and let them go wild. They would pick the flowers and root out the bamboo and do lots of damage. Once I caught a boy wrenching off a wrought-iron gate with a crowbar.

I'm rising sixty-five and I wonder what is going to happen when I die. My son loves the place in theory, but he is living in Australia. He is quite happy there, and it's hard on him to be expected to come back and settle down and make ends meet. When he comes to Ireland he is absolutely winded by the high costs here. He might be better off if I made the brutal decision and moved out, and didn't leave him hanging on the way I am now. I just don't know. The future of a house like this is probably a German or Dutchman. That's with luck. There are a lot of smaller places where the house has been sold or allowed to fall down, and the Land Commission has divided up the land.

Living here you must reconcile yourself to a certain amount of solitude. The social life is very restricted. We are sometimes lonely, and Daisy feels it. Even twenty years ago when petrol was cheap we used to drive miles to go to house parties and have a hell of a time, but those days have gone and a lot of people have left. We don't see an awful lot of the new settlers. I don't necessarily regard anyone who comes over from England as a potential friend. Although I lived over there for many years, I find myself less rigid than most English people, and I don't always find them easy to get on with.

But I also feel there is a thin bit of cellophane between the Catholic Irish and us, and it will always be there. If you are Church of Ireland a note of Englishness creeps in. I have heard people say, "Lacey, that's a very Irish name", implying that I can't possibly be Irish by the sound of my voice, and might even come from that foreign country, Dublin. I'm afraid I've inflicted the same sort of problem on my children by having them educated in England.

Then there are the people here who say "This place doesn't belong to you, it belongs to Ireland." Although we have been here in this place for hundreds of years, it doesn't make any difference. We have no right to it. We are still treated as aggressors. What can you say to people like that?

If you had asked me when I was fourteen whether I was an Irishman or an Englishman, I don't know if I would have necessarily felt an Irishman, but now I do. A great number of people who talk with roughly the same accent as me would be hailed as Anglo-Irish, and I suppose that will have to do. My blood, if you break it down, is half Irish, a quarter English and a quarter American.

You can go on about it endlessly. In the end you have to realize that the Irish Protestant is stuck with being neither fish nor fowl nor good red herring. It's a great nuisance spending all your life in a foreign country. The Irish won't accept you as one of them, and then you go to England and you're not English either, and you get very tired of sitting in the middle of the Irish Sea. When my father was brought up, all Ireland was under the crown, and there was never any discussion about the fact that we were English through and through and at the same time Irish. It was a situation that never worried me.

Let's be honest, Protestants were a very privileged minority. And of course our family were the most privileged of the lot. In the old days there was a small Protestant circle of landowners and farmers and shopkeepers who looked up to us. We used to patronize their shops, and we would get treated differently. If we were last in line people would stand aside for you and put you up in front. That sort of thing.'

The Hon Margaret Lacey, Gentlewoman. Aged 83.

Molly is in the garden, wearing a sleeveless Husky and fingerless gloves which suggests she is buying her clothes by instalments. She is dividing daffodils. She knows a lot about flowers and used to contribute articles on gardening to newspapers. To tell the truth her garden is a bit dull, full of dark green and silver plants.

She is tall and thin with the usual Anglo-Irish horse face. Her voice is old-fashioned and pure, the diction very precise. She is abrupt and inclined to be rude, saying whatever she thinks, if she considers it to be the truth. She can be cruelly funny when she is critical. She is still much involved in voluntary work with committees, the Irish Countrywomen's Association, and so on. She cheerfully describes herself as a Lady Bountiful. In addition she is active in horticultural societies.

The interior of her house is full of relics of old decency like the family minatures and the presentation carriage clock. The furniture is good, and came from the big house. She did the tapestry on the spindly gilt chairs.

Father Maguire has called to see her, and after he has been let out her old maid servant mutters, 'there's no bigotry today!' 'That's because there's none of us left to be bigoted about.' She and Kitty spar all the time.

She was brought up in Bellevue with her sisters and brothers in their own golden private world. Her father, who died in the early nineteen twenties, belonged to the generation which saw the First World War and the Troubles ending the old way of life. Although Molly always considered herself a bit of a rebel, sympathizing with Irish aspirations, she was no Maud Gonne – life was too difficult for that. Bellevue survived the Troubles to sustain another brief flowering which lasted until the Second World War. She lived there with her brother and his wife, but when he died and her nephew took over the place, she moved to the small house nearby.

★

'We were never a very rich family. We were never in the rich circle of the Irish aristocracy, and we lived very simply compared to them. I suppose the house is pretty big, and there must be about forty rooms, but of course there are, or were, plenty of bigger houses in Ireland. Friends would look at the wings and stables and say it was very shoddy, and my father was wonderful the way he closed his eyes to things falling down. He always said that the ancestor who built it did it more for show than as a practical place to live. It was never meant to be comfortable.

In my generation we were expected to keep to our own sort of background. There were some retired officers and gentlemen farmers who didn't have to make a living from the land, but we were the only big family in the area. We were born with a feeling that there was some kind of hierarchy in the world, and it went down in steps, you know. We didn't think it particularly grand, but just the way life was. The rich man in his castle, the poor man at the gate.

Some people have a very mistaken idea about our lives that we were pampered and that sort of thing. I suppose it was partly because of the huge staff we were expected to keep. All the people outside, the coachman and stables, the head gardener, foreman and steward and other people. In so many cases you needed two men to do one job. I remember watching a gardener edging the verges and the boy coming up after him on his knees, keeping up as fast as he could, picking up the grass and putting it into a barrow. All the butter and everything like vegetables came from the estate. Inside there was always a full staff and they were all our friends. There was a head housemaid and two under her, three in the pantry, the butler, footman and pantry boy, and then there were at least three in the kitchen. My mother had her own personal maid, and we had one, and there was someone who lived in a very dark hole and scrubbed the house all day. And there was a special lamp boy, because at that time everything was lamps. Lamps and logs. This would certainly be up to the First World War, and some years after it, I think.

There wasn't anything grand about all these servants, and I don't remember that their clothes were anything to talk about. All right, the coachman wore a top hat and a cockade, the butler wore butler's dress and the footmen had liveries and buttons and a cutaway. I should say the liveries were always rather shoddy and the butler looked down at heel. I don't think it was a smart house at all, if you compared it with the grander places. Now people talk about that television thing, Upstairs and Downstairs, and how the housemaids wore crinkly white aprons. Ours would wear white, and a white cap in the morning, and in the afternoon it was always black. Oh yes, there was always someone who lit the fire and polished the shoes.

I was intensely happy as a child, and I remember running out on the lawn before breakfast and thinking how lucky I was to live here. I remember that. We were brought up entirely by nannies and governesses and had our own nursery wing with our own maid to look after it. I suppose we all ended up half-educated – the girls, that is. I remember a horrible advertisement in the paper for a dreadful school some miles beyond Curragheen which said "For the daughters of gentlemen." But a place like that wasn't considered proper for people of our own background and class.

We used to get up very early and be given nursery breakfast, which was very dull. Sometimes as a special treat on my mother's birthday or something like that we were allowed to go down and talk to them while they were having their breakfast. They would be helping themselves to hot dishes on the sideboards, porridge and bacon and eggs and kedgeree and tea and coffee. We had a ferocious English cook, and I remember going one night to the kitchen when they were going to have lobsters, and my sister and I nipped all the strings around their claws and hid them in drawers, and this caused consternation. We were allowed to go anywhere in the house and to play with the servants' children. The heads to the departments were mostly English, and I suppose this was taken into account. The butler was English, the head housemaid was English and my mother's maid was Scottish. Of course our governess was English. I remember the butler played cricket with us on the lawn. The underlings all came from the gate lodges or were people off the estate.

We were taught very early about the business of service and helping less fortunate people. We took donkey loads of wood around to various old ladies and my mother did a lot of local charity work and taking things to the poor. Our toys were always taken away as soon as we had finished with them, and so were our clothes.

Sometimes we went to Cappaghglass to listen to the German bands that played in the square. It was a much more rural place then – for instance, a herd of cows was driven through the street each morning for milking. I used to see what they called "the tourist car", a couple of horses pulling a big carriage. When Dr Scott got the first motor car – gracious, long before the First World War! – it was such a sight that people were afraid to go out. I remember it down by the harbour and a crowd around it – a queer old thing, big and high, and you got in at the back. At the other end of the timescale I remember a penny farthing, and the pedals would put you over the handlebars.

Religion was more important then, and the local people feared their priest, or so we were told. They accepted everything they were told and believed it. People were terribly superstitious. I had a nurse who believed utterly that at night a coach driven by a headless coachman came up the avenue and the gates opened themselves to let us in. There were lots of Church of Ireland people in the area then. I was allowed to play with the Rector's children and the Bank Manager's children. My father was very good friends with the Bank Manager. We went to Protestant shops exclusively, except for the butcher because all the butchers in Cappaghglass were Roman Catholic.

Sunday was always considered a special day. After breakfast there were those long family prayers and everyone had to dress up. The men wore top hats or bowlers and the women wore long dresses and flowers and all sorts of things on them. You couldn't get off church if you were fit to go at all, and the pews were packed with heaps of children. In those days people had big families – my mother had a baby every year. I had five sisters and two brothers and the first lot were grown up before the others came on.

We had our own special pew up in the gallery, a little box with scarlet cushions around it and our coat of arms behind. It was so high we could look down on people's heads. There was old Mrs Wilson, a very difficult person, who complained about a draught. The rector used to have to do three services in the morning, and they were all very long. We used to refer to the Litany as the Limit.

On Sunday afternoon we went for a walk and there was also croquet and tennis. We had a tennis day once a week and I remember playing with skirts down to my heels and a big hat. My mother had an "At Home" day with her friends coming in to gossip over tea. As we got older things became more fun. What I particularly enjoyed were the long summers. There were always big house parties, and we also used to go away to a lovely fishing lodge at Garrycloyne – that's about thirty miles from here. My father had a yacht – quite a big yacht. And we went on lots of picnics. We all used to go off in a large wagonette, and when we got to the chosen place one of the servants would put a big white tablecloth on the ground and forks and knives and everything. The flies were awful. Everyone would sit around the cloth and my father used to carve the beef. The old beef joints were always on the bone, not what you get now. We would have all sorts of cakes and currant buns with tea and sometimes wine and things like a trifle. After the picnic the horses that had pulled us there would have a race, and that was always very exciting.

Horses were regarded rather like God, and it didn't matter if you could hardly read or write so long as you sat with a good seat in your saddle. Daddy was chairman of the local hunt and I think he hunted three days a week. He hated cars. I do remember my mother persuading him to hire a car and a chauffeur for the summer parties of 1912 and 1913 so that people could be taken to the mountains for shooting. He wouldn't have them for the rest of the year, and none of us had a car until we were able to drive ourselves.

My problem was that most of his friends were horsy people and the whole time the conversation was on horses. If you were literary or liked reading a good book you were regarded as impossible to talk to because you hadn't kept up with the latest thing about horses. It wasn't so much that I didn't like riding. I had an old pony when I was young and was very fond of it. But out on my first hunt I was quite terrified of everything. And right at the first fence the horse in front of me jumped wrong and was killed – and that wasn't the best introduction. But always there was this feeling that if you weren't horsy you were a flop and no good.

My father was totally unpretentious and totally unaware of class, and his main concern was sport. He tried to start a cricket team and built a small pavilion; most of the men on the estate were forced to play. Although he liked tennis and shooting, riding was his main thing.

My mother was busy running the house. I think just keeping things going took up a lot of her time. Every meal required a certain amount of organization. The dining room is a lovely room – you've seen it? There would be the butler and the footmen, and some wretched boy carrying the trays miles from the kitchen. The food had to be carried along those craggy passages and I don't know how they did it. Even when my parents were alone dinner would be seven or eight courses. They certainly didn't have anything called "starters" – my mother would have had a fit at the word. They served soup at the beginning, then fish, then meat and pudding and cheese. And we also had those enormous teas. I think the men played billiards after dinner and there was a bit of bridge.

I am just old enough to have taken part in the balls my mother gave. I remember the lines of carriages arriving at the porch and the footmen taking the shawls and cloaks and the music coming from the ballroom. My mother always invited a lot of officers from the barracks at

Curragheen. They would be in dress uniform and they would put down their names on your programme opposite the dances they wanted. It might be a gallop, polka or waltz. The clever girls always had their programmes already half filled up the day before. After each dance you were expected to go back to your chaperone, which in our case was my mother, and you had no chance of hiding away in any little corner.

The Great War started after this and the men went away, including my father and brothers. My eldest brother was killed just a month before the Armistice. Things never returned to normal. The whole atmosphere became different and there was all this sinking of ships and the dreadful list of casualties. On Sunday evenings we used to sing hymns in the drawing-room, the whole family, with all the servants standing at the back. There was Onward Christian Soldiers, and it used to end up with God Save the King. Once Mummy said, "I really don't think this is fair on the servants" and we sang Abide with Me instead.

I suppose Daddy had a good war. He was wounded, but he quite recovered and got an MC. But when he came back to Ireland afterwards things were very different, and I'm thinking of the personal thing. The Old Lord, as he was called by everyone, was the son of the house, and he had always been a great pet with everyone. It was hard for him to realize suddenly that instead of being popular with everyone you were regarded with suspicion and even liable to be shot. And you hadn't oppressed anyone. He was dreadfully hurt.

I was less hurt because secretly I was a bit of a Republican. I think they laughed at it. One way I picked it up was through the kitchen maid who was walking out with a leading Republican in Cappagh-glass, and she kept telling me these stories. How the boys were shooting this and how they were going to burn that down. I think I got it from her. Someone brought back a stone from the beach where Childers had landed the guns, and I thought that was absolutely marvellous.

Maurice Nolan, Butler. Aged 68.

Maurice and his wife, Sheila, live on the outskirts of Cappaghglass in a small modern bungalow full of china ornaments of shepherdesses, old-fashioned ladies and Copenhagen animals, photographs of his children and piles of magazines beside the large colour TV. An incongruous note is struck by the pair of giant antlers above the glass bookshelf. A gift from his former employer.

Maurice went to Bellevue in the late 'twenties when jobs were hard to find, and he was lucky to be taken on at the lowly grade of hall boy. He climbed successive ranks, ending up as butler. Like so many associated with Bellevue, he mentions Upstairs, Downstairs, and evidently identifies with Hudson. He still meets his former employers, attends their weddings and funerals and feels part of the family with whom he obtained a position of mutual trust. Although he doesn't particularly like the concept of inherited titles, believing each man should be appraised for his own worth, and not rely on some ancestor for recognition, he has nothing but love and respect for the people for whom he gave so many precious years.

★

'I always remember how vast the house seemed as I came round the drive in the taxi, and this mass of granite seemed to be blocking the roadway. I was awestruck by it because it was so enormous, and I thought it was very beautiful. Later I took a great interest in keeping it beautiful.

There was the entrance hall, the great hall and the State Rooms folded off from each other by pairs of mahogany doors. You could walk around the house without seeming to ever come to an end. There was the organ room, the billiard room and the great oval dining room which is so big that it used to be said you could drive a carriage and pair around it. Upstairs were all the bedrooms, each with its own name, the North Room, the Blue Room, the Rose Room, the Yellow Room, and there were so many you would get tired looking for them. Each had its own bell, and downstairs outside the kitchen was the yoke with the numbers on it which showed you which one was ringing.

The staff was divided into departments, you see, and each had a person in charge. The butler would be head man and you were responsible to him, and he was responsible to the Lord. The house-keeper was on the other side. In the kitchen the cook had the kitchen maid and the scullery maid under her, and so it went on up and down. Then the outside staff. In the gardens alone they had twelve men working. I suppose you could call it a small army of people. I worked it out, and there must have been sixty working outside from the steward down. They were paid by the agent on Saturdays. The heads of the departments were usually English, and so were people like the nanny and governess. I also remember a Scotch head gardener who won prizes with his flowers. Every morning the head gardener would come in with flowers and potted plants, and usually a daughter of the house would arrange them. They had a large conservatory, one of those places with a big glass dome, but that's gone now.

My first duty was hall boy under the footman, and I also had to help with the furnace. The first thing I would do in the morning was carry up coals, and then I would lay the tables for the staff. Then I would light the pantry fire and boil a kettle for the Lord to shave with. The butler would take the water up to him in a brass jug, and sometimes one of the footmen would go along for valeting.

Later I was appointed second footman and given the family livery. They also supplied suits for the men in "clergyman's grey", but when you went into livery you were sent all the way to Dublin to Callaghans of Dame Street, and they would make a beautiful livery in powder blue with yellow cuffs and a yellow collar with the family crest stamped on the brass buttons. The waistcoat would come down to about here, and there were four more crested buttons.

A second footman was a rung up the ladder, if you like. I worked under the first footman, and he was under the butler, and there was the Lord on top, and everyone liked him and he was regarded as a decent honest man. The heaviest work was in the morning, and in the afternoon you were just there dressed up to answer the bell or the front door. You were always warned as to who was coming, for people rarely approached the house without having an appointment or being invited.

Mealtimes were one of our main duties. There could be as many as twenty at the great oval table, and the butler was there officiating. The footman's duty was to carry up the meals from the kitchen and then help to serve them. We were always told that the smell of cooking should never be in the dining room, but there was little chance of this ever happening, because we had to run with the food what seemed like half a mile. Someone would be there already with the hot plates. You had everything prepared, and you ran, and if you had souflée you had to produce it in the dining room without it flopping. The minute the cook took it out of the oven a big silver cover was put over it, and then you hared along the flagged passage and up the stone staircase so that it reached the dining-room before it would sink.

I used to like waiting at table, for you would be meeting all the different people and all the big names, and hearing all the conversation. But you knew that you were in a sort of trust, and that it was always most important that you didn't blab. You had so many working in the house that you didn't go out and talk to people because they wouldn't understand anyway.

It was a nice life and I enjoyed it. I had been working there only seven years when I became butler, which was regarded as most unusual. I had gone on holiday, and when I came back I was told I had responsibility for the house, since the old butler had taken sick. He was English, and the fact that I was Irish also made a bit of a change. I can tell you between ourselves that it frightened me because what the butler said was law in the house, and you were responsible to the family for all the people under you. And part of your job was to discharge someone who wasn't suitable. The cook and the housekeeper did the same with their people, so that the people whose money you were getting hadn't anything to do with that.

I had to have a morning suit, a black coat and striped pants, the same as they wear in London – like, and stiff shirts and white bows. I knew most of the routine by then. You didn't have a conversation with the family unless they spoke to you, and you avoided running into them and that sort of thing. You didn't contact them but it was your duty to be there.

The family had their cooked breakfast at about nine, when nobody ever sat and got served, but they walked around carrying their plates. They started with porridge and helped themselves from the side table to rashers and scrambled eggs and kedgeree and sometimes they had a ham. Then at a quarter to ten the long bell pull went and I would be summoned to the boudoir and get my orders for the day. The housekeeper got her orders after, and then the cook was brought in to deal with the menu, and this happened every day.

For lunch I would have to wait at table and I would have a footman there, too, and the maid would take things to the door. It started with an entrée, and then a main course and then a pudding and fruit afterwards. Dinner would be at eight, and if there was a party it meant I didn't get to bed until after midnight. My last job was to see that the footman had gathered up everything, because there was no such thing as a washing machine in those days.

Dinner was always the big meal with a lot of work. The table had to be set with silver and a fingerbowl for each person. I had to look after the drinks, sherry, wines, port and French champagne. The Lord gave me the key to the cellar and told me what he wanted. The bottles were lying flat in racks in the cellar and there was a touch of whitewash on each bottle to show the sides you had to carry. When you brought them up they were decanted into a decanter.

To people today it might seem like a hard life, but the day passed like a wink with so much to do and the company of working with other people in the house. Top people like the butler got five pounds a week, which seemed like an enormous wage in those days. In places like Bellevue you were kept, and had nothing to buy except cigarettes. All the clothes we got, except for those stiff fronted shirts and collars. They had a laundry and even a wagonette to bring the stuff into Cappaghglass.

For the men working outside, a yard bell went at seven, and at half past ten they went into what was called the steam shed for their cup of tea. Then they were back at work at eleven, and at one they had an hour for their lunch and they finished at six o'clock in the evening. Of the indoor staff I always thought that the kitchen people had the hardest work, and on top of that they had to humour the cook.

The head staff used to eat in the housekeeper's room, what we called the "Pug's parlour". There would be the butler and the housekeeper and the lady's maid and the cook and any visiting lady's maids or valets. The place was comfortable enough, and all the staff had their own bedrooms with fireplaces. The maids had a sitting room, and our pantry was rather a nice place to sit with a coal fire always burning where we used to play cards.

You were part of the family, – they were always gracious and thoughtful and that sort of thing. If anyone was sick a doctor was called, and if you really felt ill they provided a day and night nurse. I was fortunate working for the same family all the time. They were genuine, and you were as much part of their lives and their way of life that they depended on you a lot, and as they got older they also needed more looking after.

Before the war there was always a lot of lavish entertainment and there was a yearly routine. In February or March the family would go away for a cruise, and you would give a big spring clean. Part of the work was going over the silver; each piece had to be shammied off after it was washed; I would wear a green baize apron. Some pieces had been rubbed so much that they had gone soft, and a handle might double up. When the family came back there was the Spring Show in Dublin and a few weeks after that the season in London. They always took a house in Belgrave Square, and everything was packed in baskets and brought over, silver, glassware and even the pots, for the cook always said you couldn't get proper pots in England. The heads of the departments all went and I enjoyed those visits. Once we were brought to the Aldershot Tattoo, and there was King George's coronation in 1937. We were given seats in the Mall and I watched the whole procession go by, and it seemed like a fairy tale realized. I remember writing to my mother about it. I believe it was terrible at the Abbey itself, all those ladies with coronets lying on the pavement screaming for taxis. The family kept the chairs they sat on at the Abbey.

When we came back it would be for autumn and winter and the hunting. The main house was always kept warm, and fifty to a hundred tons of coal were brought up to the basement to keep the furnace stoked. Then they had the Christmas parties, and there was a large black box from which the family and their cousins would dress up in costume for dinner. A whole dining room of generals, cardinals, kings and queens and goodness knows what else, and we would serve around. At Christmas we were given a tenant's party or "men's supper" with past and present people who worked on the estate. After eating we were brought to the great hall where the Lord and Lady started the dance and got everything going. That was a great night. The Burdys used to ask us over for their staff ball and the first time I took over the running of the house I had to ask Lady Burdy out to dance, and she'd take you off your feet. Lord Burdy used to play tunes on a saw.

Then the Second World War came and the cracks showed. The old ways were changing. You read of it and heard of it that everyone was going over to England into factories and your day's work ended at five or six o'clock. Many of the staff went to England. It was hard on the family with everyone gone and they couldn't keep it up with taxes so high. After the war they had to pull down the west wing because of dry rot – ten great rooms with a great iron hammer knocking lumps out of it, and I remember the Lord once said that the best thing would be by accident it would all burn down. It seemed to me then somehow symbolic.'

Joe McCarthy, Retired Farm Worker. Aged 76.

Joe lives in one of Bellevue's gate lodges, a very small Victorian cottage with a pitched slated roof, barge board and a niche between the eaves where the Lacey crest and coronet are displayed with a carved date, 1881. He has been here for forty years.

As a young labouring man, Joe can remember the line of men sitting on the yard wall waiting for the bell summoning them to work. 'If you left your job there was always someone outside the gate to take it up quick.' They were always conscious of their luck. Joe doesn't feel exploited. His son has taken on his old job.

When you talk to him you realize that the mere fact of possession is unimportant. Bellevue and its acres is part of him; he takes pride in every tree, every animal, every blade of grass on the estate. His own domain was the stables and outbuildings where a cupola over the archway reaches above the black and gold clock. He broke horses for the plough, worked the cattle and sheep and turned his hand at anything they asked him. Later on he worked mainly with sheep.

He retired six years ago. 'I said to myself, when I can't do a fair day's work for a fair day's pay, that's the day I'll go out. I wouldn't be pretending to work if I couldn't.' Now he does a little gardening and breeds pheasants for the estate. Perhaps his attitudes would be not so unusual in England, but in Ireland it is startling to listen to the respectful praise he and his wife lavish on the family up at the big house.

★

'I'm not a local man at all. I was reared east of Curragheen. There was an awful big estate where I came from. Have you heard of the Burdys of Curragheen, they are all gone out of it now. There's a Burdy in it, but he's not a Burdy. The Marquess of Glencullen was married to one of the Burdy girls, and he divorced her and she married a man called Campbell, and he is called Campbell-Burdy.

Oh, when you go back to the penal days, they crushed the poor, and all these things were handed down, and sure they had to leave the country. They took the crops and let them die with the hunger. There was one Burdy who must be this woman's great-grandfather. He was generally disliked, for he turned people out.

I heard old people of ninety years of age saying that when they were going to school, if a young lad didn't salute him, when the father went to pay him the rent next day, if he knew who the child was, he wouldn't take it. Or if a non-Catholic went in and he wanted a farm, the old fellow would take the rent from the Catholic, and turn him out and give the land to the non-Catholic. It was as bad as that.

Of course things changed, and I'd say 1916 had a lot to do with it and brought a lot of landlords down to their knees. All the big landlords and landowners got very nervous, because they didn't know what night they were going to get the works. The Burdys were going to be burned, and they were going to burn down the house and the parish priest stopped them.

I remember part of the Troubles. We were going to school and kicking a football in the playground, and there was an ambush in the place. And we could hear the bullets whistling over our heads, and we went and ran and told the Master. They shot two brothers sowing corn, and they shot an old man pumping water, and they fired on several lads. Our lads, too, would shoot you for nothing.

We were all poor in those days. Everyone was in the same boat except the Protestants. The landlords, big shopkeepers and farmers were usually Protestant, and we would always say when someone asked you how you were, "I'm as strong as a Protestant, but not so rich". The Protestants were lucky to be born into money, and we weren't, and that was all there was to it.

I was fifteen years of age when I got my first job. It was seven and six a week all found, and that meant I was sleeping in the house and we'd all eat together. That wasn't the rule everywhere, and in most houses there were two tables in it, one for the people who worked and one for the family.

You could go to big farmers and they were just as bad as landlords. They treated you like a dog more or less, and they hadn't any sympathy for you, wet or dry, or when we had to go out. Often men didn't get their wages, and there was no way of getting it from them if they didn't want to give it to you. The workman was the workman, and he was there seven days a week. It meant that I had no free time, and no such thing as getting up at six o'clock and stopping at eight in the evening. If I went to a market at six o'clock in the morning, I got no overtime, and sure if I didn't get to bed until the next day at ten or half past ten, I could say nothing. That was the way it was. The day was too long at that time, and it was always from sunrise to sunset.

I know one man in his old age, and he worked in this place for five shillings a week, and he went in this morning about six o'clock, and the woman of the house was going across the yard with two buckets, and she says "The day held up, Willy!" – at six o'clock in the morning. You wouldn't even have Sunday. The man in charge of the stock had to go there on Sunday, and there was no such thing as half days.

I stayed with the first man for two or three years and had a few more jobs before coming here. Bellevue was the only big place for a hundred miles that still worked in the old style. There must have been about thirty on the outside. There was never any bad feeling here. For one thing, there was the personality of the owner, and the present Lord was reared here, and his father before him, and the old fellow before that, and there was no bad points in them. During the IRA trouble no one interfered with the grandfather – they let him be. Unlike many of the others I mentioned, he was a good man minding his own business and kept clear. Like you meet the good farmer and the bad farmer just the same.

I'd say the biggest changes in farming came since the 'sixties, and up to the 'sixties it was a hundred years before that. There is a beautiful way of doing things with the machine at the present time. When I started, all the tilling was done with a single pair of horses, and the mowing too. You'd be sitting there and have the blade of the machine going along in front of you and the table behind on it, and when you think there was enough, you'd drop the table and they would put them into stacks. Then you would bring it in and make a rick of corn all around on your knees, kneeling all the shapes around in the middle. Then there was more hard work for the threshing, which used to last two weeks. First of all the stuff was brought into the haggard, then you had to haul the corn into the loft with a pulley, fill up the bags and load them on a trailer – there was no automatic way of doing it. Now they have the tank combine, and nothing to do but pull your trailer by the side of it and press a button, and it's all out.

I ended up with the sheep. They would be more or less white sheep, you know, a touch of Cheviot in them at that particular time. There's always a lot of work attached to sheep, from paring their feet to shearing which is the heaviest job. In those days I did a share of them with the hand shears and I'd do about fifty or sixty a day. But the lads from where I came would do double that amount. With sheep the machinery doesn't help. Sure you can do as much with a machine as twenty men can do, but you still have to catch the sheep, knock her down and dose her.

They were always my favourite animal. On a wet morning you would bring a little lamb into the house and feed him with a bottle. I reared twenty at one time, and when you opened the door they would be leaping around. But you couldn't pet them too much, or they wouldn't go off when they got big, and would hang around the lodge – do you follow me?

Bellevue's a big place, and it meant a lot of walking. I always wore good strong leather boots and I seldom carried a stick. I had a couple of very good dogs. If you had the right class, there was no length in training them. I'd often go out in the morning, and I'd be looking for the sheep all day, tramping around the hills and on the mountains, and down to the railway and this sort of thing – sure my head was on my knees from climbing the hills. Sometimes in winter you would lose them, particularly if there was any snow. The sheep will go with the wind, and they won't go agin it; they will go with the wind and snow and get jammed against a ditch, and if that happens the frost will kill them, for no air can get them. But then you get philosophical about the death of things, and it's the same when you send them to the butcher, and it wouldn't worry you. Although I grew fond of them, it's the same as a man knowing that he is going to die some day. You accepted it.

In the old days farming was a nice easy way of life. When you are working with a pair of horses, you are walking along fine and leisurely, but now it's a lot of rush with tractors ripping and tearing. You get very intensive. I can't understand all the needling that's done with sheep and cattle. And look at the way they grub out the hedges and leave the fields bare. This spring it was terribly bad, and I saw the poor cattle up against the electric fence in the wind and the rain, and they had nowhere to stand.

When I was young the poor was poor, and the other fellow had the big estate. My father applied to have land that was being divided, but you had to have money and everything. Rich people shouldn't have too much land. It's no use giving the land to a bank or a solicitor – that type of person that wasn't reared on land, because he isn't going to stay on it, and he knows nothing about it. You have to be brought up to it, and you have to be there, and it's your job. There's no use going off today and not coming back for a fortnight. You'll have cows calving and mares foaling and sows farrowing and ewes lambing.

I have nothing against this man here, for he's able to hold on to it. There's not an awful lot of these people able to hold on to these places. There's too much tax on them and they are a nuisance. An awful lot have been knocked since the troubled times. There was a man around Curragheen named Jacky Harte who knocked them and sold the material and timber and slates and everything. Bellevue is still there but they have been working on the house since I came here, and something is wrong with it every day of the year.

When De Valera was in power he made out that people should be happy if they had enough, and that we would never be a rich country. That was all right when we were under him, for De Valera wasn't really Irish – in no way – and people were sort of afraid of him. But with Lemass, he was one of our own, and we could do what we liked with him. People bought bigger cars and bigger boats, and they weren't too affluent when they started, but now they went back to the top of the scale. Now there's a recession, they have become nice again, and I think basically people haven't changed that much. Except that nowadays it makes no difference who you are and what you are.

I remember a time when the Lord would invite all present and past workers to a ball in the House. They would be held upstairs in the ballroom, and there would be dancing, and some fellow playing music and barrels of stout and whiskey and he would dance there himself. Then they had the hunt balls at Bellevue with no one there except the gentry. You'd know them by the way they clung together. They were gentry, sure, in their own mind. Then Paddy started going in, and money got plentiful and there was no novelty at all.

It's like in America. Jack is as good as his master, and has a good few suits of clothes and is as well dressed and he has a pocket of money of his own. The old ones wouldn't even dance with their daughters. The hunt ball is over, and the old landlord gone, and now when you go into a pub you don't know who you are talking to, for they are all dressed the same as a bank man.'

Margaret Hanly, Dairy Maid. Aged 84.

Margaret lives with her brother in yet another of Bellevue's lodges. From the kitchen window you can see the black coil of the river that flows through the land, and the swans and waterbirds associated with it. She likes looking at it, but is afraid to go on the water or on the sea. An uncle was drowned.

Her family have had a tradition of working at Bellevue which goes back several generations. Her father and brother were understewards, her sister was in the house, while she obtained her job in the dairy when she was a young girl.

She sees the past in a golden haze, and her dates are muddled. When did the old Lord get married? What year was it that his father hired a great blue open Daimler and chauffeur for the summer? She isn't sure when they returned from England after the Troubles. She is more precise about things in her own province, the obedient cows waiting to be milked and the thick cream that got turned into butter. Everything was better 'in the long-ago times.' Milk and butter tasted better then. She doesn't go out much, and hasn't been through the estate for years. She's been told that things aren't what they used to be – so many big trees cut down, the walled gardens gone to weeds.

★

'I remember the old Lord as well as I'm looking at you, and his sister, Miss Lacey, who is still living, thanks be to God. I remember their father and the rest of the family.

The time I am talking about the house was fully staffed. My father started off in the garden and eventually became understeward. His job was to look after the men and see they were there in the morning, and of course he did his own bit of work as well. The land steward was above him, and they were very good and kindly to everyone, and kindness itself. Sure, everyone had firing for nothing, and they could go up to the woods to get it. Look what you would pay for it today! Oh dear, yes.

We lived with my father up near one of the big woods, and it was a paradise on a summer's evening just to walk through it, the stillness of it, and the cleanliness and everything. Sure, everything was wild flowers there, and it was lovely. In Bellevue they had everything you ever wanted. When my sister's husband's people came down on holiday from Dublin that time, they'd love looking at it, and all the beauty. The different gardens and lovely pathways and everything. The family used to have tennis and tea in the lower flower garden when the Lord's sister, Mrs Hargreaves, God rest her soul, used to come from England and bring her servants with her of course. They used to have tea and tennis up there in the afternoon.

Everything we ate then was different from today, and there's no food now, I do say. We'd eat potatoes in their own skin, lovely cabbage, lovely turnip and lovely meat. Sure there's no flavour in the meat now and I think the fridges have it finished. The fridges take the flavour from it, and I never had a fridge until I was sick after Christmas, and I was up with my daughter for two months, and I am only back here, though I suppose I'm fifty years living here. And I was in town, and I bought a lovely bit of lamb's liver. Well, if you cooked it that day it would be beautiful, but I put it in the fridge, and when I cooked it there wasn't a taste or smell in it. I'm certainly right, sir . . . and I had a lovely little shoulder of lamb, and I had it in the fridge four or five days and it was tasteless.

When I grew up I became a dairy maid. I think I told you that. It was considered a good steady job, and our quarters were in the dairy yard behind the main house. There were many different things going on there. I remember the carpenter's yard, and the sawmill, and the piggeries, and cowhouses, and the stables with their lovely stone arches. Everything was always beautifully clean, and it would do you good to walk through it, and all so beautifully kept. The lovely pinewood compartments, and the painted metalwork, and the lovely harness room with all the harness shining – it was lovely. I hadn't any taste for horses, only the cows and the calves. I did the dairy work, and milked the cows, and that was nearly sixty years ago because I will be eighty-five please God, at the end of July. No, I was never in the main house. My sister worked there, and always said it was beautiful.

My brother and I milked twenty-five cows a day at the height of the summer. We milked thirteen in the morning, twelve or thirteen in the afternoon on a hot summer's day. They weren't troublesome, although you might get one of the young cows with her first calf, and she would be very cross for a little while. Sure, they used to know my brother, for he was very kind to them, and they would know his step and would turn their head. He was kind to them and didn't beat them and he was a long time there.

We'd start milking at about six, when my brother had them brought in. They would all go out by themselves they were so used to it, and they would be at the gate waiting to be milked. Cows don't like to keep a lot of milk, and they were waiting for you to take the milk from them. Some would be great milkers and dropping with milk in summertime.

I remember one special cow that reared Lord John. Felicity was her name . . . a well-bred cow that was his special cow, and that was the cow he was reared on. I would get his bottle of milk every day, and it was sent up to the nursery from Felicity. She was a lovely cow, and was, of course, tested.

The cows had to be done, and the milk had to be done the same as every day in the week. Buttermaking would be twice a week with whatever cream you had over. I would wear nice white overalls and good strong leather boots and my feet would be always dry. You had to have good boots in the dairy because it was all water. You were always throwing water. It was a full day's work, and churn day was always Tuesday and Friday. There were cement shelves in the dairy, and a weighing place to weigh the butter, a butterworker to wash the butter, and a churn barrel to make the butter. We also had a large horse churn outside the dairy window, and this man had the horse moving around the barrel, and it was grand.

Begod, it was a full day's work, and you would have a rest in the middle of the day. The churn was in the cowhouse, and the cows would come along, and you only had to come up and strain it into the churn. We didn't have any big carrying like that. A brother of my father's who worked there all his life, twisted the machine to get the cream. Well, if you could get into that place today, the mark of his boot would be there because he wore down the cement. I had to put a flat board to keep the foot steady. There were two buckets under the separator, one for the separated milk, and the other was for the cream, and there was little brass taps to twist so that the man who was doing it would see the cream getting too thin, and of course, he would put that off. And you'd whip your bucket away and put in another bucket for the rest.

And there were the oak tubs to keep the cream in, big oak tubs that were made for the place. They always said it should be oak, or it would taste the butter, and in the end years when the oak couldn't be got, they used big earthenware crocks to put the cream into. Then there was the butter. My father was allowed two pounds of butter free a week, and there were other people who got it, the head gardener and steward, and the land steward and some others. The rest was sold. We don't know the taste of good butter today, and I remember that the butter was also sent to Wiltshire in England, where the Lord's sister, Mrs Hargreaves lived. It was beautiful butter, and packed in oak butter boxes made in the carpenter's yard, and it was posted every Wednesday afternoon.

Afterwards you had your separator to wash, and I would also have to wash all the milk buckets and churns, and wash out the dairy. We had the kitchen near the dairy, and there was plenty of sticks to boil water, and a fine big pot. When it was ready one of the men carried it down the passage, and afterwards you would leave your separator open and all your things. If it was a nice day you could put them out in the fresh air and bring them in before you started milking cows.

I suppose the dairy was expected to pay for itself, and pay all the hands that were doing it. There were also the calves to be reared and the garden men got milk, and there were a lot of servants in Bellevue and the milk had to go there also. I never used machines. I don't like what I see of modern farming. In my day you would have old cows milked by hand and they would be as old as the hills. Sure they have no milk now after about four years, and it's too forcible or something.'

SPORTSMEN AND ENTHUSIASTS

NED DILLON   Sportsman and Retired Hurley Player,
Aged 43
DONAL MAGRATH   Harness Racer, *Aged 42*
JOHN CORCORAN   Huntsman and Kennelman, *Aged 46*
JEREMIAH KEARNS   Field Naturalist, *Aged 82*
KITTY BURKE   Museum Curator, *Aged 58*

The man who is good at sport, particularly at hurley, and who is good company, always has high status irrespective of class, his family background and even his moral character is taken into account.

The Irish Countryman, M. Arensburg.

Look at the stars! look, look up at the skies!
O look at all the fire-folk sitting in the air!
The bright boroughs, the circle-citadels there!

The Starlight Night, Gerard Manley Hopkins.

Ned Dillon, Sportsman and Retired Hurley Player. Aged 43.

Ned is a small neat man who feels much the same enthusiasm about hurley as a Gaelic speaker does about the language. He sees it as something uniquely related to the Irish character, with its roots deep in mythology. When he was younger he played for his county, something that never gets forgotten. He still has the quality of a 'star.' Everyone knows Ned and his passion for the sport, which has become legendary. He had not missed an All Ireland Final since he was in his early twenties. Generations of children are grateful for the consideration and care that he has put into the game.

He is married with four children, and teaches at the community school. Although he has lived by hurley, he is not fanatical. He enjoys watching rugby and soccer, and feels that the Gaelic Athletic Association ban on non-Gaelic games became a nonsense long ago. Even so, it is evident that for Ned hurley is more than just a game. He believes the cleavage in sport is a reflection of the conflict in Ireland and when the rabid Orangeman plays hurley with the enthusiasm of his Celtic counterpart, there will be peace throughout the island.

★

'The first thing that came into my hands was a hurley stick, and from that moment I never let go. Hurley requires more dedication than any other sport. You must have a good eye, and be able to anticipate the rise and fall of the ball, and how it instinctively comes to you, and you play it along the hurley. You look for speed and strength, but it is also no use having a headless man playing the game. You must have discipline, which I feel is the essential thing – you might as well get rid of the person who isn't going to behave himself.

The posher, more snobby schools have concentrated on rugby and football, what my father used to call "garrison games". It was the Christian Brothers who played Gaelic games, and the situation is still much the same. At my school there was never any great drive towards the academic, and it was all hurling or Gaelic football. The Brothers used to bring balls into the classroom, and teach us how to catch them, even in the middle of something like Christian Doctrine or mathematics. Of course, we were all delighted. At breaktime we were taught to develop our skills with a ball against a wall, hitting it when it came in the air or on the ground with a hurley. And it was from right to left and always keep it moving.

I still think sport is very important for a boy's development. If he can't play something like football or hurley, he must be good at something. We don't do enough in this country to find out the skills the boys have, even if it's something like billiards or table-tennis. And I don't mean this in any derogatory manner.

For someone like yourself, who doesn't know or understand hurley, it's difficult to explain just what it means. It all goes back to Cuchulainn and Finn McCool, and all these other fellows in mythology. They didn't have the game we play today. They hit the ball from field to field, and from one townland to another, and there might be a hundred men driving it around. I think it was always regarded as a national game, and the hurley was the sign of rebellion. Even today the Protestants won't play it. After the Norman occupation it was banned by the Statute of Kilkenny, and only in the last century the GAA helped to revive it. For someone like Michael Cusack, one of the founders of the Gaelic Association, the idea was "to bring back the hurling". Those were his exact words.

I think the GAA created respect for national games, and their famous ban on foreign sports like cricket and rugby helped the people to stand on their hind legs. Of course the ban was part of that nationalistic tradition of the time, and only became divisive later on. You can still get the old diehards on the County Boards – "Wrap the green flag around me, boys" – but young people today are totally gone for that sort of bunkum. It is bunkum, and every intelligent young person realizes that. It's totally wrong when you tell someone he has to play hurley, but he can't play soccer. Now that the ban has gone for a number of years, you can see that it has made a difference. Lots of people thought that everyone would play rugby instead of Gaelic games, but in fact that hasn't been the case, and I think hurling is stronger than ever before. If you ask me, I think that if there is still a ban, it comes from the other side, which is, a matter for themselves, of course. I have known only three Protestant players, and it isn't taught in their schools.

If Gaelic Football is the more popular, hurley is recognized as being the more traditional game. There's more "dash" in it. This doesn't mean physically assaulting a man or anything like that, but putting your body into it. Like rugby, there are fifteen players on each side, but unlike rugby, you try and finish the games in the summertime. The biggest game in the year is the All Ireland Final on the first of September. I have seen twenty-five All Ireland hurley finals, and in all that time, I've never seen any violence like you see every day in soccer matches. All right, fellows might say this or that to each other, and there might be a lot of abuse going around all day, but they would end with their arms around each other. If it ever became professional, it would finish it, I would say.

As I said, I grabbed a hurley stick almost from the cradle, and I have been involved with the game ever since. They say that you reach your peak at about twenty-eight, and that may well be so, but last year I played in a sort of geriatric's team, and I am well over forty; some of my friends thought I was mad. Of course, hurley is really a young man's game, and first of all you must be courageous. If two fellows clash, you mustn't be afraid to come in close, for there is no fear of the hurley hitting a person then. There are many other skills, like sensing where the ball is going to drop, and after grabbing the ball to be on the turn, so that you are inside the other man . . . that's another of the arts.

When I was a boy we had great crowds, and they sort of uplifted you. After a game everyone gathered around, and gave you a slap on the back, and you felt great. Now of course there is television. A Captain hasn't a big part in Gaelic games, and he is usually looked upon as the fellow who takes the "cups", and that's all. You'll find a popular fellow is usually appointed as captain. For a local club there are three selectors and you might be put on the county team, or you could be dropped after a few weeks. Some fellows become "stars" at eighteen, and I've seen it happen, while others might take another five years to mature. But whether you become a "star" or not, you get to know many people, and even today I can salute them in the street. Of course if you do well, it won't harm you, and it's the same with any sport. I know a good few reps around Cappaghglass who got their position through being good at hurley. If they are not still gods, they are looked up to. "I know him", if you like.

Soccer is taking over a bit from Gaelic football, but I think hurley will always hold its own. Any kid of four or five can boot the ball along the ground, while something like hurley is a much more skilled and difficult game to teach. I've always thought that there is something distinctly Irish about it, and it's a funny thing that unlike so many other games, it doesn't transplant at all. They played it in New York, but it was really only a ghetto game, and even in England it's dying out because there is no emigration. I teach it and coach it after school sometimes. While soccer is the game of the future, I think hurley will hold its own in rural Ireland almost like religion. I suppose that's an opinion that reflects a bit my father's talk of English officers playing rugby. But I happen to believe that by playing hurley you are demonstrating that you are Irish. I wouldn't say it in public.'

Donal Magrath, Harness Racer. Aged 42.

The meeting was held in a field a few miles from the town. Trailers and cars spun in the mud and the smell of chips from the mobile stall hung over the gathering which was dominated by men in crumpled hats holding sticks. The cold March day was blustery with wind. Some travelling men ran a small merry-go-round in the field. The scene was like an early picture by Jack Yeats.

The first race, diminutive boys clinging to saddles, came unexpectedly over a furze hedge. Then came the turn of the harness horses and the sulkies which was the main event. Eight or nine prancing around the field to the blare of music and shouts from the two bookmakers. Donal was one of the jockeys. He told me afterwards how his first horse was used by his father for ploughing. In the evening after it had been brought in he would take off its harness and trot or gallop it around a field, jumping it at obstacles. When he was sixteen his father bought him a 'Dublin mare', and from that time horses had been his passion. He also races greyhounds; there is not a week when his horses – and his dogs are not competing in some event.

He and his family live in Cappaghglass, but the country is beside them, the fields coming down almost to the main street. From the front his shop presents a conventional image with its large plate glass window and the shelves inside stocked with merchandize. But when you open the back door and walk into the yard, you are in a different world. Half a dozen dogs jump on top of you and there are so many stabled horses. From the street to the yard may be twenty yards, and behind the yard again fields stretch down below the line of scraggy hills.

★

'They all drive fair like, and there is no such thing as holding a horse, or driving a horse to suit bookies, because if you started doing that you could be fined. And they don't pull across each other. There is a great skill in driving, but the weight or the age of the driver doesn't count in harness racing. A friend of mine is over seventy years of age, and he's just as good as ever.

The first race is on New Year's Day, and it goes on most of the year around. In winter the road racing or saddle racing is more popular. At a meeting everyone has a colour, a helmet and a number. There is no weighing in and you get big fellas driving cars.

I still drive myself. I go once or twice a week whenever the races be coming up. The most important thing for any good driver is to know the feel of the rein, and just let him at it if you are able to. You can give him the whip in a sulky, and there is no bother at all about it, but you must also know the type of horse and what it will do. If you are driving a horse, and there is a horse ahead of you, the horse in front must do a harder pace. You might have a horse that might like to take the lead from the start, or you might have a horse that would come in from the back, and you just let him at it. I had one horse that I bred myself and he ran seventeen races, and out of the seventeen he won fifteen.

I breed them and sell them. There's the occasional horse fair here, but that's mainly for hunting horses or free jumpers. Mostly pacing horses are sold by the ear, and not in the sale, and you have a fair idea of what he might be worth. The best horse I ever had won £200 in prize money last year, and you can see his trophy. Mostly prize money isn't much, not even enough to run the car. You might win two hundred pounds for a first and fifty for a second, and that's only the petrol home. But I don't do it for the money. It's really the sport of winning and having a good race.'

John Corcoran, Huntsman and Kennelman. Aged 46.

John is not a native of Cappaghglass, but he is visiting his wife's people who live in the town. He doesn't think much of this area because it no longer has a hunt. He has always worked with horses, buying, breaking or hunting them – the hunt is the thing. During winter, Wednesdays and Saturdays are sacrosanct.

His small farm in a good hunting area about thirty miles away is dominated by the horse – the actual farming comes a weak second in his activities. He has been known to leave a cattle sale abruptly rather than miss a meet. The farmyard seems little more than a haggard full of horses which he is in the process of training, the only money that seems to come in regularly is from helping his friend, the Master, in what they both call The Sport. Help includes being a kennel man and whipper.

★

'Plenty of farmers have a mare and a foal and they break the horse and then hunt him. It's always been like that with me, to have horses and make them, hunt them and sell them, and aren't we a selling nation before anything else? Usually I break a horse in September and hunt him in the opening meet on the last Saturday in October or the first Saturday in November. Then I would keep the horse to hunt for the winter, unless I get a lot of profit out of him.

I used to buy horses cheaply. The first my father bought me cost £25 and we sold him for £175 after a season's hunting. Today you would pay £1000 for a young horse that's not made, and for a good hunter you would pay around £3000. A friend of mine hunted a horse last year with the fox hounds and got £6000 for him, but he's a show horse and a hunter all combined in one animal; he would make a three day event horse more than likely. The market is still good for the right article, and that's like everything else; if you buy the right horse you will make a lot of money.

For me fox hunting has always been the best; you watch the hounds seek her out and look for the fox and they find the scent and "Tally Ho" him away. Then the huntsman blows his horn and the hounds come out of cover and open up, and the music of them is excellent. And the horse under you will begin to shiver with excitement to get going.

I will be out hunting every Wednesday and Saturday during the season. I think the main job with the Master is to be very nice to everyone and even the tinkers down the road. He always stops to chat with them which means he knows everyone and everyone knows him. And that's only good manners. I started off with him as a groom, if you like, and over the years became a kennelman and a whip. I have always found it interesting and rewarding work, and I suppose that sort of thing is born in you.

I don't see any argument for these anti-blood sports people. The only animal I wouldn't like to hunt is the deer because I feel sorry for him. As for fox hunting, I don't see any cruelty in it at all. Would you sooner be in a country where you knew every fence and perhaps had to run for your life a couple of times a year, or be poisoned or shot? The other thing they don't raise any fuss about is snaring, and that's an awful game. I had a dog caught in a snare, and I think that's a most brutal sport. The amount of foxes that can be killed hunting, especially in close country, is minimal.

When you are working for a hunt it means a sort of dedication; you wouldn't want to be doing it unless you really enjoyed yourself. At the start of the season you have to take out the hounds and keep them fit. We have twelve couple at least, which is twenty-four hounds, and there might be some pups in the yard of six months old. One of my jobs is to go around and collect meat from the farmers – it could be an old horse that has been put down, a diseased cow or sheep that no one wants, and I will have to skin them so that the hounds will get their raw meat with their bread. Mostly it is free and we don't have to buy anything.

Working with hounds takes a lot of your time, for every one is different and has a character in itself. You remember their names when you see them. It's like meeting somebody at a show that you haven't seen for a long time, and you only remember the person's name when you see them. We started off with names like Ginger and Spot until the Master thought of giving them the names of politicians he disliked. We have had almost the whole Dail at one time or another. I remember the leader of the Opposition some years back was a particular brute. In any pack there is usually a rogue dog that will get killed. Usually he is a growly sort of dog, with the hair going up on him and looking for a fight until his luck runs out. One day you will hear a battle going up in the main yard, and you run, but mostly you are too late.

The hunting round our place is very varied, so that a horse that hunts with us would be able to hunt anywhere. We have everything from a fly hedge, post and rails, a stone wall to a bank. We get to hunt most of the winter – this part of the country is mild most of the time. We have to stop now and then when there is snow or a hard frost. The best day for hunting foxes, and even a drag, is wet windy weather, which you might think would be the worst.

Last year the Master had to restrict the field and cut down the subscriptions because he felt that the hunt was getting too big. Now we have a waiting list of people who want to get on. You might think that the membership fee of £85 might stop people, but there aren't any poor lads around when it comes to hunting. What has happened is that we are getting a new generation of town and city riders who come out to hunt. A lot of people start hunting after going to some riding school without having a clue about it. They haven't an idea of how to behave in the field and how to ride with hounds. And now that everyone has a horsebox, and hacking is a thing of the past, there is also a lot more drinking. More than often they start at some public house, and also finish at one.

In any hunt you have a lot of strict rules to follow, but now no one takes any heed of them, and they don't know what you are talking about. A simple one is "Hold hard". You must put up your hand and shout it out, and the people in the back are supposed to stop to allow the huntsman to work the hounds. With a big field, and even with a field master to help, no one can see what's happening. The first lot of horses might be four fields away, and then there would be others behind them and a few others lost. A rider would always walk around the headland of a field and not cut across it. Sometimes a person misses the other horses, and goes across the middle of it, straight into the hounds. They catch hold of the saddle and away they go. The Master will shout and bellow and go mad, and he'll find a few others will be following him and there is no way to get them to stop. Sometimes it's very funny.'

Jeremiah Kearns, Field Naturalist. Aged 82.

He hasn't been well, and now has to get used to the idea of immobility. He's always been a restless man, hating to be confined after years of exploring the area. His family have been here for generations, and he knows every inch, he says – the best place from where to watch fulmars gliding, a shelf of rock hiding a rare plant, foxes holes, badger sets. For most of his life nature has seemed inexhaustible, and in between farming, he has observed it obsessively. But things are changing for the worse, and he has seen much destruction of the things he has loved. However, nature has a pretty big apron, and old men like himself have always been filled with regret for what has gone.

★

'I think it was because my family have always been farmers that we always had a great interest in nature. My father was a great bird man, and when I was a boy I soon knew every bird in the Irish list. I think we had three times as many birds as we have today, and the same with fish and everything, and I just don't know exactly what the cause of their decline is.

There were wheatears in rough ground, and corncrakes were also very common. They never nested in corn, so why they were called corncrakes I could never understand. They would insist on nesting in the hayfield, which meant that very often when the hay was cut, their nests would be destroyed if it was early. That was one of the reasons they can't nest here anymore, for the farmers are out now for silage in the last week of April and the first week of May, and that's when they were always nesting.

I remember a lot more game about. One of our pleasures as children was to go out hunting. I used to shoot a good deal of snipe and woodcock, and perhaps on Sunday morning we would take a couple of dogs to chase the rabbits or hares. We rarely caught them, and anyway we didn't want to catch them for the trouble of bringing them home. The great thing for us was finding them and giving them a fair run.

One of our problems was that we were never taught to use our eyes. A subject like biology was regarded as taboo, for to teach biology you must also teach sex. And so they were both out. But of course this didn't stop us learning. The big difference today is that people will help you. That's one of the reasons that when someone says to me "I wish I had learnt it in my young days at school" I try and explain as best as I can.

In the old days there was no such thing as ornithologists coming down here, and if one had turned up people would have thought him a bit screwy. But my own family was a little different – whether it was a bird or a wild flower or a butterfly, my father always took a great interest.

One of my early memories is going out with him in his yawl to do some fishing. There would be shoals of fish everywhere and we would meet flocks of razor bills and guillemots in big clusters catching the bait. The rocks would also be covered with these birds laying their eggs on the edges. And gulls nesting – once I saw a punt leaving one of the islands with two men in it, and there were hardly room for themselves in it, for it was so filled up with gulls eggs. I have eaten them myself; they are all right if you get them fresh and don't boil them, because you might have half a chicken inside. I believe some people eat puffins and gannets as well, and of course those old French sailors would eat any old thing so long as it moved. Their stomachs must have been like lead.

The first thing you must have for observing wild life is untold patience . . . Oh Lord yes . . . and also an inquisitive mind and a knack for observation. You can't be taught that, and over the years you just pick it up. Take myself. When I am out in the country I never look where I am going, and it must be a thousand times I was lucky enough not to be killed by a car. You have got to be able to use your eyes and concentrate on some bank or hedge. If I see something like a caterpillar, I stop to look at it, so of course some people think I am mad poking about at the bottom of a hedge. It's the enormous variety in nature that always interests me, and I could never be one of those specialists who are only interested in one particular thing. I put down my attitude years ago to just walking round the farm.

If you are looking for seabirds, or migrants like warblers, and that sort of thing, the early morning is the best time. I love the seabirds; I can sit for hours on a clifftop and watch the gannets diving or the fulmars gliding up on a cliff and you are thinking they are going to crash, and "whish", he's over the top without an obvious wing beat, and I think that's marvellous. One of my particular hobbies is watching the migrations. After a while you learn how to count the numbers of birds more or less, so that you can say "That's a hundred fulmars" or "There goes a hundred and fifty shearwaters". Some people use counter things, but I found my thumb was going all the time.

I like to think of myself as what they now call a field naturalist. That means I know a little of everything and am probably also a master of nothing. When young people down here ask me about something, I always try and help them as best as I can, and this gives me the greatest pleasure. I don't know why it is, but I find people who are interested in nature somehow much more genuine and you won't find lads being rowdy or vandalistic shall I say? One boy I was teaching became an expert on marine life, and another got interested in butterflies and is now a recognized authority on them.

Although I am not much of a botanist I have also always been interested in wild flowers. This isn't much of an area for rarities, but you find the odd rare flower like one little species of helianthemum on the Western headland, and there is one patch of an autumn flowering orchid which I think is unique in Ireland. I am more interested in the commoner miracles – to me it is extraordinary that you can bring a plant from one country to another, and in completely new surroundings it will grow more vigorously than at home. Around Cappaghglass there is that garlic with the triangular stem which people think is a form of white bluebell. When I first saw it I thought I had discovered a rare new plant, but now it's everywhere. Then there is the Australian dock and the wretched Japanese knotweed which is the devil altogether. My mother was actually given a present of it and it spread and spread. Fuchsia is also extraordinary in the way it spreads. It never seeds itself, it blossoms beautifully, but never produces a seed. Perhaps never is not correct, for once or twice it will, in a very beautiful year. But generally it spreads by roots, and of course people plant it all over the place.

You can say the plants are holding their own, but it's sad to me how the wild creatures are going. There are a lot less hares, and I'm sure one of the reasons is the way they are trapped for coursing. And because rivers get polluted and the amount of fish gets less you see a lot less otters. That little river below Ballybrack that dries out at low tide leaving a little stream in the mud – you often used to catch sight of otters beside it on the mud flats looking for trapped fish. I haven't seen one for years.

And the birds. When I went down in the fields in the old days I might see thirty kestrels, and now they are rare. I spoke about the corncrake, it's gone like the dodo. Come to think of it, with its bottle-shaped figure it looked a little like the dodo – you could have it for a symbol of what's happening. The lark and the yellow hammer and the green finch and a lot of other birds like yellow pipits that live in the field seem to be vanishing. It's a change in growing patterns of course. The farmers have got so expert in growing grass, and there are no dandelions or the weeds that sheltered field mice and other things. Now you see nothing but truncated hedges and pure grass. You suddenly wake up to it one morning, and realize how there aren't many birds left.'

Kitty Burke, Museum Curator. Aged 58.

A notice says MUSEUM. You approach through a dip in the hills beside fields with thick hedges and down a rough lane to a whitewashed tiled cottage which has a view of the sea. Outside the door is a pile of odd shaped stones and a couple of round quern stones. You pull the little bell rope for Kitty to let you in. Inside are piles of objects crowded around the parlour and kitchen. You notice an old-fashioned bellows, a rushlight holder, a cannon ball. Upstairs more little rooms are bursting with everyday treasures – pieces of lace, shawls, old dresses and other things Kitty has rescued.

Her collection has been gathered from all over her farm, and she values it for the light it sheds on the past. She remembers with affection the old farming life and the company of the old days, which is why her museum evolved. History is not something dead; wherever she turns she can see it around her house.

★

'I remember when we were children my father found some old stone with markings on it which he put into a wall he was building. On a hill farm like this there are always mounds of stones, but that was the first time I became interested in where they came from. From that time on I had my eyes open. Once I counted fourteen foundations of houses in the fields on this farm, and I am sure there are a lot more underground.

When I was a child so much of the old life still survived. Like the man reaping away with a scythe and making a lovely sound with the swish of his blade. I used to lie down on the ground and watch him for hours. I can remember going to the well for a gallon of water. Now it comes in pipes, which is an improvement, but not so interesting. My father used to work a horse threshing machine, and one of my earliest memories is sitting on the shaft and the horses going around and around. There were so many small jobs that always had to be done, like fetching water, filling the oil lamp, trimming the wick, cleaning a glass globe and pumping the Tilley. When my mother had a free moment she would make clothes for us, or do crochet – there's a skill that has gone. We were much more together, and people would talk about simple things. Now they have more money, and the old family life has gone.

I suppose it was a sense of tradition and continuity between one generation and the next that got me interested in history. My father kept these old books, and would never destroy anything, but would always put them away. He told us we were descendants of ancient Irish kings, and this made us very proud. I learnt Irish at school, of course, which was very useful. Most of our fields and places are still called in the old way, although no one speaks the language any more. There's a path that the old people called *cúm na gcathair* or the path of the stone settlement. There's a kileen, and a hill called *carraig na ngabha*, the hill of the blacksmiths, where we were told they had lived. We also have a "chamber" field; my mother always used to say that old ruins are buried under it. I don't know if she was right, but I do know that from a child I grew up with this sense of history being all around me.

Old buildings, old stones and stories of long ago took hold of my imagination so that many of our neighbours used to say that I was "stone mad." I used to bring back things to my father, and we would sit down looking at them and wondering what they could have been. But he was also superstitious, and if we found anything like a stone axe or a hammer, he would always put it back where it came from. I suppose all this gave me an idea of starting a museum one day for all the bits and pieces that were lying around open to the world. What made me do it was the fact that people had lived and worked in and around our little farm since bronze age and stone age times, and it was the thought of all these people that made it seem very exciting. I mean, here was this small place that had seen all these changes, while I, myself, had seen the last of them with the disappearance of the horse. That's why I begin with the stone age and end with the horse and plough.

When I opened this place six years ago, I made it a point not to buy anything. Everything you see comes from the farm or from the immediate neighbourhood. I hate any commercialism, and it was an odyssey of love, if you can call it that, to rescue and preserve the ordinary things of life that would otherwise be forgotten. That's my idea, anyway.

I suppose you might think that everything is a bit of a jumble. I don't like cataloguing things too much, but prefer to leave them by. If I find something like a flintstone scraper, I leave the bits of earth on it as I picked it out from the soil, not cleaning it too much. I think that spoils the effect it makes. I have things like quern stones, a broken metal torque, plenty of axe heads, a piece of an eleventh century plough, bits of pottery and so on. The best time for finding things is in the winter, when the land is clear and there are no weeds.

I used to be able to divine for water, and later on I got this knack of finding metal; many other diviners can do the same. It's a sort of headache. By walking in the direction, the needles are pointing in my forehead, and I can find bits of metal hidden under the ground. Now I wait for them to start, and I know that iron is there and where to find it. I have collected old fish hooks, spades, an eighteenth century pike, and seaweed hackers. The cannonball came from near the old castle on the rocks which was besieged long ago. The furze cutting machine was in use not so long ago. The famine pot I discovered on the bottom of a well.

The other things I have are all these household domestic articles which I found in the house. Either my family has always been very poor, or they hated throwing things away. When my father and mother died, I found a whole lot of old boxes that were bursting with clothes and everything. Here is a piece of lace made by the nuns at Curragheen, a bit of "frize" and a ball of linen cloth that I found in a cupboard. Look at the jet beads and the tortoise-shell comb. And I have some greeting to my grandmother sewn on silk. There's kitchen things, of course, butter churns, an earthenware bowl for skimming milk, rushlight holders, candle snuffers, pot ovens, all sorts.

I enjoy histories, and although I respect all nationalities, I also think that to be Irish is best. I know we had those wonderful monks and holy men that gave us the Ardagh Chalice and the Book of Kells, but we also had the ordinary people who lived and worked on this farm for all those years. Sometimes I feel that these people are very close to me, and I touch the same stones and tools that they used, or walk down to the standing stone which the cattle still scratch their backs against, and only half a mile away is the fairy ring with its banks and moat where the children pick blackberries.'

EMIGRANTS

PATRICK EGAN   Returned Emigrant, *Aged 72*
JOHN GOOD   Prospective Emigrant to Australia, *Aged 23*

In relation to their own families farmers thought that emigration was a satisfactory solution to the problem of clearing the house and believed that job opportunities would always be in the more urban areas . . . Strangely the majority of farmers thought that there was no future in farming and that it was not a secure or rewarding occupation. In their opinion, only one boy or girl who was not capable of doing anything else would choose to remain on the land.

Limerick Rural Survey, 1956.
Edited J. Newman.

> I'm bidding farewell to the land of my youth
> And the house I love so well
> And the mountains so grand in my own native land
> I am bidding them all farewell,
> With an aching heart I'll bid them adieu
> For tomorrow I'll sail away
> O'er the raging foam for to seek a home
> On the shores of Amerikay.
>
> *The Shores of Amerikay.*

Patrick Egan, Returned Emigrant. Aged 72.

As the youngest of a fatherless family Patrick didn't have an easy start. His childhood was hard, his youth was hard and America beckoned. Although he arrived in New York in the year of the Depression he prospered. He married an Irish girl and brought up a family of three girls. He often thought of Cappaghglass, the green fields and the sea. 'I tell you, no matter how long you are away you would always like to come back. Oh God, you would.'

When his wife died and his children had grown up, Ireland re-claimed him. Today he lives in a modern centrally-heated bungalow overlooking the village and the sea. It contains a deep-freeze and he has a trap in the garage to remind him of his love for horses. Why did he return? 'I love it here.' He won't say a bad word about the States, but feels that it's no place to die in. 'There's pressure, pressure all the time and I can't eat.'

Arthritis makes him hobble as he gets up to serve you American coffee out of a tin, 'not like the water they sell in this country'. He has a Bronx accent and says 'I guess' a lot. He likes brightly coloured shirts and enjoys meeting people. He sees regularly a few old friends from the distant past, survivors, and they talk about Cappaghglass fifty and sixty years ago. On his sideboard are photographs – himself in miner's rig and helmet, his daughter in graduation gown and cap standing beside a swimming pool. An old Cunard liner with smoke belching from her funnels.

★

'I was born in December 1912. There were six in the family, four boys and two girls, Johnny, Jim, Charlie, myself, Mary and Sheila. I was the youngest. My father died when I was a small child.

I often think how hard it must have been raising such a large family on nothing at all. My mother used to go scrubbing and washing floors at one shilling and sixpence a day, and of course there was never any money. Sometimes a man would give us a little fish on the pier which we used to bring back and that would be a treat. Neighbours were always kindly and there was hardly a day without some person coming to our house with something.

No one had any education then. I didn't like school at all, for the Master used to kill me. He would hit me with a form over the knuckles and you'd see stars. There must have been ninety-five children going to that school. After we got out we used to help our mother picking up sticks for the fire, for every house had a fire. I used to get them in a little brake and pull them with a bit of ropeen, and sure, a crow would bring in more.

Later on I became mad for horses, for there were horses everywhere at that time. I learnt to break and ride them and I'd drive them to fairs and sell them for a man. He gave me a little money for that. But the only job you could get was breaking stones for the road. They had to be screened through a wire mesh, you know, before the steam rollers came in. When that bit of road was finished there would be no job.

I was the youngest in the family and hadn't thought of emigrating. There was no one in the small house except myself and my mother. But there were no jobs and the chance came to get a ticket. It cost twenty pounds and that money was provided by my sister Mary who sent the money from New York.

I can remember the day I left very well. It was Saturday the 16th of August 1929, the day after the Fair. A few of my friends came to see me off. There was also a girl from Cappaghglass going the same way. I went out on the Franconia, the Cunard Line ship, and it was grand, to tell you the truth. We left Cobh in County Cork and she was packed with Irish from all over the country. It was the last time the Irish could travel like that before the restrictions on emigrating came in. It was all dancing, eating and drinking, but some of them were so seasick they couldn't eat at all. So I had everything on the table. I wasn't used to so much food at the time, but it seemed very good. I didn't see many families go. They were mainly single men and girls, and like me without any trade or qualifications. Whatever job you would find you would have to take.

The journey took us about a week and when we got there everyone separated. Many were going to Cleveland, some to Boston and Buffalo and the devil knows where. I never saw them again, not even the girl from Cappaghglass. My sister and my brother met me in New York and I got lodgings with an Irish couple who ran a boarding house. The man was one of the first men to take a horse over Brooklyn Bridge. You would get a lot of Irish dishes, the very same thing.

Potatoes, meat and cabbage, carrots and parsnips and pigs' feet too. Oh God, yes. I had good teeth, not like now.

The first time I made money I sent a pound back to my mother. A pound at that time was a lot of money. It was five dollars or something. But it came back again because there was no one to claim it. She was dead. I guess that settled me from wanting to return home.

Work was very scarce and the labouring man was regarded as nothing. And it got worse during the years of the Depression. But I was never out of work, for I don't give a damn what job I'm doing. I would prefer to work for ten dollars a week rather than to stay idle. My first job was with the Metropolitain Engineering Company in Atlantic Avenue. The money was cheap and there was always the lay-off. It was my first experience of living in a city. In Cappaghglass there had been no electric light or water and only a few cars, and it took time to adjust. The lights of Broadway dazzled me. There was the green light to go ahead, the red to stop and you wouldn't have a notion. You would get killed like a flash.

I liked New York, to tell you God's truth. I played football on Saturday and Sunday and the people were grand. The different races never bothered me. I was working with a coloured man and he told me that he would never work with the Italians, but only with the Irish. The only thing I didn't like was the climate. Those hot New York summers when if you stopped working for five minutes you would stick on the pavements with the tar. And in the winter it would get so cold. I remember catching a crowbar and I couldn't let it go for the cold. It burnt my hands to the bone.

The best job I ever got was with horses, for it was all horses at that time. I was staying with my sister, and one day she said there was a man looking for me. He was superintendent of a large dairy. I'll never forget him, a big rough foxy man. He said, "Egan, what can you do?" I said that I could do a lot of things, but my main interest was with horses. He said, "Have you a dollar?" I said, "I have not, sir – bad times." And that was the truth. So he gave me the dollar to pass the doctor and I was very lucky. What charm I had, I still don't know. It was my first good job, taking care of horses and feeding them from a large box full of crushed oats. All the milk went out on horse wagons then. After waking up I used to get the horses ready at two or three in the morning, and I'd watch them plodding round the streets of New York. I think your first good job is always important, for it sets you on your feet.

Later I must have changed jobs a hundred times. I worked on

buildings, I worked for the Utility Company, and even took a job as a miner for a short time. Most of the time we lived in a flat in New York, and when I married I brought up my family there. My main interest was always walking around. My kids would say, "Dad, is there something wrong with you to be walking around like that?" I put it down to my rural background and always thinking about home, for you always have strange thoughts in your head. America is a bad place to grow old in, they don't give a damn.

I had been in the US for more than thirty years before I thought of coming home. My brother Charlie had gone to England, and then he came back, and took over the old home. Now he died, and I went back. They knew I was coming, but didn't know what time, so there was nobody in the house but my niece who I had never seen. I just walked in. It was raining like the devil, and the main street in Cappaghglass seemed so narrow and everything so quiet.

That's how I came home. Eventually I bought this house. The worst thing about this country is the climate. It's damp all right, and I have arthritis. If there was a man who could cure that he would be a millionaire. Any man that does heavy work will show it when he gets on in years. When I came home here, now, I got a kind of rash on my skin. I went to Brendan Hurley – do you know him? Christ, a grand man and a grand doctor. Now he said to me, "Paddy, what's the matter?" "I don't know what's the matter. If I did I wouldn't go to you." Did he laugh – honest to God. "Do you know what you have? Arthritis," he said. "And it's in the blood. Sweat brings it out."

I don't go near whiskey or rum or brandy or any one of them. Guinness would kill me and my poor head would burst open. I have blood pressure as well, you know. I take pills for my arthritis, but they are not much good to me, especially on a foggy mucky old day. I get as sore as the devil in my joints and knees. I used to go to town once a month, but since this damn thing hit me I don't go there at all. I still see a few people from the old days and we talk about old times. If it weren't for the arthritis – I guess it will stay with me till I go down six by two.

Occasionally my family comes over and visits me. They don't understand why I wish to bury myself in Cappaghglass.'

John Good, Prospective Emigrant. Aged 23.

John wouldn't leave if there was a job available here. However, he is looking forward to joining his brother in Australia. He has already paid a short visit there, and what he saw makes him determined to go again. He thinks Australia is a country geared for young people where there are great opportunities for anyone who wants to advance himself.

He is a good-looking young man with flaxen hair and blue eyes. He likes engines and mechanical things; after leaving school he tried unsuccessfully to start his own small business. In spite of the greater prosperity and the higher education Cappaghglass cannot offer him a job. Next month he will be flying into the sun, leaving the grey town. He plans to review his situation in four or five years. His decision to stay permanently in Australia will depend on such ponderables as a good job and maybe marriage.

His family supports his decision to leave and everyone regards him as a privileged person. Many are called, but few are chosen by the Australian Department of Emigration. They expect to see him often; air travel forges easy links.

★

'Today it is very hard to emigrate from Ireland, because no one will have you except England. It's almost impossible. When my brother got married in Australia I applied for a visa and they refused me. Then I re-applied for a six months visa and only when the plane was about to go, I got one for two months.

I think that changed my life. It was the different life-style and being so much outdoors, the climate and everything. There were also much better jobs. Of course I would have preferred to stay in Ireland if I could advance, but there's no opportunity for that. Many of my friends who left school with me are still without jobs, and even if they had degrees and honours and papers, it would be the same thing. And if you start a business a lot of people just don't want any competition.

I have a permanent visa now for what they call full emigration. My friends envy me and I know I was very lucky. There is a points system before you are accepted. You get twenty-five points for having a relative over there, ten to fifteen for having a trade, and everything must add up to at least sixty. I would say that seventy per cent of people who apply don't get in.

I'm not fussy about what I do. I hope to go into the brother's business, for he's settled down now and married. You have to have the attitude of making a go at things and sticking it out for at least five years. I met an Irish fellow who would have given anything to come back after only a year, but I thought that was the wrong attitude.

A ticket there costs six hundred pounds return depending on the season. When I get there it will be the middle of their summer and I imagine it will be very hot. People make three or four hundred dollars a week and the standard of living is much higher than here. They have lovely houses too. Once I looked at Australia on the atlas, but never dreamed I would be going there. They talk about Irish scenery, but there's nothing the equal of the Barrier Reef and the desert. Its really a marvellous country and you could fit Ireland into it and you wouldn't even see it.'

MEDICINE

DR BRENDAN HURLEY	General Practitioner, *Aged 48*
EILEEN O'HEHIR	District Nurse, *Aged 56*
COLM CARROLL	Faith Healer, *Aged 48*
TOM O'BRIEN	Bone Setter, *Aged 45*
JIM SLATTERY	Vet, *Aged 32*

It is recorded in several writings that Josina the ninth king of Scotland was sent by his parents to Ireland to be educated among the physicians and surgeons there. These early physicians were not only well versed in the theory of their art, they also possessed the attribute of common sense so essential to success in medicine.

Dr Brendan Hurley, General Practitioner. Aged 48.

Dr Hurley lives in a solid two-storeyed house on the outskirts of Cappaghglass. You don't have to see the brass plate to recognize that this sort of place must belong to a doctor or bank manager or a similar steady professional man. The large garden has raked gravel paths and some wind-blown palm trees. A child opens the frosted pane front door and announces. 'He's out on call.' Behind her you can hear the telephone ringing.

Dr Hurley's medical parish, which he shares with one colleague, stretches over a hundred square miles of hills and mountains into some of the roughest and most isolated parts of the country. His red diesel Golf is a familiar sight. It may be seen driving up a boreen in first gear in winter-time to a lonely farm house. 'How's he keeping?' 'Much better after what you gave him the last time.' Arthritis or the spring flu is alleviated. The visit takes a short time, but there is the cup of tea and a chat before he leaves. Another long road, bad visibility and eight more miles before he returns home for a quick tea and then down to the clinic.

The daily clinic and the constant commitment of keeping in touch with the nearest hospital forty miles away increases his work load. He steals time for the occasional game of golf or fishing trip. In spite of all, he enjoys his work and wouldn't change.

★

'I was born in a small village which is why I like living here. Most of the city doctors who come to this part of the world go bonkers. I've seen this happen time and time again. They practise beautiful medicine, but in six months ninety per cent of them are raring to get out. The young lads who do a "loco" here will treat a disease better than I can, but they will forget the impact of the disease on the family or on some old person in the house.

In any rural situation you have to wait and see – you can't put your finger on it in five minutes. You have to know that Johnny is related to so and so, and who was the grandmother and the aunt, and it all takes a long time. Very often if you go to someone with flu or a pain or something, and you don't bother to spend enough time with them, you'll find out the pain isn't the real reason why you are called out. There's some other problem.

The days of the single-handed practitioner are numbered. The old boys who worked here before me were not only doctors, but father confessors and everything else. I'd say they didn't charge ninety per cent of their patients, and that was in the days before any free medicine. It was not only a job, but a vocation, and maybe this indoctrination has passed over to some of the current rural GP's. But it isn't going to last. The new generation of doctors isn't willing to give their whole three hundred and sixty-five days of the year completely to their job. They want more family life and more free time.

I work under contract to the Health Board. Theoretically I'm off from one o'clock on Friday until nine on Saturday, and I'm off again on Sunday to midnight, and that's my short week. And of course you can be on call at any time during the night or day. One of the other problems is the amount of paperwork and the way the State makes us do the gathering for them. That's the sort of work they should get accountants to do, but they don't, so that we are almost like unpaid Civil Servants.

My colleagues who work in city or urban areas think I'm mad. They are used to a casualty station sitting around the corner or some hospital within reach where you can send acute cases at once. Their work is almost all in group practices. Their patients come in mostly to see them, unless it's something serious.

Here it's quite the opposite. We have a small ageing population scattered over an enormous area. That means you go out all the time on visits. Last month a friend of mine who works in England came over to see me, and I asked him what he would do if he was called out at eleven o'clock at night to an island where a woman had developed some obstetric complication. He said he would retire – and he put it a lot more fluently than that. He just could not believe that this would happen. Although he has a country practice in England, his nearest general hospital is six miles away and he has helicopter cover all the time.

I have responsibility for many things which are taken for granted in big towns and cities. Another friend stuck his head into the surgery and saw me bottling up blood. He couldn't see why I didn't send the patient to the hospital for a blood test until I told him that the nearest regional lab is seventy miles away.

A doctor like me must be dedicated. I know that sounds an old-fashioned word, but you must accept the fact that it's a very inconvenient life. I don't agree at all with nurses going on strike. I once had a locum down here who insisted on being paid six pounds before he'd even visit a patient. That made me feel sick. I believe it was nothing short of criminal, and we are here to help people. When I worked in voluntary hospitals, I was always impressed by the way people stuck to their job. You'd see it in small things like the matron taking the trouble every day to talk to each patient and ask them how they were. People appreciate things like that.

Around Cappaghglass we have the exact opposite of a city practice. In cities they have a zooming young population of under twenty-fives, but here most of the people are on the wrong side of sixty-five. If you ask me I would call it a geriatric practice. It means a different type of medicine. I have two health nurses who go around to old people, who are really our eyes and ears. Every Tuesday morning we have a meeting and go over our respective lists, and I have a list of calls a month ahead.

There are many problems with old people apart from the purely medical ones. Someone living alone is more likely to become ill and depressed than someone who lives in a sheltered environment without stress and without loneliness. And when they are wandering, senile, and not orientated for time and place they need special geriatric care.

Of course you know Ireland has one of the highest rates of schizophrenia in the world. I blame much of this on three things – clerical celibacy, enforced celibacy and enforced isolation. Behind it all there's the good Christian tradition of keeping things going. You have the situation where an unbending set of religious values is forced down people's throats.

Take the man who is living out in the back of beyond and had a bad thought that he was committing a sin. Or perhaps he went to Dublin for a weekend, and he's damned for ever more, and there's a mission every couple of years to remind him that he is damned. All that has had a most ferocious impact on mental illnesses. Then there's the policy of keeping old people in rural areas. Think of living seven miles from the nearest village with your crochety sister. That sort of situation won't help along your clinical depression.

There's a culture of its own in looking after old people. It's not so much prescriptions or things like Meals on Wheels, but also just going in and working out what the problems are. Sometimes it's not so easy, and you have to be so careful. Take, for instance, a newcomer from a completely different environment who's doing her best to be kind. And they come in and bring an apple tart or something. They are trying to be helpful, but what they are doing can also be taken as a desperate insult. Old people have this hatred of charity, and this is a tradition that comes right back to famine times. I would advise any newcomer to talk to a person for maybe a year rather than this "overhelp" to a next door neighbour. Retiring English people, people fleeing from city life, they are the ones that make these sort of mistakes a lot, through the best intentions.

Things have changed admittedly, but in the old days most doctors used to be Protestants, and people felt they didn't want to be under any obligation to what was then called the Ascendancy. Old people bore their illnesses more stoically, and a person was absolutely dying before the doctor was called in. They were afraid that the neighbours would hear of it, and there was this feeling of shame. So a lot of herbs and a spot of poteen was tried first of all. Modern medicine and the use of antibiotics which can make such a dramatic improvement in an illness has given people different attitudes.

In future an increasing number of people will end their days in hospitals and homes, in spite of the fact no one wants to. There's still a tradition of caring for the old, and many of the younger people are superb. I've seen young wives who'll put their backs to the wall rather than see the old ones moved unless it's medically necessary. But times are changing, people like that are becoming fewer, and less and less are available to look after the old. The rush and bustle of modern life just isn't leaving the time. So what happens? More and more are being sent to these places, and although lots of us feel guilty about it, we seem to have no choice.

In the old days under the dispensary system the doctor was given a district to look after. The pace of life was much slower. Now people have cars and are a great deal more mobile, and only if they can't come in do they send for the doctor. We hardly ever have a house call to see a baby nowadays – they wrap them in a blanket and bring them to the clinic. It's the old people that account for all the travelling.

I like to feel that people regard me as a friend and that they can call me at any time of day or night. I always carry intravenous stuff and a full range of drugs and Interdox, which is an anaesthetic thing. I may not be very civil at four in the morning, but I think people know me well enough at this stage to say "He blew the head off me, but he is coming." On Fridays, which is my half day, I often go fishing, but even then people know where I am.

I think all medicine should be free, but not like the NHS in England, which has turned everything into a paper mountain. The majority of my patients have a medical card, and there is a means test, but they change the regulations every bloody week. The only advantage of paying money is if you are having some operation. Then, if you pay, the waiting list is much shorter. Apart from that, I can see no advantage, as we treat everyone the same. The service that we give them has more to do with the changes in medicine than in society. There are all the new drugs. When I first qualified all the beds were full of diphtheria patients, and now that's wiped off the earth. TB is another thing that used to be very common, and now I see only about five new cases a year.

One of the biggest changes was the establishment of the College of General Practitioners in the 'fifties. That's an organization that runs a general training scheme for doctors going to rural areas. The only drawback is that after about three months in a place like this, they return to the city and never want to come back. I suppose you can't blame them.

I've talked a lot about the indigenous old – the victims of the 'thirties and 'forties and waves of emigration, if you like. There are other categories of patients that are something quite new in a rural practice like this. I mean these new retired people. Perhaps they have got tired of the vandalism in the cities, or they have visited the area in the summertime and found it a charming place. Anyway they decide to come and spend their old age here. Unfortunately, many of them don't take into account their isolation from friends or even from something small, like the opportunity of going to a theatre or a cinema. After three long winters down here it can be quite a different thing, and I see the effect of this at my clinic. They might develop ulcers, migraines, psychosomatic things, but if you take a look at them, often all that is wrong is that they are desperately unhappy. They are missing their grandchildren and their old friends, and the strange thing is that they cannot admit that to each other. So the symptoms develop – depression, alcoholism. Many of them would be much better to up stakes and go, even if they were to lose some money.

Another new factor, and this affects young people, is the side effects of unemployment. Many of the unemployed get depressed and they start drinking, not to enjoy life, but for other reasons. Alcohol is always a problem if you look upon it as a psychiatric illness, and of course Ireland has some of the worst statistics for alcohol abuse in the

Western world. I find there is no way I can blame a boy who cycles five miles to town and gets smashed at night, because there is no possibility of him getting a job. During the summer there is more money about, and I find people are drinking younger. As a doctor I see the blunt end of this.

I mentioned to you some of the diseases that have vanished. In general people live longer and are far healthier than in our parents' day. There is less chronic illness among the young than there was twenty or thirty years ago. Because of things like psychotropic medicine they can be returned more quickly to the community. But the backlog of chronic patients who are now ageing and will need hospitals gets longer.

If housing and nutrition have improved out of all recognition, we still have heart conditions, strokes and of course, cancer. Cancer is the biggest fear without any doubt, and for the old it's *the* horror. The media push on cancer frightens old people, and they are not used to being told to look for signs of things. I think this causes a great deal more anxiety and tension. They would prefer to wait until it comes.

There's still the respect for the doctor and I find most people very appreciative of any little service I can do. To become a successful GP you have to be accepted, not only in your own field, but as a person. I think my drug bill is about twenty per cent less than average, and I put it down to the amount of time I spend talking to people. Just simply that.'

Eileen O'Hehir, District Nurse. Aged 56.

Nurse O'Hehir lives in a modern bungalow on the outskirts of the town. In her hall there is a white painted wrought iron stand with potted plants growing up to a pyramid. Her drawing-room has a brown leafy carpet with a brown draylon suite and matching brown curtains. A huge fire burns in her pearlized tile effect fireplace. She gives me a stupendous tea.

She is as familiar a figure in Cappaghglass as the doctor. Seeing the changes in the countryside during the last thirty years has taught her not to be too dogmatic in her opinions. She thinks people are more disorientated and selfish now, but yet there is a lot of good in them.

'My father employed people, which made me a real little snob. My aunt would say, "Your ancestors never emigrated and never took the soup." That made us feel better than most other people. Emigration was not a slur, exactly, but something for people who weren't well off. So when I told my mother I wanted to go to England and become a nurse she sat down and cried. Because I was the youngest daughter the onus was for me to stay. But in spite of everything there was no stopping me.

I had a happy childhood. My father brought us up with horses and one of my first memories is of taking the pony and the little round trap to school. We used to leave it with a relation and take it home again, the two or three miles, and that was a wonderful experience. We didn't learn very much at school, because there were too many scholars for one teacher, and she just hadn't the time. But then later I was sent to a boarding school under the nuns.

I loved the nuns, and didn't find that they were lesbians, like so many people say now, or that they forced religion down your throat. I knew nothing like that, and the only thing about it was that boys were taboo. We wouldn't be allowed to look at a boy when they were in the next school, and if you did you got a good thumping. We never mixed with them at all. My mother was also very strict all the time. If you saw a boy along the road you couldn't talk to him. If any girl smoked she was a tramp. The boys were ignorant like us too. And if one went off with a boy and something happened, the family was disgraced and the child would be put in a home. When I look back on these things – and they talk about other countries – I think it was terrible in Ireland when I was growing up.

My mother always used to say to us about Protestants – we called them Church of Ireland, never Protestants – "I wish you'd take a leaf out of their book", for they never misbehaved and were in time for church, while we were always late. Church was full of people dressed up, they had navy suits and red faces and after Mass everyone met and talked. We were terrified of the priest – if we met him we would run away. Nowadays, they'll say, "Hello Father, how are you?"

I was only seventeen when I went to England, and the war was on. My wages were ten shillings and I never thought I would be able to spend it. We never had big pay, but ten shillings would take you to a lot of places.

I trained at a big London hospital where we were shown how to use the gas mask and all that sort of thing, but nothing happened. Then one day there was a raid, and everybody rushed out to see the planes coming, for they weren't used to war. We just looked at them and we were all young nurses, and it was about four o'clock in the afternoon. And all of a sudden the bombs dropped. I was on a woman's ward at the time when somebody called for a drink of water. I went to the door of the kitchen, and there was just a big gaping hole. Then the electricity and everything was off, and we started moving the patients. All night they worked on them in the big casualty department. The water was cut and everything, and we had lamps rigged up for light. I think ten of the staff were killed as well as some patients. That was the start. You know, I never liked Germans. Even now when I see German tourists in Cappaghglass I have the feeling they are different and aggressive.

I must say I can't speak too highly of the ward sisters who looked after me. Indeed they have been a guiding light to me through all the years of my profession. I still think that training was the best in the world.

After the war I returned to Ireland because my mother had become ill. It was expected of me. If it wasn't for that I would have been quite happy to stay in England for the rest of my life. When I came back I did my midwifery, and after my mother died I became a district nurse.

My parish, for that's what I called it, was north and east of Cappaghglass, and consisted of about six hundred people living between the sea and the rocks. Most of them would have been classed as small farmers and fishermen making a difficult living. In those days people didn't look for material comfort. They expected nothing, and they weren't disappointed when they got nothing. They never felt hard done by. They had their own vegetables and their own cattle, and I couldn't see any real poverty. They were lovely people and all seemed very happy and industrious. It was quite a different world.

I was given an old Raleigh bicycle, and I took everything with me in a bag. If it was night time they often sent a car. I can't tell you what pleasure it gave me visiting all the different homes, mostly small farms tucked between the hills with all the poultry, pigs and cattle around the yard.

Apart from general nursing, one of my most important duties was as midwife. Most babies were still delivered at home. Of course, if the labour went on too long, the doctor would have the woman removed to the nearest hospital. Very often there were no amenities like running water, and the electricity didn't come until I had been working a few years. The usual light was paraffin or candle. How well I remember the homely atmosphere inside with the old wooden furniture and a flagged floor and a blazing fire. Mostly the patient didn't have an anaesthetic. After the birth there was always a cup of tea and a bastible roast of warm bread and butter.

I got paid one pound ten shillings a week – only after four years was it raised to over two pounds. This was quite accepted. There were the religious orders, too, of course. You didn't do nursing for the money, but to help people, and I think this stemmed back to Florence Nightingale. Now it's a different thing. There were no office hours and people would come in at any time. Even if it was Sunday you were expected to give an injection. Nursing always required strenuous physical work. Sometimes when there was no doctor, you had to take extra responsibility, and the equipment we had was very poor. In the old days people only went to the doctor as a last resort, but when I started this was beginning to change. You could educate them, although there was always a certain amount of fear. Perhaps many of their families had been wiped out by things like TB or diptheria and they had been through very difficult times.

I must have cycled every lane and road around Cappaghglass and knew every house. They were all personal friends of mine. Tuesday would always be the dispensary day, and I would go along to get instructions from the doctor and tell him the condition of the sick people. Then the following day we would usually have a polio clinic, and I would help with injections. There was a bit of everything, even helping the dentist when he came to the school. We had a dental chair and he brought his own equipment and all the children loved him. He would tell them the most fantastic stories as he pulled out their teeth.

The most important part of my work has always been geriatric. When I started we still had a lot of emigration, and the people who remained behind were getting old. They were mostly in their late sixties. Today you will find old people at least a decade older than that. At that time not only were you expected to nurse them, but also to lay them out when they died. You wouldn't see a young nurse doing that today.

The most important thing with old people is to be conscious of their dignity and to remember you are always just a visitor to their house. Another thing, while some people mellow as they get older, it is also true that childhood faults can become more apparent. Many old people now have telephones and they all have TV which is super for them, but it can also be very confusing. They may find it very hard to accept soap operas and American things. To use that phrase, there's culture shock.

The vast majority want to live in their own place. If they dig in their heels and say no, that's their prerogative, and my role would be to make them as safe and comfortable as possible. They are adamant about not going to a home, and are more accustomed to quietness and their own company. They will cheerfully say, "Nurse, if anything happens to me, you'll find me down where I am."

But it often happens that there is just no option and they have to go to homes. The men can settle down in the day room and enjoy a pipe, but I think the women feel it worse. After managing their own house all their lives, they suddenly find themselves with nothing to do. And those who stay at home with their families are often given separate living quarters. I don't hold with that at all, it must be very demoralizing. They have reared their children who have been the apple of their eye, and there is a feeling of rejection. I think it's a breakdown in accepted Irish life.

We have eliminated diseases to a large extent in children, and you can say that preventitive medicine caters from the cradle to the grave. Most women who have children now go to hospital. More women are working, but I believe that a family should come first. The young people have a much better way of life, don't you agree? Perhaps the biggest change for anyone who knew the old days is not seeing any Wellington boots beyond the back door. If you ask me what I find oddest about country houses today, it is the number of men you will see walking around the house in their socks.'

Colm Carroll, Faith Healer. Aged 48.

He is a small wild-looking man who has spent most of his life in healing. He lives by himself. In the sitting room a large tinted photograph of Padre Pio gazes down from a wall. His visitors receive a card with his name and address. 'A service where your health is important' is written underneath.

He is a natural talker, and the words bubble out of his mouth, as he describes how all his life his hands have healed. He is trying to heal my dog who is blind. He talks gently to the dog, who follows him to a chair and instantly falls asleep. The pain must be in the eyes, Colm says, but there's a little sight left. The vet had told me there was none. Colm gives me some papers and tells me to run them over her eyes for the next few days. If I liked, I could make the sign of the cross, but that was not essential. I may not have done it right.

★

'Everyone in the town knew that I was the seventh son of a seventh son, and that can be very tough. People were always expecting great things from you, and my mother used to hide me away in the room when anyone called at the door. A pain in the back and a pain here, and at the time I was only four or five years of age.

I don't know how we managed and that was something of a miracle itself, for we were very poor, and my father had a very small wage. The seventh son has always been looked on as something different, and even somewhere like India he turns out to be a Guru . . . someone blessed or something. You feel different from other people. At school you are going to be considered a freak, so that means you have to do far more than others to be normal.

The strange thing is that I never had a child's mind. I could pick up the papers at three years old and read out to my father. And then I had a queer sort of birth. First of all I was born by breech . . . and I came feet first. Then I was born with a caul, which is a thing around your face, and then to be the seventh son of the seventh. Then my grandfather was a healer and my aunt a herbalist. I had two uncles who were herbalists and my grandmother was a fortune teller. In the name of God I had it every way.

From when I was a small boy I was automatically a doctor, and they would be saying to me, Dr Carroll do this, and Dr Carroll do that. They would come up to me in some sort of pain and say, "Holy God, what disease have I?" And this can be very tough because they are expecting great things. "Why don't you go to hospitals?" some people used to say. "There are sick people there, and you can do a lot of cures." Surely to God if I were to go to hospital and put myself on people and say "I'll cure you", then I am becoming God. It has to be a request to do the thing . . . they have to need help. And there's not one person who comes to the door, but that they do need help.

And the other thing you must have is a sense of humour. Because you can mix a very serious thing with a good sense of humour. For who wants a person with a long face coming to the door with someone dying? Other healers have secretaries taking money from you, and what are they giving you? Charging a fee for something that has been given free. In all the 35 years that I have been doing it I have never charged a fee. It was always up to the person, what they gave. You can't buy health.

People get sick for all sorts of reasons. Of course cancer is more prevalent. Look at the food and the fertilizer that goes on everything. All you have to do is to take the tinned peas and when you open them, what do they do but turn black. There's an acid in the tin, but that goes down into your stomach and it's all poison.

Another reason why people are sick is because we are suffering from older generations of people. Those who wished harm on someone, those who went around putting eggs into hay and wishing envy. For instance, how many times did the priest get into the pulpit in the old days and curse some individual from the altar? If we are human we cannot all be saints, and something will upset us. "Oh God I could kill them" you might say; but you see, the curse of people is put on others, and it's on the children, and they suffer for the guilty. So illness does come from the older generation, and Christ has nothing to do with it.

When I was young the person who had the greatest influence on my life was Padre Pio. I got a relic from him when I was thirteen, and from then on I fell in love with him. I would say it was love, but not the sort of love you feel for a woman, but a burning thing that consumes you, and I have never felt the same for anyone. I visited him once, and at that time there was no sort of commercialism like £5 for a Mass and £5 for relics, and everything was very simple. I stayed with him in a room for more than an hour with an interpreter, and his words to me were "You are born with a gift that God has given you, and use it for the suffering souls, and never think of yourself above another person or being special."

I have been very lucky with priests and with doctors and the medical profession. I have been recommended by the medical profession and by the clergy. I don't infringe on the religion, I don't go around with a candle in my hand. I don't get you to say prayers and give you penance, I don't give you medicines or herbs, and another thing I don't go round drowning you with holy water on a frosty day.

Healing is a most individual thing and it's no use coming along and saying, "Christ can grant you a cure". You cannot be trained to heal, but have to develop it yourself. As regards religion, I don't mind if you are a Protestant or an atheist or believe in a stone, or if you come from the deepest jungle. It has nothing to do with me. I never ask a person his religion, and the only name I get out is their first, and not the second. I have heard some people say that you have to have faith in curing because of the word "Faith Healer" – but that's a ridiculous thing. To come on any journey is faith enough, and the only person who must have faith is the healer himself. If Christ has put you on earth as an individual, to my way of thinking, he has also put you there for some purpose. The healer must have undying faith that something is going to happen. If a person walks in at the door and says to me "I've no faith in you – you are a fraud" I will say thanks be to God, for he has given me a test. I have seen people jump off the floor with the shock of having been cured.

I treat with everything from mental illness, alcoholism, nervous complaints, gangrene and cancer. Anything, it doesn't matter. For the last six months the greatest majority of people have been coming with depression because of the way the government is treating them. It can't be good. I think the greatest thing I possess is the diagnosis, and recently I was put to the test in a lecture. A young man had asked me what illness he was suffering from, and I said to myself, "Holy divine God will tell me what illness he has." And the minute I said it, I put my hand straight to his stomach. I said, "You have got ulcers and do you know, that your sister has them also", and he nearly dropped stone dead, and there was a great rousing cheer.

I have been at it for 35 years, and do you know what? If a man or woman comes to me and they are not sick, I would be depressed. If I don't see sick people I am sick myself. I love people, I love sick people and I prefer the challenge of someone with cancer and two days to live, rather than a toothache. I have Mass cards for cancer that I have cured, and I never take no for an answer. The nuns and priests may say that it is "the will of God" to be sick. But in the name of God, if you happen to be the mother or father of a dangerously sick child, wouldn't you go to every end to save him?

I do postal healing as well. I get letters from all over the world, and that means working on my typewriter all night. Today is a quiet day because Thursday I keep for animals. I have no fear of animals, and in the name of God I have never believed that a horse should be shot because he has broken his fetlocks. If that's the case, and we break an ankle, why don't they shoot us? I was put to the test the other day, and was given half an hour to get a horse up where a stick had gone through his leg, or otherwise he would be put to the humane killer. So I went in and talked to the horse, and I have never met a more intelligent animal than a horse. And I was frightened seeing him so quiet in the stable, and said, "If you die I lose . . ." and on the third attempt to get up, he made it. So the vet went off and didn't have him killed, and when the owner came to me I said, "If that horse doesn't win a race before the year is out, you can take the humane killer to me."

The worse a thing is, the more I like it as a sort of challenge. After I was holding a meeting in a hotel I said, "Holy God, will there ever be a miracle taking place?" for it had been a tiring day. And at that moment a blind man walked in aided by his wife, and I was sort of waiting for this thing to take place, you know. Anyway the wife brought him in, and he was totally blind, and I put my hands on his eyes three times, and he looked around and ran out of the room. I was sitting in a chair and almost fainting. And then the owner of the hotel gave me a gulp of whiskey and didn't that go to my head, and I went to the toilet and cried for two hours, and I had to go down a fire escape. Do you know the people in the bar were blind drunk when they heard that a blind man had got his sight, and it wasn't for hours they sobered up. And after all that the blind man was grand.'

Tom O'Brien. Bone Setter. Aged 45.

The man who introduced me was sceptical, even though his own daughter had been cured from a pain in her back; one sharp wrench and it was gone. Tom is a self-effacing countryman with a strong fleshy face, and a dialect difficult to understand. He has a manner that suggests a medicine man at a fair rather than someone associated with a power that is tinged with magic. He has no medical training, he has never studied anatomy, and he regards his ability as a gift. His father, whom he doesn't remember, practised bone setting, so did his mother and grandmother. He doesn't advertise, and doesn't charge, and isn't particularly religious. He is emphatic that his powers are not associated with faith healing. It's merely a question of touch.

★

'The first time I can remember it happening to me was when I was about seven or eight. We were all playing in a field, and the next thing was this fellow shouting with a bad knee, and anyway I caught it and it goes away fine. It didn't happen again until almost twenty-five years later when a friend who had gone to England came back, and his little girl had hurt her back. What happened to her was that she was leaving the school bus, and the bus went on, and she fell. You could slip your hand under her shoulder blade. I fixed it. She got out of bed and walked away.

My father was dead when I was only five and I didn't know my grandfather or see anyone else doing it around me. And it isn't something you can do by training, for I was doing it unknown to myself, and it was a thing that just came through by touch. There is a tradition going around that it follows a particular family. When someone dies the "good" will always hit someone else. I had an uncle who could do it, and he wasn't long dead when I got it too.

I never send a fellow away if I could help him, but you wouldn't want too many coming in or it would kill you. I get someone almost ever day – you would be surprised how it goes around like wild fire. With some people it's much harder than a week's work, with the sweat pouring off you, and it takes the world out of you.

What I think is that the back controls everything, and if it goes, everything suffers. Even doctors keep away from it most of the time and they will find something else to be done. There are three discs in your back, and they control your hands, and if one of them is gone, your hand is locked. I don't only treat backs – I treat everything from the back to any sort of joint, broken ankles and wrists and anything. I sort of size them up on the spot, and everything depends on how I feel. One day I might be full of worries, and on another I might meet someone and be as free as a whistle, while another man would come along and leave you dead.

I had a fellow who came from Boston, who had a bad toe with a special guard for it at night, and he said no one could touch it. But I caught it, and do you know what happened? I put it back, and he never got any trouble with it again. It's like a carpenter taking off shavings. With any dislocation, you can fix it with no bother.

A lot of people come to me complaining of arthritis, but I don't believe it exists. They show me X-rays which they say shows the arthritis, but when I've finished with them it has gone. Where did it go? If they go to a doctor and settle for arthritis – that's that. I won't touch people who have left it too long, if you understand me. They have adopted nature, and you can't do much about it. But if you get an old person who has kept good and active, and has been knocking around, that's no bother. When they are over sixty, the joints wear away. Before that there's a bit of room to fix him. There are plenty of clergymen I have straightened out.

In my grandmother's time they gave luck pennies, and now they give whatever they feel. I don't charge any set rate, but if I don't get something it's the worse luck going on, for I imagine they would take your luck away from you. Quite a lot of my work is with animals. I take no notice of vets and good luck to them, for they are the best in the world. But I treat animals differently. I remember one time there was this pacing horse, and after an accident the vet said he should be put down. But I wasn't with him ten minutes when he stood up, and three weeks later he won the country championship.

About seventy-five per cent of racehorses are strained in the back. This is what happened to a horse called Laragh Princeling, and he couldn't turn to the left. Sometimes I dream about a place that I was never in, but when I get there I am no stranger. I saw this big stables and the big tree in the middle of the field for weeks before I went down. When I got there it was exactly the same. It only took me a short time with him, and he was perfect. When you put your hand on his back, it didn't go down, and he stayed lashing. That's the secret. Always get him to lash out, for he will clean his own back then; kick out with the front two legs, and then roll over. After I fixed him he won many races, and a big race at Leopardstown, but later got killed at a hurdle race in Gowran Park.

Much of the trouble people get now is from the way they live and eat. They don't know what they are eating, they don't know the taste, and in a few years I think we will all be poisoned. That's what I believe. But before I start on food I'll tell you what causes bad backs, or most of them at any rate. Whenever the back is bad, you have something wrong. The old people knew a thing or two, and always had hard wooden seats to sit in, and when they went to sleep they were on old spring beds with the hard bottom to it. Today if they are not sitting in cars, they fall into the couches to watch television with their knees up in their mouths; and how can that be good for you, and all the rest of the softness?

The modern food is something which I have strong opinions about. I don't approve of it in any way. My stomach is like a detector; give me something in a tin and I'll reject it straight away, and a fridge is the most dangerous thing going. If you put something like meat in it, you could swear that it was never bled. Those frozen vegetables make my stomach turn.

I am very careful in what I eat or drink, and I share that with the hippies, for they have it right. Look at all the natural food they eat, and they run on things like free range eggs, brown bread and goat's milk. At one time every farm in Ireland kept a male goat, and if he urinated in a pail of milk it was considered very good. What I particularly like eating is fresh fish, and things like liver is very good. If you go out in the harbour, the water is polluted, and even a pollock's liver would have a red cast on it, but when you go out into clear water, it is soft and creamy. I keep a bottle made from the entrails which is one of the oldest cures from the Bible. If you have a bone that is chipped or a weeping joint, it will clear up with no problem.

It's no use saying that we are going to wake up in time and know what is killing us. I gave up growing cabbages and bought them in a shop, but always felt rotten after eating them. So now I have planted a hundred of my own with seaweed on them. Now you can be sure that the beef is rigged with injections, and everything we are eating is contaminated by fertilizers. I think fertilizer is where the trouble starts. I had a pony once that slipped on an old fertilizer sack that had been spread on an icy patch of the road, and immediately got poisoned. Then there are those black spots on carrots that rot out, and I met a farmer who told me that his bonhams were dying, because of a weedkiller that had been sprayed on the barley. And that's why I am off drink, for there are too many sprays in everything.

In the old days it was accepted that when you became seventy you were put into the kitchen to die. There might be nothing with them, but when they were seventy and got the pension, that was the end; it was as simple as that. Now they want to fight it, and the doctors back them up. Every day there is a new drug on the market and they pump buckets of it into people like they used to do with cortisone. That's finished now. If you ask me, they are curing one thing and starting up something else.'

Jim Slattery, Vet. Aged 32.

The telephone call is from a farm about ten miles away. Jim grabs a cup of tea, throws a few things into a bag and climbs into the red Ford Escort which has a radio telephone. After the main road there is a turn off into a wilderness crossed by narrow country lanes that spread through the hills like gossamer. Unless you know them you are quickly lost.

The sight of sun breaking over the sea reduces the petulance of the early morning start and gives Jim a feeling of well being. He takes pleasure at the sight of early spring gorse or a bank of primroses. The farm he is visiting was once part of a landlord's estate. Most of the trees have gone and the high stone walls are punctured and levelled. The farmhouse is a bungalow built a short distance away from the gaunt ruins of the old mansion. The farm equipment is modern, the milking dairy and sheds, the silage pit and yard where the tractor and machinery are kept. Jim drives past the line of cows walking down the lane from their milking, each ear neatly tagged and numbered. The farmer waits with a sick calf. The day has begun.

The problem is too much work. The car phone is constantly ringing, and even at the weekends there is little opportunity to stay at home. For the moment Jim covers an area similar in size to that of the doctor. But while many of the doctor's patients come to him, Jim has to go out to nearly all of his.

★

'When I came to Cappaghglass I just put up my plate and from then on there was plenty of business. In fact now I would welcome more competition as I have more than a thousand farms to cover. I think everyone calls me by my first name now, and that's far better for everyone. You know they are more direct with you. People still call out a vet quicker than they would a doctor. For one thing there's none of the stigma of a doctor coming to a house and everyone saying, "I wonder what's wrong with the family, they must be on their last legs."

Normally there are just two openings for vets in Ireland, private practice, or the Department, which makes you a civil servant. If you choose private practice it means giving yourself day and night to the job. There is very little time to see your family or even to sit down and read the paper. We work a twenty-four hour day, particularly in spring time. The phone will go in the morning on average at about nine o'clock, and before that there will, of course, be the emergencies. Occasionally the phone literally goes bang, bang, bang until lunch time.

I don't have a partner. Sometimes I can get a colleague who will relieve me and I will do the same for him. If a farmer rings up from a long distance away I will give him the name of a nearer vet, but I don't think that you can ethically refuse any work. Sometimes a farmer won't tell you that another vet has been treating an animal and he just wants a second opinion. But I will always go. I don't think a vet would ever go on strike. We have a Hippocratic oath and it would be a very poor man that would fail to go out to a sick animal.

I remember one St Patrick's night, and I will never forget going out at two o'clock in the morning for a calf with diarrhoea which is a very small job. The problem that night was the farmer who lived on his own was mental, and I remember saying to myself, keep facing the man. I didn't know how far he had flipped his top and was going to hit me or whether he was just worried about the calf. He was fine actually, and quite happy, and the only thing we did was to charge him a fee for going out at night. We usually charge extra after seven o'clock.

I don't have any set hours for clinics, and if people bring their dogs or cats or whatever they just have to wait. I think it's far better for them waiting for me than me for them. I might come in from the country and find a bitch whelping . . . and just as I come in my radio telephone rings for some emergency like a Caesarian . . . I will have sterile packs prepared, but you have to treat one animal there and then afterwards rush out to another call maybe fifteen miles away.

The travelling is terrible. My link with the base is the radio telephone, which is the eyes and ears of the rural vet. Fortunately I love driving, but I still regard the car as an instrument of work like a stethoscope. It has to do its job, and if I batter it in an accident that's part of the job. I have a sort of rota system if nothing else interrupts it – maybe TB or brucellosis testing one week and maybe clinical calls. I particularly enjoy small animal work. It's nice to go to your clinic and do orthopaedic surgery. I think the big change in skills in surgery came in the seventies. The new graduate coming out felt that to do a Caesarian on the farm was a routine thing. Before that there had been a big scare of infection.

In Ireland we are lucky we still haven't rabies, foot and mouth and some of the other diseases you get in Europe. But we still have TB. And there are problems with drugs that appear to be on the increase. The frightening thing is how the bacteria are becoming increasingly resistant to antibiotics. You might find an animal is sick and you send away a swab to get a bacteriological test done, and when you treat it with the appropriate antibiotic there's no improvement. The level of antibiotics in our food is altogether terrifying. Up until now a farmer could buy his drugs in any hardware shop which meant that he could make a mess of everything. Of course you have to allow a farmer to treat his animals, because there is no way that a vet can get to every sick animal. He will recognize a lot of ailments, and if he knows he can use penicillin or something, there's no reason why he can't give it just as well as the vet. But the problems and the overdosing arise from ignorance.

My father kept ten of everything, ten cows, ten sheep, ten pigs. But now a farmer would have twenty, and that would be a basic for survival. But of course there are still many of the old timers left who I visit. The more progressive man often borrowed money and built half-acres of concrete, and is now finding the banks wanted the money back. His neighbour did nothing, and people now praise him for his good sense. One farm I visit, you'd risk your life every time you go and see the cattle. The facilities for holding them are non-existent.

Living in the country you always have something to look forward to, and if you don't enjoy the scenery you would go crazy. I might be driving for an early morning call – and anyone in his senses would be in a bad humour – and you might see an early sunrise or something. There's autumn and winter when things quieten down for a bit and you have the long evenings. Maybe music at a local pub. And there's pleasure to be got when you are out on call. You'll be half-frozen, hungry and discontented with yourself, but inside the place there will be bliss. The kitchen will be swept clean and there will be something to drink and a lovely fire. You can have rich-poor people and poor-rich people, and I always prefer the latter. They can be very happy although they have only a few cattle and very little money. They get up may be at eleven in the day and do a bit of work and go to the pub at night and sing and dance and then they come home and are happy. To me the modern farmer is a victim of progress. All right, he doesn't do much manual work, but if he buys a tractor at around £20,000 that will put a terrible pressure on the man.

One of the problems about being a vet is that you have to be very money-minded to survive. You are thinking about a sick animal, also about the lowest fee that you can charge. For the farmer it's a matter of simple economics. If he has a cow and I can guarantee that after £100 worth of drugs it will respond, that will be fine. But if I cannot make that guarantee he will probably save his money rather than run up a bill. New drugs can be very expensive, and unlike the doctor's patient, a farmer has to pay for his sick animals. One of the troubles is that vets have to use very strong drugs when they go on a farm, because more often than not the farmer has used all the weaker ones with the wrong dosages and the animal won't respond to anything that doesn't pack a big punch.

We charge a minimum of £5, but this can vary. Say a farmer whom I haven't seen for months has a bit of bad luck and all hell breaks loose on the farm. I might visit him every day for a week and the drugs charge could cost more than the worth of the animal. Then if the animal dies you can only charge him a percentage. You are getting an average fee, and it's a varying fee, and you don't know when you will get paid, and if the people can't afford to pay you your income becomes less. Usually the small farmer around Cappaghglass likes to pay cash in hand if he has it. With the bigger farmer you have to send in bills. But there is nothing that is what you call normal. You're thinking of the animal but you are still thinking of money. And you always get the man who says, "That fee is too big."

Most vets have strong views on cruelty and I am no exception. I think there is a lot of cruelty to animals in Ireland, but it isn't intentional. People feel that the animal has no feeling. A farmer might respect them all right, but if he is driving them in for a TB test he will tend to belt them. Take something like dry stock which are semi-wild, and when the farmer has to catch them they struggle and fight. It's a normal attitude to retaliate. It's a very big question, and as a vet I'm conscious of the problem the whole time.

I don't like veal calves being locked in small pens or animals and hens being force-fed. But I can see it's a matter of economics . . . If a man is going to make money out of something like battery hens the only way we can help him is to reduce the cruelty as much as possible. There must be so much heat, air circulation, light, space, and it's the old story that there is a right and a wrong way of doing things.

I also feel that while I personally don't like factory farming it's no more cruel than semi-detached suburbia is to humans. And a lot of nonsense is talked about the advantages of free range eggs. They are just playing on people's views. Don't tell me that the free range hen in the yard doesn't pick up a lot of parasites. It's the same thing in the country when people will say on a frosty morning, "A fine healthy morning" when actually it's far more unhealthy than a fine summer's day.

People say to me, "You treat a sick pig and go home and eat a pork chop" but I don't correlate the two. I enjoy eating meat and would never be a vegetarian. I think there is a reference in the Bible to animals for food, and it's better for the starving millions in the world to have beef rather than to have them starving.

But of course it must be done properly and humanely. There is international legislation governing the transport of animals and if that is enforced they are able to travel as well as humans. Again they should be put under veterinary supervision. I don't object to the slaughter of animals if it's done humanely. With the humane killer there is no cruelty. But I am aware that there are slaughter houses in this area which are sub-standard from the point of view of hygiene, and possibly even in their method of slaughter. If I saw one I would certainly speak to the person concerned – there would be a moral responsibility on me.

I haven't much time for people who go overboard for their pets. To me it's sickening. I remember going to one person who was lying on the ground beside her sick poodle and crying over the animal. When you work with animals you must put them in their proper balance. Have you ever watched the seal culling on television when you see the baby seal clubbed over the head? Against that you have to make up your mind that a humane killer would be impractical and if you used a gun the bullet would richohet over the ice.

Some people latch onto religion, some latch onto animal protection and if anybody says anything to them they get more and more entrenched. They can't see the wood from the trees and they keep going down this little avenue all their life. I don't mean by this that in Ireland we should be complaisant. As a vet I have seen far too much ill-treatment and suffering.

I think coursing is a cruel primitive sport, and I regard hunting as decadent. I've spoken to colleagues about hunting, and they say that's nature's way. I don't agree. People believe that a hare has no feeling. Recently a farmer told me how a fox was cornered one Sunday and put in a bag to be released again so that it could be chased by dogs. I feel vicious towards people like that. Or the man who was expecting me to call, and when I told him that there was a sick badger that needed my attention first, he nearly died laughing.

Of course people's attitudes vary. Take something ordinary like a dog. To many farmers around here he's a working animal and when he gets sick or breaks a leg he's regarded as useless and drowned. But this isn't always the case. Only the other day a sheep farmer came to be with a sheepdog which was ill and I said it was doubtful if it would pull through. I treated it and he brought it home and late that night phoned me. I could tell that he was absolutely intoxicated. He said that the dog was much better and had eaten some bread and tea . . . he rang me again next morning he was so concerned about it.

I think there is dignity to life and it doesn't matter to me whether it's animal or human. I'd even respect flies or rats. We kill what we think is our inferior, but in reality something like an ant runs his life and commune in a more civilized way than we can and with better standards. We seem to regard ourselves as something very special. And I suppose in some ways we are. I believe that all animals and everybody has a soul, but just that our soul is a different type to an animal soul. I mean if there is a Maker of all of us I reckon he would have a hard job programming the animal as He did us.'

RELIGION

FATHER DENIS MAGUIRE	Parish Priest, *Aged 60*
FATHER GERRARD O'SULLIVAN	Priest, *Aged 65*
EDWARD HUMPHRIES	Church of Ireland Rector, *Aged 46*
WILLIAM PARKES	Shopkeeper, *Aged 22*
CATHERINE HUGHES	Christian, *Aged 24*
TIM SULLIVAN	Pensioner, *Aged 80*
BILL GIBBS	Bachelor Farmer, *Aged 83*
BRENDAN O'DRISCOLL	Returned Emigrant, *Aged 60*
JERRY GALVIN	Undertaker, *Aged 70*
MARY O'HALLORAN	Teacher, *Aged 30*
JOE O'SHEA	Churchyard Attendant, *Aged 62*

The dominant theology expresses itself in a nationalistic rhetoric and a desire to preserve a highly idealized rural past.
Contemporary Irish Society, Michel Peillon.

The days of man are but as grass: for he flourisheth as a flower of the field. For as soon as the wind goeth over it, it is gone; and the place thereof shall know it no more.
Psalm CII. 15

Father Denis Maguire, Parish Priest. Aged 60.

'What did I do today? I got up at 7.30 and held Mass an hour later in the church. Then I had breakfast, which I cooked myself, and wrote three letters before going out on calls . . .' There was the old lady whom he had visited the night before with the sacraments, distant parishioners wanting to talk about a family problem or just waiting to see him. Saying Mass, hearing confessions, attending school – his day is his own. If he wanted he could spend it by the fire and nobody would say boo to him.

The fact that his parish has a large ageing population is something he likes. The old people have the politeness of their generation and a high regard for their priest, and will always give him a warm welcome. Not that he liked the old style. 'When I first came here I was the lawgiver, I was God the Punisher's representative in the parish. Even the children ran away!'

He lives only a few yards from the church in a large matching presbytery built in similar Triumphalist Gothic. When he first came he worked to get new carpets and heating, insulation for the roof and to transform the cavernous empty rooms so that they acquired a new function and importance for the Parish. The old-fashioned drawing-room with its carved marble mantlepiece is now used as a meeting room, the dairy has become an office, and he has plans for the yard outside which once lodged cows, hens, turkeys and pigs. He would like to convert them into flats which could be used by young married couples waiting for a new home.

Father Denis sees himself as a liberal and progressive priest. He welcomes the problems which other colleagues fear as dangers to the church. He even welcomes the recession, believing that good comes from evil and that the present generation of lads look into things more intelligently than their predecessors. He is not afraid of educational advances. If there is a loss of the old structured piety, there is a corresponding gain in religious awareness.

He entertains me to tea, cakes and rhubarb tart in the sitting-room which he uses as a study. He smokes a pipe. He is a small, talkative rubicund countryman. You could imagine him at the creamery talking away to his friends. Rural life is changing, he says, for the priest as well as for everyone else. He is glad that priests are no longer expected to chair every committee and can have the time to concentrate on more important spiritual problems. Spiritual fulfilment, marriage breakdown, unemployment, illness, old age . . . the list of things he has to deal with is endless.

*

'There's a plaque on the house which says it was built for the officiating clergy of Cappaghglass, and so it was always the priest's house. Both the presbytery and church were built on a bog, which was the only land that the landlord of the time would allow them. The wood for the two buildings came from an oak wood on the same estate – Bellevue – and the walls were made four feet thick, like a castle. When I first came here the house was being kept up in the old ways. You had the Parish Priest, his curate, a housekeeper and assistant housekeeper, and outside there was a yard man and farm hand just for starters. There was a fleet of servants in the blooming place, and that was an industry in itself. We might have been the Pope. I still have a housekeeper and curate but everyone else has gone.

My first job was to make this place livable. The plumbing was uneven, the wiring dangerous and the former PP never lit a fire in the twenty years he was here. He sat down here in front of a radiator, and there was actually a hollow in the floor where he went through the carpet and all with his two heels. And he never slept winter or summer but with only a sheet over him. He didn't know what cold was, and that was that.

I have brightened things up and rationalized the whole heating system. There was no heat in the back and too much heat here. I had to cut off the radiators. There was a big room where the clergy dined, and everything was brought up like in Upstairs Downstairs, all very formal. Now we have opened up the dining-room for parishioners, and they can have choir practices in the winter, board meetings, or perhaps it can be used for a novena. I think big places like this should be used for the benefit of everyone in the area.

How did I start? Well, when I first went to school I had no idea at all of becoming a priest. My father was a shopkeeper and my mother gave her life for teaching. The strange thing is that although watching her put me off teaching, I ended up in a calling where a lot of my life consists of teaching and being at the beck and call of anyone who comes to the door. Just like she was.

In the old days the priests usually came from what were considered the middle classes; strong farmers, comfortable farmers, teachers and Guards' families. The poor person didn't have a look in. There was the old tradition of respectability with its three hallmarks, you know – a pump in the yard, a bull for your cows, and a priest in the family. It was just that chaps didn't have the opportunities otherwise, for in those days unless your parents could afford a boarding school you hadn't a chance. You came through the Diocesan seminaries and then on to Clonliffe and Maynooth.

I had a cousin who was pressurized in this way, by fond parents or aunts or whatever. I think his vocation was rather shaky. But they would go on saying to him, "What are you going to do with your life? What do you want to make of it?" Being a priest seemed pretty practical, for there weren't many options for a young lad. You could become a doctor or a soldier and it was almost the same – we drifted into seminary in a casual sort of way. We actually used to say to each other that it was either Maynooth, the junior ranks of the army or the Guards, and that was that. Other jobs didn't cross our minds. Out of a class of thirty in my time there might be five or six for Maynooth, a dozen or so for the Missions and a few became doctors, civil servants or Guards.

I think it took almost eighteen years from first entering National School before I was ordained. In the old days priests didn't retire; they died with their boots on. They got a lad to do the work for them, and sat around the fire and made life hell for him, you know. For six years I was what they called a "reader" and looked after the old fellows for two pounds a week, and it took me almost thirty years to get my own parish. Almost a lifetime.

When I started the rural priests would still see themselves in the old role, and they were a bigger shot than the Pope. They were stuck on every committee but didn't necessarily go near them. It might be rugby, hurley, Tourist Week or anything else. The old priest lived well. He played bridge or penny poker and had a good meal and put his toes up at the fire with a good punch. As a Dean of Maynooth once said, "The horse would always leave you home." At that time, too, the priest only associated with educated people like himself, and if the odd one went into a labourer's cottage and had a mug of tea, he would be regarded as a bit of an eccentric. Thank God that's long over.

People who see me working at Cappaghglass must think that here

goes the normal PP on his usual business. There's the morning Mass at
eight and half-nine, there's the Sunday Mass and confessions and
there's always the sermons to be preached and schools to be visited.
Preparing children for confirmation, visiting sick people, and you
must not forget that every day there is some office work to be done.
Every day is different – it's very hard to plan ahead.

One of the first things I did after taking over the duties of Parish
Priest was to make the church comfortable. You can't bring a congregation into a cold church nowadays, you have to have adequate
heating, the best of lighting and the place must be clean and bright.
Practical details before you open your mouth at all.

And today with a more educated audience you must prepare your
sermons well. What people want is practical morality and practical
living brought home by the Gospel. Any religious text has a message
for me today – what am I doing with my life? If the subject is violence,
it's no use giving a tirade about the North. That's what you think
you're going to say, but you're not. You say, have you any violence in
your own house or in that of your neighbours? That's bringing the
whole thing down to Joe Soap and his neighbours, and that's what
they want to know.

A priest must know his people. I mean he must know about
unemployment, dole queues, mortgages, paying debts, fighting with
the neighbours, quarrels over land, husbands beating wives and
driving while drunk. A Christian ethic is to love your neighbour, but a
step above that is love one another as I love you. That's what Christ
said, and that's a different thing from just loving your neighbour. It's
the universal word of God to all men.

After so long in an area you get to know the people like your own
family and just as the doctor regards his work as essential for people's
health, I have the same attitude for their souls and salvation. I enjoy old
people, particularly visiting those who are housebound, bringing
them the sacraments and afterwards sitting around for what I call
"apostolic gossip." Another thing that brings me joy is house stations.
I see the station, not only as an important religious expression of the
people, but as a link between religion and ordinary life. The big
Corpus Christi processions are an outward expression of religious
faith. And funerals, of course. If wakes have died away, and most
people now die in hospital, funerals are still great social events. "Two
funerals today" a publican said to me last week, and he was rubbing his
hands! They were good for his business.

I would say that the family thing in Ireland is the strongest in Europe and that's not just an opinion of mine. People are saying to me, "For God's sake preserve it and make it stronger." I see my role here to help improve relationships between parents and children, husbands and wives. I think I am a more understanding person than I was when I began. In the old days parents didn't talk about the sex business and that kind of thing. Do you know that one of the best prepared couples I came across recently for marriage had lived together for a year to see if it would work out? These people are human, and it's not for me to judge. Even if they are not married, I still have a heart for them, and it's for me to get them going in a better direction.

When I look back on things I wonder am I the same man who became a curate thirty years ago. I remember how a rumour was spread that I was seen out at night with a blackthorn stick chasing couples in the area! Chasing couples isn't the way of preparing them for marriage anyway.

In a rural parish like Cappaghglass you get all the old problems thrown at your head. Married people are one thing. The majority of men won't admit that they don't communicate with their wives. "Isn't she all right? What the hell is she grumbling about anyway? Didn't I buy her the coloured television?" He gets the set and it's him who's watching it and she's minding the kids in the kitchen.

Another problem is the bachelors. That's partly due to attitudes in the population, long standing attitudes. All a fellow wants to do is to have a piece of land, get a white-faced bullock, sell him, do a spell of drinking . . . and what good is a wife for? Then there's the lad who stayed at home to get the farm and mind the parents, or the girl who's left on the shelf.

But marriage problems are the ones that crop up over and over again. The old situation was that you were married and that was that. If it broke down you stayed put in the same house anyway. You just accepted it and motored on. And that is one of the reasons why it's better to get in there and stop the marriage drifting apart before the damage is done. Unless your family is sound, you have no community, and unless the married couples are sound, you have no family. The children who never experience love and security are going to be violent, and maybe they are going to be on drugs, although that isn't a problem in this area, thank God. The home where there is security produces the stable person.

I think today that education is instruction rather than education. You know that the word is from the Latin root, meaning to lead out. Leading out the person to be a full person, and surely you can't lead out the body and leave the soul behind. Education will involve religion, for you are developing the child as a whole person, and you can't develop the body without the spirit.

I think there's good and bad things about Irish life. As I see it, it's not the education, but the life-style that makes the difference. Take the 'sixties. The big value of the 'sixties was what the pay cheque might be. Parents driving kids to get good jobs that paid big. You asked kids if they were going to be priests, and they would say, "That doesn't pay enough." Now there's a swing back from the 'sixties, and away from material advancement. Not what's good for themselves, but what's going to make this a better place to live in. And there's a huge increase in vocations.

I spent a year with a group of boys and girls doing Leaving Cert, and talked to them about relationships at home and with one another. I was astonished by their mature attitudes to religion, to their priest and to people in general. Five years ago the same blooming crowd would have knocked everything we said. They would be cynical and wouldn't even listen to me. A little bit of recession and apparent hardship has made people stop and think.

There's no reason why there should be a rigid demarcation between priestly duties and interests in the community. You remember how a lot of the social changes and farming movements were started by priests. They took an early part in the co-operative movement. But nowadays there are so many societies, that priests have been anxious to ease themselves out of those positions. What I am saying is that first they should do their spiritual work, and only if there is any time over, do the other lines.

In the old days a priest spent a lot of his time getting people jobs. He might go to the local bank manager and say, "I've a good lad here" or to a shopkeeper "I hear you were looking for a decent chap." But now you have employment agencies. I don't see any value in organizing youth clubs and that kind of thing, for that only makes a priest a glorified baby-sitter. I suppose I have had my bellyful of organizing things, but it's different now. You wouldn't keep a fellow quiet nowadays by asking a priest to be president of a football club. When we came out of Maynooth, that was the thing. I remember an old priest telling me "Sure, every young priest should give one summer to Duffy's Circus, and he would learn skills there he wouldn't learn at Maynooth."

I try and stay optimistic, but it isn't always easy. Some things depress me. Take a country parish like this one. It's most refreshing to find a family nowadays that would go down to the river bank on a Sunday night or through the woods and chase rabbits or look for birds' nests the way we did as children. Now it's the lads from the town that go out fishing. It drives me mad to see teenagers around and saying "There's nothing in this place, only the pub." They have football, hurley, tennis, just to name a few of the sports. But they would rather go into a pool hall and watch the television, for the whole thing of mass entertainment is laid on.

However, it's by no means all bad. The old Emergency was a great leveller and finished the scars of the Civil War and of gentry versus peasantry. It didn't matter who you were or how you spoke, everyone was there defending the country. I thought it was a marvellous thing – the start, if you like, to a change in attitudes. Today there are other things which impress me. A lot of the younger crowd now will organize something like a disco and give all the money they make to some third world country. Or just send out some money to a Mission. It's terrific. Before it would have been organized by the teachers and the priest. Now they do it themselves.

For someone like me who was trained under the Council of Trent and worked for fifteen or twenty years in that atmosphere, it's an amazing change to find yourself post-Vatican II and in an expanding and explosive situation. When I was ordained we all had a very different attitude. There was a feeling of complete trust that has gone out of life. Take the Missions. We Irish priests had a very colonial approach, and just took over a Mission and that was that. And you stayed there and told them how to behave. Nearer home people often had the attitude that once they went to Mass they could do anything else for the rest of the week. I did my bit, so now leave me alone. Aren't I all right? I've chalked up enough credits for the Lord. It's all a little less pat nowadays.

Another development from Vatican II is the growth of ecumenism. One has to start from the top and slowly filter down, and this will take time before all the different churches are one. But I believe this will happen. You still get hardened attitudes, such as Catholics are superior to Protestants and the other way round. Some priests may find it awkward to get on with the local rector, and all they will do is perhaps meet in the supermarket and wish each other good day. Last year I read the lesson in the Church of Ireland church and Mr Humphries and I regularly visit each other. If all the Christian churches are doing the same thing, there is a far greater chance of them coming together and having one big community. Already there is a greater understanding and coming together, which I think is very fruitful. I think it was the way we were brought up that we thought the other one had horns . . . a terrible fear, you know. We have all experienced that kind of thing.

People are always asking me about my attitude towards the North and what is happening there. I think the politicians are approaching the whole thing from the wrong way altogether. They should forget about unity. Unity is not possible at the moment. The problems are too great. If you had a poll down here in the South, the majority of people would accept that.

A few months back I met a Church of Ireland bishop, and he was a grand chap. "I'm going to tell you one thing," said he, "there are men on my side and men on yours, and they won't listen to each other." And he was dead right. There's no Christianity in the violence, wherever it comes from.

Although I can see no outcome or settlement, I think the despair of things will lead to something stronger. Both Catholics and Protestants ultimately are going to be enhanced by it, and have a greater regard for each other. Just think of Poland, which came through a tremendous persecution, and the strength of religion there. If you are a student of history at all, you will know that the worst thing for religion is when a country goes soft and materialistic.'

Father Gerard O'Sullivan, Priest. Aged 65.

Father O'Sullivan was born and brought up in Cappaghglass and returns every year for a short holiday, staying in the same guesthouse, in the same room. He is a familiar figure during certain weeks in July as he walks down the main street. 'Hello Father, how are you?' people call out as the tall figure passes. He lifts a hat, smiles, and from time to time stops for a talk on the weather or a mutual acquaintance. For all his long absence from the town he has kept closely in touch, and seems to know everyone who is not a visitor.

He is an old-style priest who concentrates his ideas on virtue, good living and morality, which, he says, are getting despised as old-fashioned ideas. The wasted activities of modern man are a favourite topic. The subjects of divorce and abortion arouse real anger. Little that he sees around him gives occasion for good cheer. He looks sadly at the hippies and good livers with their long hair and loose morals who have fled out here from the cities and from England and the Continent. They symbolize the slide from ordered civilization which threatens the Christian world.

The greatest threat to the Catholic church is not Protestantism, but what he calls 'existentialism' that pervades the world. He argues passionately against the role of the individual as a free agent determining his own development. What does he think of ecumenism? Not much. Too many words, gestures and political attitudes. He believes in a slow process of change, very slow. If you have a belief, don't water it down for anyone. While he can sympathize with the attitudes of the minority, the Irish people have always kept their faith. As a historian he knows about the Penal times when thousands would crowd a hillside to hear Mass in the rain. He has read about the Famine and the struggle for Catholic Emancipation, and believes that Irish people owe it not only to themselves, but to past generations to preserve their religion.

★

'Did you know that the Pope himself apologized to the bishops for the rate of change that came after Vatican II? Everything happened too quickly. In the ecumenical thing you have to work on the outside, and some of the changes are paper changes which are only on the surface. It's a long business and you have to start by eliminating offensive phrases. In other words, you have to progress step by step. I would compare it to the old Irish custom of matchmaking where you don't rush your fences. There is no point in putting on a false front and telling people that union is around the corner. I know in my heart that it will never happen.

Much of the talk I hear could be put down to the "garden fête" area . . . a cup of Protestant or Catholic tea and not much else. If you ask me, I also believe that fifty years ago there was a more open relationship between a priest and a clergyman. Their Roman collars would never have touched.

How can things change, if one really is honest? There are far too many prejudices and far too many dark areas that need to be cleared up. As a committed Catholic I believe in the fullness of the Catholic message that has come down through the Catholic church. Nothing can change that, even with the best intentions.

What I see today is the danger of a more secular society in which both the priest and the church have little role to fill. The liberal humanist element has brainwashed quite a number of people. They are getting glibly educated, but whether they are educated in the true sense is a debatable point to me. They are inclined to swallow clichés a bit too eagerly. I will take one particular example, the idea that we should have divorce facilities in the South in order to make ourselves more acceptable to the Protestant majority in the North. Now I really can't see the logic behind this approach at all. I don't think it's going to work, for people won't respect you for sacrificing your principles in order to satisfy everybody. The way I look at it is that if a minority of farmers want to import foot-and-mouth disease, you are jolly well going to fight it. It's the same with divorce.

Another thing that annoys me is all this talk of mixed schooling. There is a Catholic and a Protestant ethos, and I would say that these two things cannot be forced together. There is nothing more ridiculous than an individual brought up in one tradition forcing himself to accept positions on the other side.

What worries me is the decline of absolute standards. Someone has called it "the age of the shrug" and that's the way it is. One is dealing with a generation that has been better educated, but has also been drastically changed by things like television. The priest used to be regarded as a rather fearsome character, who commanded respect from young and old alike. But now when I go into a room full of younger people I am almost ignored. Even at Mass they are not listening to you, and I think they are in danger of losing their faith. The child that leaves Primary school at twelve years old in June and whom I know personally won't say hello by the time Christmas comes along. That's what the bus and secondary education are doing for Ireland.

Today people are prepared to accept lower standards and of course every crackpot minority has its voice heard. You have the women's "liberation" movement and the men's "gay rights" movement, and I have even heard of a "Man–Boy Love Association" in America. These degrading developments arise from the idea that people have the liberty to do whatever they like or whatever they feel at a particular moment.

I think there is a case for some kind of censorship, but you must strike the right balance. I mean, if you think something is worthwhile, you will definitely have some sort of control. If an architect designed a house for you and said afterwards "I have made a lot of mistakes" that isn't going to be much comfort. It is too late then. Dilys Powell, the film critic of the *Sunday Times*, started off as a great campaigner against censorship, but before she had finished she had changed her attitude completely.

While I can see values in liberalism and a liberal education, there is still a vast amount of secularism. The media, drama and literature are dominated by philosophies of existentialism which will militate not just against the Catholic Church, but against any dogmatic framework. These forces presuppose things that are diametrically opposed to our beliefs. They are man-centred rather than God-centred. I think the real threat to the western world is a complete breakdown of any absolute standards, and this covers everything.'

Edward Humphries, Church of Ireland Rector. Aged 46.

Eddy, as he is known, is small, dark and smiling. He worked in Africa for a relief organization before deciding to take holy orders. He became Rector of Cappaghglass eight years ago, and is generally popular. For one thing, he is a local man, and his uncle was a clergyman here before him. He knows about farming and fishing. 'That boat was held together by putty and three Hail Marys' he will say about a ramshackle fishing smack, and everyone knows what he is talking about.

The new Rectory is a modern bungalow which makes up in comfort for what the old one offered in threadbare graciousness. His wife, Mary, is grateful that she never had to live in the fine draughty Georgian house which was sold off to a German couple years ago. The bungalow is a family home, bubbling with life and laughter, especially during the school holidays.

Church attendances fluctuate wildly from a short summer high, when the congregations are swollen by visitors, to the normal winter low, when in many churches outside the town the phrase 'two or three gathered together in Thy Name' has a repeated dismal ring of truth. The majority of blow-ins who have settled in the area who might be presumed to have some sort of affiliation with the Church of Ireland, are not church-goers. Eddy has in his care eight rather decrepit churches, most with tiny congregations, and on Sundays he visits a lot of them in his small car. Amalgamation – dreaded word – constantly threatens to reduce their number.

He isn't discouraged. Churches may vanish, but there are some small signs that the number of Protestants in the area is slowly increasing. He isn't even discouraged by mixed marriages. More disheartening is the problem of keeping religion alive among people who don't want to know. Is education the death of religion? he often wonders. But then something will restore his confidence, some charitable act by a neighbour, a demonstration of old-fashioned piety or goodness. He likes his job, his way of life and his religion, and in theory he can stay here all his life. But country clergymen tend to leave their parish after nine or ten years, and he has been here longer than that. The fact that he says it at all makes you wonder if he would like a change of scene.

★

'I remember grumbling to someone that I had a terrible big parish to get around, and he said, "Your uncle did it on a bicycle." But then the old boy had only a third of the area I have to cover. In those days there was a clergyman within thirty-five miles of the next one. My uncle always had a fishing rod tied onto the bar, and if he saw some nice pool or stream he would get off and fish for brown trout. That was the style then. Everything was slower moving when the parish was separate, and of course everyone was his own man.

In those days Protestant society was different. There was the gentry and landlords and army. Then there was town and country. Country was strong and not-so-strong farmers – the acreage was never big around here. The town was shopkeepers and professionals. There was always a Protestant bank manager or even two bank managers, and solicitors. They weren't exactly the Ascendancy, but they were people who were able to get to schools and colleges. Many Protestants were educated for jobs like the bank, but the majority of RC's never got beyond the National School.

Now the Protestant town people have entirely disappeared and I can't really tell you the reason. I have the Cappaghglass register, here, and if you go back in it you will find that at one time all the trades and crafts were Protestant. No one can say that they were persecuted, boycotted, ignored, or that business was not all right. Mixed marriages isn't the whole story by any means. The likely explanation is that after the founding of the state, many could see no sense of hope or future, and educated their children for export. It may have been something dating from the tensions of the 'twenties and the feeling of being forced to live in an alien state. I can't put my finger on it.

There were more restrictions then. Catholics weren't allowed inside a Protestant church and at a funeral they were forced to wait outside. Now they pour in. When I was a boy you weren't allowed to mix or play with an RC, and somehow you were brought up to believe you were just a little bit above them. I don't know why. The Protestants were considered to have more go about them and did things the RC's didn't do. They were not really Irish, but they became Irish.

In the old days the Protestants were mostly landlords and nearly all the RC's were serfs or whatever you liked to call them. I think that in the North of Ireland today they are too equal in numbers, and at the same time are completely ruled by the Protestants and that's where all the troubles come in. When there is a large majority the minority have to keep quiet, which is what happened here. We are less than five per cent.

Around Cappaghglass the worst period of the parish was in the 'sixties when the congregation reached a sort of valley. The clergyman of the time feared for its very existence. Since then the numbers have crept up a little and there are slender grounds for hope. Many of those who went to England in the 'forties and 'fifties decided to come back and have a go at things. Some took up farming and others went into trade, and now we have about fifty people in our main service on Sunday.

But the decline has been dreadful. Twenty years ago there were three clergymen administering six parishes, and now there is only myself and a lay reader who helps. Also in that time, two of our churches have been closed and another will be closing soon. In recent years there has been a tendency not to keep the church going for the simple fact of keeping it going. I think the people might, but to the clergyman this isn't always the highest priority. The church may be cold or damp or getting into bad repair. There may be no music, and that's no good either.

You have to balance things spiritual and material. I know that if I closed down two of my churches whose winter congregations can muster less than a dozen, they would find it hard to get to Cappagh-glass. Many parishioners are old and infirm, and it is still easier for me to go down there and hold a service than for them to come up. And when people are confronted with a sermon they will come to it. Of course this means a lot of charging about, and I do around eighteen thousand miles a year. A parishioner said to me once, "It's very hard on you doing all this driving on Sunday," and I said, "Oh yes," thinking that it's very nice of him to notice. But he added, "Particularly when you are not used to it during the week."

It used to be said that one of the many problems of the country clergyman was underemployment, but I don't think they can say that any more. I am as busy as I was as a curate in Dublin. On Sundays I take four services and that's a very tight schedule. My first one would be at Cappaghglass, eight o'clock communion, and then I drive quickly to Ballybrack for a service at ten-thirty, then back to Cappaghglass for the big twelve o'clock service, and then a later service at Briarstown at six o'clock.

Like an RC priest I am paid by the people, though more indirectly. The system is known as the assessment. What happens is that the assessment is paid to the Parish Treasurer who pays it to the Diocesan Secretary, who pays it to the Representative Body who sends out the salary. But basically it is the congregation that pays the priest. You can imagine that with that system and small congregations, the Church's finances are a matter of strict housekeeping.

One of the difficulties that arises out of belonging to such a small minority is the conflict between one's duties to your parishioners and the fact of being a Christian. They shouldn't conflict. I mean, when I first came down here they were still running socials to get our young people to mix, and RCs were kept out. It didn't work. Now there's a community hall and everyone is together. The problem, of course, is mixed marriages. Most young fellows are marrying RCs and I often say "Why can't you get a Protestant girl?" and he'll say "There are ninety-five RC girls for every Protestant I meet."

This area used to be stricter than many other parts of Ireland, and every Protestant that married an RC had to sign his children over. But in recent years there has been a bit of a change. Although there is still pressure to make them do this, young people are tending to make up their own minds about clerical interference. I don't think dividing up families is a bad idea. It used to be done in the old days. Children don't find it odd that boys go to one place and Mammy and the girls go to another. There used to be plenty of rather homespun arrangements like that in Ireland long ago.

If you ask me what I think will happen in the future the honest truth is that I don't know. Ecumenism has been a help, and since Vatican II it has been a reasonably respectable thing. I get on well with Father Maguire, but then, my uncle was always friendly with the Parish Priest in his time. Some of the older style priests don't accept Vatican II and would like to get back to the old days. I think there are some Roman Catholics high up in the hierarchy who are dragging their feet very hard, and trying to resist the changes.

It's understandable. You can understand that people feel loyalty to their churches and religion and don't want to go too far in breaking down the barriers. And the RCs aren't the only ones to put up difficulties. They are very close to accepting our orders. But if they do get round to accepting our orders, and then we start to ordain women – what then?'

William Parkes, Shopkeeper. Aged 22.

'I'm Protestant, but I gave up going to church long ago. My mother and my two sisters still go. The last time I was there it seemed to be full of geriatrics. Looking at it the other way, my friends who are Catholics are just going for the sake of going, and they are losing their faith too. They are there because their mother and father want them to be there, and they are conforming because people would be talking as they always do in the country.

In twenty years you'll see divorce introduced and you'll find lots of other changes. Now they pay lip service.

If we depended on the Protestants for doing business, I wouldn't be sitting doing very much anyway. They died or got old or sold.

I might marry a farmer's daughter but of course when you are a Protestant and you are marrying a Catholic there is no question that you have to toe the line. In places like Dublin they may be cosmopolitan and look at it in a different light and make up their own minds about it. But here is Cappaghglass with farmers and fishermen, cripes, their opinion is strong. You must be a Catholic and have the faith. The weaker fellow always gives way.'

Catherine Hughes, Christian. Aged 24.

Her faith and sense of salvation are the things that fill her life. 'Are you saved?' she asks me over a cup of tea. 'Will you go to Heaven?' I'm not sure. My replies puzzle and alarm her. She is a dark girl, whose expression varies between seriousness and melancholy. She and her parents live a careful rural life between farming and praying in their small mountain farm. Praying comes first. I am offered freshly baked bread, scones and home-made blackberry jam in the kitchen which is made a little bit too warm by the Esse. The lino shines so you could see your face in it; on the walls are texts, 'Lo, I am with You Always' . . . etc. There is no television in the house.

★

'What I am saying is that Jesus has shown me that He is the Way, the Truth and the Life. You either belong to the world or you belong to the Lord. I asked Jesus into my heart when I was about ten years old. Do you want to go to heaven? I'll tell you that if you do, you must free yourself from worldliness and become changed like me. I was brought up here at home, and my mother taught me that we need to ask the Lord Jesus into our hearts, or we won't be able to get to Heaven.

When I was at school a lot of people thought I was crazy when I found the Lord. Most young people I know of are just looking for a good time and getting the most out of life because they can't see anything else. I enjoy the freedom of the country life, for you have time to think, and you have God's creation all about you. To me the city is nothing, but many of my friends want the excitement of it and all the social life. That doesn't appeal to me.

You need money to live, but to me money isn't of any importance because of the simple fact that Jesus is everything. And when I have Jesus I don't need any of these things. I think people have become too wordly, buying expensive clothes and spending money on things of the world that will vanish. There are treasures in Heaven, but God doesn't tell you. The clergy should satisfy their need, not their greed.

We don't do things of this world like dancing and drinking. We don't go to whist drives or pubs, and I would be very strict with myself not to fall into temptation. I don't say I'm a martyr or anything, but just a sinner saved by Christ. Religion is man-made and I keep away from religion altogether, and read the Bible every day. I just open it and read it anywhere. I like St John's Gospel best, but there are things in the Old Testament that I feel depressed about . . . things that they say.

Answer me now, where do you go when you die? I have to tell the people the truth, that they are all lost and that they are sinners. Some people might think they are going to Heaven, but how can they be sure? Sin is in people's hearts, and you know yourself that the root of all problems is sin. I believe that the Lord is coming back soon as in the days of Noah. I go back to that verse the whole time that Jesus is the Way because he died on the Cross for our sins. I am a born-again Christian, and you can be the same yourself.'

Tim Sullivan, Pensioner. Aged 80.

'Oh God, the faith of the Irish is frightful, you know. Oh God almighty they thought the priest was king. Whatever the priest said it was supposed to be right. They were a sight to the world, but listen, things have changed. If you were seen talking to a girl and a priest comes, you'd go through barbed wire – you'd be gone as if you were a hare. When I was going to school, when I saw the priest walking to school, I'd go inside the ditch with the sight of him. Now I see him there with the youngsters and they are giving him backchat.

When I was young I'd be afraid to go into the Protestant church that I would be dragged down or something. And a Protestant woman, Annie Phillips she got talking and she said they were the same. They were afraid of going inside the door of the chapel.

Mind you I'm saying that we got on well. We figured out from the Prod men and women that they were better – more genuine – anyway you like, than the Catholics. They were much more truthful, more honest and more upright than the Catholics were in their way.

First and foremost they did their best to help. Where I lived there were no vets. There were no vets anywhere. You couldn't get a vet in

Ireland and you treated your animals yourself. Willy Phillips and John Watson they were great cow doctors. And anytime you would go for them in the night and even if it was the summer, and crops with the wheat falling off the head, they'd go away with you and stay with you. A Catholic man wouldn't do that for the world. The cow doctors could do anything with an animal. They were really brilliant men in their own way.

I went to the Protestant dance at the Protestant hall. The first time we went we got a great welcome. The second time we went, it was strange, there were no Catholics there and we went away. There was some order of the priest and I think that started it. We were all going to the Protestant dance and he wanted them to go to his own. And then the clergyman would allow no Catholic in his dance. Romie Callaghan tried to go, and the clergyman came up and took him by the shoulder and ordered him to leave.

The Catholics weren't that bad. They weren't as strict at all. I'd say the Protestant could come if he liked, but you see, he got sour. It was ourselves that started it.'

Bill Gibbs, Bachelor Farmer. Aged 83.

A very old man, small and wizened, stands by the range, boiling milk. He has spent his life scraping a living from the little farm, and all the time wanting to read books and write. He keeps his papers, some newspaper cuttings, others beautifully written out in long hand, in an old biscuit tin. He shows me an article he wrote about the coming of the Danes to Ireland.

He lives in the same old house which the IRA raided in 1920. Outside birds sing and the sun shines down on the gorse and heather, but he prefers to remain inside pottering about in the gloom. The dark kitchen has a flagged stone floor, the old metal range, a table covered with blue checked oil cloth, some dusty chairs, a good many dampish books and a photograph of the Lusitania. Sitting in his chair, his woollen cap pulled over his head, he gazes up at the ceiling and talks ten to the dozen. 'You should read it,' he says about a book. 'That man knows what he's talking about,' he says about another.

He is grateful to the government for his old age pension. In his old age he seems relatively tranquil in spite of loneliness and a persistent melancholy regret. The bitter religious divisions and the slavery of the farm that soured his life are things of the past.

*

'My grandfather was a great historian who could do any amount of cypher writing, and he was a great scholar, one of the best that ever went to school. He said that hundreds of people around here died with hunger during the Famine, and there was no distinction between Catholics and Protestants, they all died together in a heap.

He knew about evictions too. The worst he ever heard was the eviction of John Doyle and his cattle from the land. All the cattle were put in the pound, then they were all evicted from the farm, every one of the Doyles. The Sherriff's name was McCormick, and he was a Protestant, and when he died the Doyle family tore up his coffin in the middle of the night. They threw it on the surface, and were about to throw it into the sea, when they were disturbed in some way. The story was that they heard any amount of noise and saw flashing blue and red lights, and they ran for their lives, leaving their shovels and everything behind them. They were in full flight after attacking the graveyard, my grandfather said. No one did anything like that in my time, and people sobered down and got very united. When my brother died it was two Catholics that opened up the grave for him.

I had a very tough old life. I never wanted to be a farmer. What I would have liked was to have been a journalist writing for some newspaper, that's what I would have liked to have been. But my father hadn't the money to educate me, and anyway he didn't like the idea at all. It was no bother for me to be a journalist, for I had always a great knowledge and love of Ireland, and I used to write articles for *Ireland's Own*. I was always interested in the towns, and the famous Irish families, for they had a wonderful great history to them. Half of Ireland belonged to the great Anglo-Norman families that came here from Normandy. I wrote a history about Cappaghglass, but have only one copy. I did a lot by an oil lamp and sent it to the papers.

Although I was brought up on a small sized farm with only four cows, we came from a very aristocratic family. At one time we owned half a village and a lot of land, and one of the jobs my grandfather had was to act as pilot to all the shipping. I remember he had a big long glass, and it was set out that length, and when he saw any ships flying their flags, the pilot boat would bring the ships back here into the harbour. They used to come from France, Italy and Germany, and all over the world, and he got £5 for every vessel he brought in. Sometimes there would be so many that they would have to stop outside heaving on their anchors. There used to be eighty to a hundred ships inside of Cappaghglass harbour.

We started at a Protestant school, and then went on to the Catholic one because it was better. The only thing we had against it was the religious teaching. At half past twelve it was "Hail Mary full of Grace, Blessed art though among Women" while we shivered outside in the playground. When the Master heard that he had Protestant boys, he would round us up, for he didn't want us to listen to their religion. He was a bigoted man, like the Orangemen in Belfast, he was a Catholic man and didn't want us to hear it at all.

At about the time that I was going to school my mother got two nice little girls from the Protestant Orphan Society. She had asked the local clergyman to get them for her, and they were about three or four years with us. I have their photographs always above in my room. They were about the same age as me, and they did all the work for us. One of them would bring up messages from Cappaghglass, and the other little girl would bring in the water, and she would milk the cows and feed the calves for us, and she would feed the pigs. These two girls used to walk with us every day to school, and they were great company. But when they were sixteen you had to pay them, and my mother let them go.

One of them married a Catholic, and we went to see her. She had a photograph of the priest stuck on the wall, and she said, "This is the girl who is preparing for her First Communion now." That's what happened to one of them. And there were four or five Protestant fellows here, and they were madly in love with her. But there was only one she wanted to marry, and that fellow wouldn't marry her at all. He never married nobody, like myself, and he lived until ninety.

We had about a dozen coastguards and their families living near to us, and they were all Protestants. They were pensioners from the British navy, and they had very much the same uniforms with bright yellow buttons and the white cap. They were hardly doing anything at all, but watching the ships coming in. They were great customers of the shopkeepers, and were for ever buying tea, sugar and cigarettes, for they had a good salary from England.

When the war came things were very different, for the Germans at that time were sinking twenty-five or twenty-six British merchant ships every week. The Lusitania went down too, and all the people that were lost in her, one thousand, four hundred and eighty-five lives. I remember what they called the Dreadnoughts with their three funnels. They were all woodburners, and painted an Atlantic grey – that is a darker grey than the Mediterranean fleet, and they had two white bands painted on their funnels. At night we could hear their fifteen inch guns practising away, and they made a voice like thunder.

The war affected everyone, and there were any amount of Protestant boys that joined the army or navy and were all killed. It was very dangerous joining it. I knew a man down in Cappaghglass, and his warship was torpedoed, and I did hear that his son joined the English navy too, and his ship was also torpedoed, and the two of them were lost, the father and the son. Did you ever go into the Protestant church and see the list of all the fellows that were killed because they had no other employment but to join the army?

I went down once to the Coast Guard Station, and the head Coast Guard said, I suppose you have come to join the Royal Navy, for they also recruited people. They would take your name and address, and then you would be ordered back for a medical examination. You didn't need much education at all so long as you passed the doctor. You had to have good sight, good teeth, good hearing, and they would strip you naked. But I was too young to join up, for the minimum age was sixteen.

My cousin who had gone to Portsmouth in August, was dead the following year by March, and two of my uncles were killed. Another uncle came home in a nice khaki uniform, and he had got a sniff of mustard gas, and he could hardly draw his breath with it. One of those who was killed fought in the great Jutland North Sea battle in May, 1916, under Admiral Jellicoe and Admiral Beatty. I remember about all the great battles, the battle of Neufchappelle, the Battle of Arras, and the taking of Verdun, and the long lists of names of those who were killed in the First World War. Did you ever see Islandbridge in Dublin that's in memory of them?

I remember about the death of Lord Kitchener; he was going to Russia, and he was torpedoed in 1916 by the Germans. The schoolmaster read us all the world news, and read the death of Lord Kitchener to us. And he was a Kerryman too. The Irish are the best fighters in the world, and not afraid of anything. I knew the names of their generals and regiments, like the Irish Guards, the Connaght Rangers, the Royal Munster Fusiliers and many more.

1916 had come along, and after the war people turned very black and bigoted. Before that there was nothing. The Catholics wanted their independence and the Protestants didn't and they were a big majority, you see. We had to submit to them whether you live or die. There were twenty Catholics to one Protestant, and we were only a daisy in a bull's mouth compared to them.

In 1921 they raided all the Protestant houses and took whatever was inside. They knocked on your door and came around collecting money for the arms fund. The Rector told us to pay no money at all to them, and I declare to goodness that because of this all the Protestant families around Cappaghglass were raided at the time. They were all armed with revolvers and pistols, and they fired shots through the windows, and took our Sunday clothes and Sunday boots, and even the spy glass belonging to my grandfather. They took my brother's silver watch, too, and his bike, and they swept it all away. They didn't go near the Catholics at all.

My mother was very frightened, for a good friend of my parents was killed one night. His horse had bolted, and he was thrown on the rocks, and he was all mangled and broken, with the blood streaming out of his nose and mouth.

Cappaghglass had been a Protestant town, but when it was all over many of the families began to leave and go to England. It was a great difference, because if you were not a Catholic, you would not get a job. My brother tried at one time before he went to England, and asked one of the Catholics to give him a job unloading a steamer, but he wouldn't give it to him because he was a Protestant.

What made things worse was at that time everyone was very tight on religion. Are you a Catholic yourself? My mother was a desperate woman against mixed marriages, and my grandmother was the same too, and the Catholics had also their parents against such a marriage. The priest always had them well-instructed, saying that anyone who turned over from their own religion would be damned, and that they would never get to Heaven. He was putting all that stuff in, and you might as well be carrying a "phuca" in a bag as trying to get a Catholic man or woman to turn a Protestant. There was a desperate shortage of Protestant girls, and people were marrying their first cousins.

An uncle of mine married a Catholic girl and had to turn his coat. The first thing she did was to take him to the priest, and she made him renounce his own religion. And she said that it was a rule in the Church, that if there was a mixed marriage, the whole family should turn Catholics. But his father was so demented and mad with him, that he made out a will and cut him off to one shilling in the week, and he wouldn't give him a house or property or a single bit belonging to him because he married a Catholic girl.

That's how it was with us, and I could tell you many other stories of the same thing. Another friend of mine, whose father was a black Orangeman, wanted to marry a Catholic, and her own father fought tooth and nail against it until he drove the daughter out of the house. I declare that the greatest thing that she could do for herself and the young man was to go to England. She was waiting ten years there before her father died and they could marry. And that was the kind I was myself, because I couldn't get a Catholic girl, and the Protestant ones were so scarce that they were picked up like hot cross buns.

I began to go *scoraicht*-ing down in the village, and you could meet many shop assistants, and they were very nice girls. Then I used to go over to the crossroad dancing, what they called a pattern at the roadside, and my brother was a great player on the violin who used to play all the Irish tunes in the world. I suppose there would be up to two score of people there, but I didn't see any Protestants, they were all Catholics. I got to know a lot of Catholic girls to marry, and one would have been great company anyway. But if I brought a Catholic girl home, my mother wouldn't let her inside the door, but blew up like the atom bomb.

If a Protestant man marries a Catholic girl, he is for trouble because his parents were down on him, and they wouldn't give you land, or a house, or a shop if you married one. And there was also quite another thing about it too, that Irish girls hate marrying farmers, and when they marry one, it's grudgingly and against their will. If a girl married someone in a bank or a shopkeeper, they had a fine easy life, but if they married a farmer they would have to work as a slave. They were out picking the potatoes, cleaning mangles and turnips, and taking out buckets with potatoes mashed up inside to the pigs. And they were very tough to milk, the old cows. I've seen several girls get a four pronged pike and throw out the dung and manure from underneath the cows; it was very slavish, and very hard work.

I remember one time we had two Protestant schoolteachers down here, and plenty of men wanted to marry them, for they had a nice clean job, and they could get the ready money. And they got plenty of offers from farmers, but wouldn't look at them at all. And they stayed old maids rather than marry a farmer.

We had an old book about Ireland which gave a very poor account of farmers, and my mother used to say that farmers weren't worth

reading about. It was only "roll his bones over the stones, and he's
only a pauper that nobody owns."

Catholics or Protestants or Jews or anybody, the money was always
very important. If a girl hadn't got money to marry with, she would
be disowned and never got married. The girls would have to go to the
bank and take the money out of it. And my mother had to do it too,
and my two aunts had to do it, and my sister was a schoolteacher, and
when she got married, she had over three hundred pounds, too. But
there was no girl and no money for me here anyway, and I was busy
looking after my mother till she died. I would bring her tea and cake
and look after her room, and I was working on two fronts. I might be
out there in the big hay field, and the fire would be out, and I had to do
it myself and sweep the room. When she died, I didn't worry about
marrying then.

The other night I was thinking in bed of all the Protestant bachelors
that was living around here and could never get a girl even if they had a
bit of land. In my own case a lot could be blamed on religion, for I
could have married plenty of Catholic girls, but I would have to turn
over and join the Catholic church. They would make you do that like
my uncle who married a Catholic girl because he couldn't get a
Protestant. But I wouldn't like to change my religion, and even the
Pope gave it out a few months ago on television that in any mixed
marriage the Protestants will have to turn their children over to the
Catholic church.

Most of my friends are dead now. I have seen that the Irish
government took it down that the amount of bachelors that were
living like myself in the house were a hundred and sixty thousand in
the twenty-six counties. If it hadn't been for religion or politics or
economics most of them would have married.'

Brendan O'Driscoll, Returned Emigrant. Aged 60.

'I think basically what holds people together is the church and religion,
you know. I find that the people down here are not interested in world
affairs. Eighty per cent of them just don't want to know about people
like President Reagan or Margaret Thatcher. I suppose it's nice for

them because they have never travelled and they don't know any different. They believe that when they die they will go to Heaven and they have no worries. I envy their happiness. If a person dies they are quite convinced that he won't be going to Hell and they will be joining him. They are sad, but it's a kind of happy sadness. I believe that there is a Heaven, but if there's a Hell, I just don't know. I try to believe and I want to believe, for that would make me happier. They believe that they are going to Heaven, but I won't be going there. If there's a Hell I'll get to it, or else I'll rot.'

Jerry Galvin, Undertaker. Aged 70.

The word Undertaker is written in discreet black letters beside Grocery and General Hardware. The shop sells things like calendars, teapots, biscuits, delph and writing paper. Behind are the living quarters and behind them again the workshops. A stack of coffins and some black silk linings lie beside a cupboard full of plastic wreaths. The ancient sewing machine on which the old cloaks were once hemmed is a treasured possession, now used to make coffin pillows. But Jerry's business has its roots in job carpentry and woodwork of all kinds. He averages about twenty-five funerals a year, and as people are dying older this number will get less.

★

'I do about half the deaths around Cappaghglass, and the other half are divided up between the two other undertakers. I suppose I get the lion's share. I went into the business at about fourteen and now I'm an old man. I can tell you, I have seen a few changes. When I began everything was hand-made. The shoes were made by the cobbler and handmade suits cost £2.10. There were carpenters, masons and a nailmaker called Jimmy the Punch.

The main thing my father made was cartwheels and butts – the common butts. Everything was done by hand with a chisel, mallet and plane, and you couldn't use anything else for making wheels and fitting the spokes. My father was a brilliant cartwright and could make a wheel in a day. There were three blacksmiths who did all the metal work on the carts and what they called the box. The cost of the whole cart came to about twelve pounds.

My father progressed into the coffins, and I came after. Because it was my father, I just picked things up. Cutting wood into boards, learning how to fit coffins and that sort of thing. Although wheels and carts were important, the funeral business was always there. You can't miss. There are three big occasions in the life of everyone, baptism, marriage and death, and that's where we came in.

The most important thing was making the coffins. There was plenty of good native wood, elm and oak. Today all the coffins are ready-made from old chipboard. But before we never had ready-made coffins. When someone died we had to work all through the night to get it ready. You would start away with the old box and do the best you could. It would take two fellows about eight hours to make it, and you would have to have it ready. A good coffin cost about fifteen pounds, but there were higher prices. I often had lead-lined coffins. Nowadays plastic will do that much better.

Everyone had a wake, Protestant or Catholic. The person was laid out on the bed and there would be someone in the family beside him the whole time. Everyone would say their prayers over him. There would be whiskey and beer and plenty of eats, and when I was young everyone had a clay pipe. They would crack the stem off and keep sucking away and if there was no roll or "twist" as they called the tobacco they would even smoke tea. And there was a special kind of red seaweed they called dilskey. For a penny you could buy a whole pocketful and keep chewing away.

They had horse hearses then. There was a carrier in the town which hired out sidecars and carriages and horse hearses. They had two on the road. The driver would wear a white sash called a cypress, and a top hat with a little band on it and the horses would have little plumes. They had crêpe on the doors which were all shut, and the procession would depend on what standing the man had and how popular he was and how strong the family was. There would be up to two hundred and fifty cars at a big funeral – side cars and traps and bicycles and horses following behind. In my father's time at least a dozen horsemen would be at the tail of a procession on a big funeral. I remember the covered car and the side car, and then the farmers coming along with the traps and bicycles. I heard of keening but never saw it.

We had our first motor hearse before the war. During the war most people kept horses, but we got petrol coupons for the hearse. They would all be looking at us and saying, "Who's dead?" Sometimes we would take the hearse to a party or picnic, and I remember bringing a man who was ill to the doctor. "Where are you going with that blasted thing up to my door?" he bawled at me, "Take it away as fast as you can get out of it."

After the war the wood got scarce. The last man I buried in an elm coffin was Captain Stanly. That was the most expensive funeral I ever did. He was an old sea captain who wanted to be buried at sea, and it took so much lead to sink the coffin and all the valuable anchors that went down with him that his poor widow was broke.

I've done a lot of funerals, and I'll tell you something. Honesty is the thing. I will always tell a person exactly what it will cost before I start the business. It's most important for people to know where they are, for some prices are ridiculous. You know the old saying, "you don't go to heaven until the coffin is paid for." Some would pay direct, or a fellow might say, wait till I sell a cow at the next fair. I have even had them bring me a bag of spuds as a sort of deposit.

Nowadays a funeral can vary from two hundred pounds to a thousand, but in the old days you could do the lot for twenty pounds. The funerals have changed. Now people can enter each other's churches without having to stand outside in the rain. The white linen scarves that the priest or clergyman wore vanished in the 'seventies and so did the bag of hay to cover the coffin.

When I was young everyone wore black if a person died. Did you ever see that? The men would wear a black tie and a black banner on the arm and the girl would wear black clothes. I know a woman whose husband has been dead these forty years and she's in black still and never wore anything else, even a white scarf around her neck. And there was no such thing as going to a dance for after a person died you were in mourning for a year. I remember it myself. It was regarded as a most natural thing that everyone should do it, and anyone who didn't was talked about all over the country.'

Mary O'Halloran, Teacher. Aged 30.

Mary lives and works in a country district about thirty miles north of Cappaghglass in the mountains.

*

'I was raised in the city and until I came to work here I had the usual middle-class constipated attitude towards death. The fact that this area still has wakes has demystified death for me certainly. It has made the whole aspect of the thing much easier to take. We need the opportunity to live with our dead, and I don't see it just as an old custom, but the way things are practised here.

I talked to the priest about wakes and laying out dead people, and he sort of nodded in his chair and said, "It's a wholesome thing to do" – to lay out a dead person. Graves aren't opened here on a Sunday or a Friday, so if somebody dies on a Friday, the grave will still have to be dug the next day. There are two expressions people use: there's readying it and there's digging it. Readying means that you take the sod off, so that if someone dies on a Friday you can ready the grave, but you can't dig it until the Saturday.

When a person dies the mirrors get covered by cloth in the room where the dead person is, and they don't take anything out of the house. You will get a laugh at the wake by looking under the bed to see if the bucket of water is there that they washed the body with. A neighbour told me, "I remember now when my mother-in-law died . . . the Lord have mercy on her . . . and sure didn't I keep the bucket inside for three weeks until it began to smell, and only then did I throw it out."

A wake brings all sorts of people together into the house, and it works here that the men tend to stay in the kitchen, and the women stay with the body, and you'll have jokes and talk and all that. Everyone who comes in is offered tea. They will sit at the table and there will be ham and bread, butter and cakes, and maybe you might have seven sessions of tea before midnight. At midnight the rosary is said, and then an awful lot of people will go – people who aren't immediate neighbours. At the last wake I went to the next of kin put the bottles away until the boozers were gone, and it ended up with about fifteen people staying for the night.'

Joe O'Shea, Churchyard Attendant. Aged 62.

The old church and graveyard are beside the sea. The church was first
Catholic, then Protestant and today it is a roofless shell filled up with
graves. People still come down to bury their dead here and pray for
them as their ancestors did a thousand years ago.

Joe keeps the grass cut, deals with applications for new graves and is
responsible for maintenance. Like Jerry Galvin he can remember the
old long funerals. From his grandmother he heard stories of 'Hullabol-
ing' or wailing that accompanied mourning a century ago. Traditions
concerning the dead have been changing during the past few years, but
he disapproves of the innovations.

*

'It was the usual thing that the man who brought the hearse could only
go to the door and wasn't allowed any further. From then on friends
and relations helped and there was no such thing as gravediggers. The
respect they had for making a grave was a big thing. They would take
up bones that may have belonged to some person's grandfather. Then
they are settled there in a nice heap, and are all put in at the head of the
coffin. The next day the first thing the clay is put in and all levelled up.
Then they would put the sod back on top and make a cross of the
shovels and spades. There would be no laughing, no grinning, nor
sneering and that kind of thing. Then you would bring home the
shovels and go into the first pub and have a drink there and go back
into the house where the funeral was. And maybe have a meal there
and a few drinks more.

Now it's left to us to do the digging. People want to be buried where
their ancestors were buried around the church. You will find coffins
going into the same grave over the years, just one on top of the other.
After they are buried the coffins are usually gone in six or seven years,
and then there is a room for another one. But it doesn't always happen.
In very dry ground where the churchyard slopes the coffins usually
last six years, but in the flat places where there is deep earth they could
be a lot longer than that. Sure we have experience of having graves

opened and seeing the coffin intact after thirty years. It depends on moisture. In the dry ground there is no moisture to keep the wood alive and dry rot sets in.

I remember an old schoolmaster called John McMonagle who knew where everyone had been buried for generations. He would take up the breastplates covered with clay and read them. "There's Michael Donovan gone down there" he would say, "and below him is Seamus his father, and below that again the old man who was born before the famine." He was greatly respected, but you wouldn't smoke near him. I often went to the school and he offered me cigarettes but I wouldn't take them. If people came to him in schooltime asking about who was in a grave he would be delighted, and the children would be delighted for he would be at the graves, and not come back for two hours. One day he said to me, "Come over to this grave." And he says to me "There's one John McMonagle gone down there, and that's my father. And there's another, gone down there, and that's my cousin, and another John McMonagle is going to go down there and that's myself. Think of that, Joe," he said. You'd be afraid to go home after hearing him talk.

When I began it was three pounds for two graves or one pound ten shillings for one. But I'll tell you it was a very slow sale because they were mainly burying their dead in the surrounds of the churchyards – the old places all around where there was a church. I think they were so poor at that time that any sacred ground would do.

You see that little row of plots. There's a space there for those babies – the ones that go to Limbo. We have spaces as well for washed-ashore people and them that die who have no one to claim them if you like. Travelling people and some who die in the County Hospital. The Stranger's Corner they used to call it and this space was reserved for those sort. We have seven graves here. A few are cases from the 1939 war of airmen and bodies washed ashore. There's a headstone up to one person, he was from Tipperary.

In the old days if a person wanted a grave they would buy one and get a receipt. Any person around could say I want to be buried there, and I'll buy this grave. They'd be near their relations if possible. Do you see what I mean? He'd buy the grave, and he'd give orders to the undertaker to bury him there, and I'd get the receipt, and I'd mark it out for them. And when the man came to die or whenever it would be – or the man and wife generally – I'd point out the graves to the undertaker from the map, and that's all there would be to it.

What you see now is the old style graveyard divided up between

Catholics and Protestants and those children. But with all this ecumenism things are going to change. There's going to be no more segregation in the old way. When a man dies a priest or clergyman will consecrate the ground and they are buried one after the other. The position is you won't get the grave until you die, but there will be plenty of graves available.

Speaking personally I prefer the old way. We are all Christians together, but people still like to be with their own denominations. I'd say the old tradition is strong – you'd follow the trend rather than to be changing it. It hasn't happened fully yet – it's on the borderline of a switch.

They are all bought headstones now. There were stones when I started. I think if I was an engineer in charge of a graveyard I'd disallow any high crosses, big crosses and that sort of thing. I'd keep them down, and mind you, with these regulations today about those big headstones, you have to go down with a base of eight feet which is a very costly thing. But what I propose is that they have a small headstone that one or two could just take together and leave enough space on it to write their names. I hate those shiny black things. They are only a made-up cover on the stone. I've seen the rust coming through some of them lately. Coloured marble chips are going out. I think gravestones should be uniform, small, not more than three feet high, not very high, like, because the way they are now you can have some of them higher than that car there.

Wreaths have become more numerous. I hate them, because they cost money, they are put down here, and in a few weeks somebody tramps over them and they get broken up in pieces and they look very ugly.

Oh, cremation is a long way off. I don't see anything wrong in it, but I wouldn't like to be cremated myself, even though I wouldn't feel anything. I'll be cremated soon enough when I go to the other side.

The pensioners put away money for their burial. They don't want for anyone to be losing by them, and that's crucial. Their pensions are good and they are not extravagant. They put away a little money, maybe into the bank, and we never have any trouble. Many are saving for their burial away back twenty years. The grave would cost £45 and the tombstone about £50 at least, and the grave digging would be costing £40 more. With the coffin and the hearse, that would come to around £500.

It's important, the funeral. The people are always intimate with each other, and if there is a funeral you are expected to go. In the cities you could be dead for a week and they wouldn't mind you. But here they would miss a person for a ten mile radius. They would miss anyone who wouldn't be there.'